Money Demand in Europe

Contributions to Economics

http://www.springer.de/cgi-bin/search_book.pl?series=1262

Further volumes of this series can be found at our homepage.

Nico Heerink et al. (Eds.)
Economic Policy and Sustainable Land Use
2001. ISBN 3-7908-1351-6

Friedel Bolle/Michael Carlberg (Eds.)
Advances in Behavioral Economics
2001. ISBN 3-7908-1358-3

Volker Grossmann
Inequality, Economic Growth, and Technological Change
2001. ISBN 3-7908-1364-8

Thomas Riechmann
Learning in Economics
2001. ISBN 3-7908-1384-2

Miriam Beblo
Bargaining over Time Allocation
2001. ISBN 3-7908-1391-5

Peter Meusburger/Heike Jöns (Eds.)
Transformations in Hungary
2001. ISBN 3-7908-1412-1

Claus Brand
Money Stock Control and Inflation Targeting in Germany
2001. ISBN 3-7908-1393-1

Erik Lüth
Private Intergenerational Transfers and Population Aging
2001. ISBN 3-7908-1402-4

Nicole Pohl
Mobility in Space and Time
2001. ISBN 3-7908-1380-X

Pablo Coto-Millán (Ed.)
Essays on Microeconomics and Industrial Organisation
2002. ISBN 3-7908-1390-7

Mario A. Maggioni
Clustering Dynamics and the Locations of High-Tech-Firms
2002. ISBN 3-7908-1431-8

Ludwig Schätzl/Javier Revilla Diez (Eds.)
Technological Change and Regional Development in Europe
2002. ISBN 3-7908-1460-1

Alberto Quadrio Curzio/Marco Fortis (Eds.)
Complexity and Industrial Clusters
2002. ISBN 3-7908-1471-7

Friedel Bolle/Marco Lehmann-Waffenschmidt (Eds.)
Surveys in Experimental Economics
2002. ISBN 3-7908-1472-5

Pablo Coto-Millán
General Equilibrium and Welfare
2002. ISBN 7908-1491-1

Wojciech W. Charemza/Krystyna Strzala (Eds.)
East European Transition and EU Enlargement
2002. ISBN 3-7908-1501-2

Natalja von Westernhagen
Systemic Transformation, Trade and Economic Growth
2002. ISBN 3-7908-1521-7

Josef Falkinger
A Theory of Employment in Firms
2002. ISBN 3-7908-1520-9

Engelbert Plassmann
Econometric Modelling of European Money Demand
2003. ISBN 3-7908-1522-5

Reginald Loyen/Erik Buyst/Greta Devos (Eds.)
Struggeling for Leadership: Antwerp-Rotterdam Port Competition between 1870–2000
2003. ISBN 3-7908-1524-1

Pablo Coto-Millán
Utility and Production, 2nd Edition
2003. ISBN 3-7908-1423-7

Emilio Colombo/John Driffill (Eds.)
The Role of Financial Markets in the Transition Process
2003. ISBN 3-7908-0004-X

Guido S. Merzoni
Strategic Delegation in Firms and in the Trade Union
2003. ISBN 3-7908-1432-6

Jan B. Kuné
On Global Aging
2003. ISBN 3-7908-0030-9

Sugata Marjit, Rajat Acharyya
International Trade, Wage Inequality and the Developing Economy
2003. ISBN 3-7908-0031-7

Francesco C. Billari/Alexia Prskawetz (Eds.)
Agent-Based Computational Demography
2003. ISBN 3-7908-1550-0

Georg Bol/Gholamreza Nakhaeizadeh/Svetlozar T. Rachev/Thomas Ridder/Karl-Heinz Vollmer (Eds.)
Credit Risk
2003. ISBN 3-7908-0054-6

Christian Müller

Money Demand in Europe

An Empirical Approach

With 33 Figures
and 46 Tables

Physica-Verlag
A Springer-Verlag Company

Series Editors
Werner A. Müller
Martina Bihn

Author

Dr. Christian Müller
Swiss Federal Institute of Technology Zurich
Swiss Institute for Business Cycle Research
ETH Zentrum WEH
CH-8092 Zürich
Switzerland
christian.mueller@kof.gess.ethz.ch

ISSN 1431-1933
ISBN 3-7908-0064-3 Physica-Verlag Heidelberg New York

Cataloging-in-Publication Data applied for
A catalog record for this book is available from the Library of Congress.
Bibliographic information published by Die Deutsche Bibliothek
Die Deutsche Bibliothek lists this publication in the Deutsche Nationalbibliografie; detailed bibliographic data is available in the Internet at <http://dnb.ddb.de>.
Dissertation, Humboldt-Universität zu Berlin, December 2001

Physica-Verlag Heidelberg New York
a member of BertelsmannSpringer Science+Business Media GmbH

http://www.springer.de

Softcover Design: Erich Kirchner, Heidelberg

SPIN 10925010   88/3130/DK-5 4 3 2 1 0 – Printed on acid-free and non-aging paper

To Barbara and Walter Müller

Preface

The first of January 1999 marked the beginning of a macroeconomic experiment without precedent in modern history. For the first time eleven European countries agreed to abolish their local currencies in favour of a single one, the Euro. Not surprisingly, the necessary preparatory process has been accompanied by an intensive discussion about the best way to manage the new Euro currency properly. To spur on that discourse was the principal motivation for this thesis.

The introductory chapter attempts to bridge economic and econometric views on money demand analysis. It should help to motivate estimation procedures and to standardize interpretation techniques, hopefully initiating further discussion in that direction. It intends to make the following chapters more accessible.

In this thesis I approach the general subject in two principle ways. In chapter 3 I consider technical issues dealing with time series with shifts in the mean. Two years ago, Helmut Lütkepohl and Pentti Saikkonen asked me to join in on a related project which became the cornerstone of this chapter. I have very much appreciated the highly instructive collaboration with both these scholars.

The other approach is mainly an empirical one. It can be regarded as an offspring of a series of research projects which have been conducted within the

National Research Centre (Sonderforschungsbereich 373) at *Humboldt University Berlin.* Chapters 4 and 5 directly address key problems of monetary policy conduct in the European Monetary Union (EMU). To that aim, two separate studies on the demand for money function were carried out. Chapter 4 scrutinizes monetary policy in France before the dawn of the Euro era.

Research demanded significant revision of an earlier article on French monetary policy, eventually leading to an understanding of the initially very puzzling features of the French demand for money function. In this regard, I am quite confident that the new results clarify those issues of the French case which remained unsolved, and which have not yet been answered elsewhere in the money demand literature.

The fourth chapter is an extension of a previous publication of Elke Hahn and mine on the behaviour of macroeconomic time series at the European level. This work would not have been possible without the outstanding support of Katja Rietzler and her colleagues at the *German Institute for Economic Research (DIW)*, Berlin who helped collect the data. Here, the most important motivation was to mimic the situation in which the European Central Bank (ECB) would find itself once the Euro was introduced. The main innovation in comparison to the original paper is the extension of the analysis beyond 1998. It turns out however, that not all results can be perpetuated.

Acknowledgements

Patiently and craftily my supervisors Prof. Dr. Helmut Lütkepohl and Prof. Dr. Jürgen Wolters kept the error correction mechanism going, which made me stick to the route finally ending at the Dean's office to hand in this thesis. I am especially indebted to them for their generous support and encouragement during the more than three years of my graduate studies.

While working on this thesis, I have benefited from the creative and inspiring atmosphere at the department of econometrics at Humboldt University in Berlin. Apart from my supervisors, Dr. Jörg Breitung, Klaus Müller, Carsten Trenkler, Elke Hahn, Ralf Brüggemann, Dr. Bertrand Candelon, Ulrike and Dr. Ulrich Busch, Susanne Kademann, Christian Schleyer, and Ute Hasenöhrl have read parts of earlier versions of this work. Claude Million made a special effort to turn the blueprint into almost legible English. All their comments led to many improvements. Needless to say, the remaining mistakes are my own.

The result at hand has been produced while I was a member of the National Research Centre 'Quantification and Simulation of Economic Processes' (Sonderforschungsbereich 373), project C4. It provided me with financial and organisational support, and gave me the opportunity to present parts of this thesis at seminars not only at Humboldt University, but also in Santiago de Compostela, Brussels, Lausanne, and Florence. I am particularly grateful for the granted research leave which I spent at Stockholm School of Economics, and for the hospitality I enjoyed there at the Institute of Statistics and Econometrics.

Last but not least, I would like to thank my parents and my dear Suse who gave me the emotional support, and all the invaluable things that finally made me accomplish this academic assignment.

Zürich, 10th February 2003 Christian Müller

Contents

1

Introduction

Conducting monetary policy in an area as colourful as the one represented by the eleven founding members of the European Monetary Union requires a few more considerations than just thinking about a homogeneous single country of comparable size. This need arises from differences in the histories of policy conduct, including monetary strategies, transmission mechanisms, communication, degree of independence of individual central banks (CB), data aggregation methods and data definitions and so on.

The objective of this thesis is to investigate the conditions for monetary policy making by looking at money demand as a central mechanism transmitting monetary policy action. It is noteworthy that the existence of this transmission mechanism is not only necessary for a particular monetary strategy like monetary targeting, for instance. It is also a very common and important ingredient of macroeconomic modelling in general. Moreover, investigating demand for money functions is not of a purely academic interest.

The ECB, as has been made clear at a very early stage, follows a monetary policy which rests on two premises, the so-called two pillars. The first premise concerns the monetary aggregate. The ECB announces a reference value for the growth rate of the monetary aggregate (harmonized M3), whereby actual deviations from this value (somehow) feed back into it's interest rate decisions. Although this setting to some extent resembles the official monetary targeting strategy of the German Bundesbank, the notion of two pillars implies that a second consideration guides monetary policy too. This second premise is "a broadly based assessment of the outlook for . . . the risks to price stability" (European Central Bank (1999b), p.47). Obviously, the two pillars are another term for the ambiguities the ECB faces when taking policy actions. These problems are at least twofold. First, the member states of EMU are far from being homogenous in their economic, legal, cultural, let alone their monetary policy history. Therefore, committing to a single recipe for achieving price stability does not seem justified a priori. Second, even though the German Bundesbank conducted a policy which earned the bank a high reputation and the Deutschmark low inflation, a lively discussion has erupted as to whether better alternatives might exist. For example, Svensson (2000) advocates the use of more transparent and direct policy objectives, namely inflation targets. These arguments are put forward before the background of successful inflation targeting, by the Bank of England for example.

For this thesis however, the contrast of monetary targeting and inflation targeting is not the main issue. Instead, the focus is on the central mechanism for both these frameworks instead, i.e. the demand for money function. In other words, knowing the properties of the money demand function will be of indispensable value to monetary authorities, independent of what strategy they choose to apply.

This thesis approaches the problem in two principal ways. In a methodological section unit root tests are investigated which allow for the possibility of a structural shift in the mean of a univariate time series. For European monetary policy analysis, the relevance of the problem is given by the fact that many of the countries involved have experienced shocks which may have led to structural shifts. Among those are the German unification and, as will be argued in chapter 4, the change in the exchange rate regime in France. Moreover, the introduction of the Euro currency itself may be such an event which eventually may invoke the need for appropriate testing procedures.

Chapter 4 is an empirical study in the tradition of country-by-country (cbc) analyses of money demand across the whole of Europe. The idea of the cbc approach is to confirm the existence of stable money demand functions in all EMU countries in order to justify the exploitation of that relationship for monetary policy purposes on the EMU level. Anticipating the results, it turns out that the exercise fails in the case of France because a more stable money supply function dominates the market for M3. A detailed empirical investigation of the German dominance hypothesis and a short reference to related theoretical concepts help to understand the outcomes.

Chapter 5 looks at European money demand matters from a different angle: It assumes that the ECB will have to decide about its policy on the basis of an aggregate of information from all EMU member states. To that aim, the relevant national data series will be aggregated to yield EMU variable series, and a demand for money function is estimated for these artificial data. Contrary to many other studies, the properties of the function derived, only rudimentarily resemble a money demand function.

[illegible]

2

Economic and Econometric Concepts

2.1 Introduction

Laidler (1999) points the finger at a long standing dilemma when he notes that:

> Differences between monetarists and Keynesians on transmission issues were . . . about where it was most fruitful to simplify the basic framework in order to bring it into contact with empirical evidence, not about fundamental questions of monetary policy. (op. cit. p. xvi)

To overcome some of the unavoidable frictions between economic considerations and econometric tools this chapter tries to establish some links between what economic theory suggests and what econometric methods are able to confirm. The point of departure is a mainly technical one, however. Therefore, no particular money demand theory serves as a null hypothesis, although the approaches can be traced back to Meltzer (1963) who primarily considered monetarist views. Likewise, the concept of money itself will be treated as a technical issue.

The remainder of the introductory chapter presents a scheme according to which demand for money functions can be discovered in a systematic, theoretically founded manner. The views expressed are mainly a blend of standard textbook presentations such as Jarchow (1993), Issing (1993), and Laidler

(1993). Furthermore, Sriram (1999) gives a useful overview. The quantity theory of money serves as a starting point which will then be augmented to incorporate more general approaches to money demand while focussing on how to transform them into econometric models. Next, the economic considerations are complemented by presenting econometric concepts with the focus centring on system analysis. The chapter closes with a suggestion to categorize potential econometric results and their economic interpretation.

2.2 Economics of the Demand for Money

2.2.1 A Specific-to-General Approach

We start with a concept inherited from the classical approach. Thus, the starting point is the identity

$$Mv \equiv QP \tag{2.1}$$

where M stands for money used for transactions, v is the transaction velocity of money, Q the volume of transaction and P the price level. Since in modern economies all income is measured in terms of monetary transaction the volume of transaction can be substituted by income and the identity (2.1) holds by definition.

However, few additional assumptions about the nature of the variables M, v and Q will turn equation (2.1) into a backbone of theories of the demand for money. The following sections present those sets of assumptions and relate them to their respective theoretical concepts.

The Quantity Theory of Money

In its basic form, the quantity theory of money draws apart the real (production, consumption of goods) from the nominal side of the economy (money and prices). The former are determined without having any relationship to the other, reflecting what is called the classical dichotomy. Therefore, money could not matter less for the origin of income, and its exogeneity in conjunction with a static economy implies that the price level is directly linked to the stock of money in circulation. Put differently, with Q, v, M being determined exogenously and independently of each other, the price level is determined by the ratio of money stock to real activity

$$P = \frac{\bar{M}}{\bar{Q}}\bar{v}. \tag{2.2}$$

The bar above the variable signifies the exogeneity assumption.

Despite its various weaknesses, including lack of dynamics, the postulation of full employment always and everywhere, the quantity theory of money can be regarded as a very basic and rudimentary form of a demand for money function: "The quantity theory is in the first instance a theory of the *demand* for money. It is not a theory of output, . . . or the price level." (Friedman (1956), emphasis as in the original). It is regarded as a function because under the assumption that $\bar{v}$ is fixed (2.2) acknowledges the systematic link between the stock of money (demand for money) and the transactions (determinant) taking place in the economy.

Neoclassical Demand for Money

The neoclassical theories of the monetary sector provide dynamic versions of the classical models. They aim at explaining adjustment processes within the economy following exogenous shocks like increases in the money supply. The main idea of Patinkin (1966) was to assume real financial assets including money to affect demand and supply behaviour on the real goods market. As a consequence, exogenous increases in the money supply temporarily lead to, for example, an increase in the demand for real goods (real balance effect). This excess demand is met by an increase in production and an increase in prices up to the point at which the initial shock to real balances is countered by the rise in the price level.

Yet another neoclassical stream of literature, the Cambridge school led by Marshall (1923) and Pigou (1917) focusses on individual choices rather than on market equilibria. It raised the question, how much real balances agents would wish to hold given that money holding was needed to pursue transactions. Thus, in contrast to earlier views, the v becomes a behavioural variable rather than a technical constant linking the need for transaction to the desired level of real balances. Furthermore, assuming this relation to be constant in the short-run at least, and holding other things equal, a formal structural expression can be given as

$$M = \frac{1}{v} PQ \tag{2.3}$$

where equilibrium on the money market is assumed (money supply = money demand). Moreover, $\frac{1}{v} = k$ is the famous Cambridge k. The Cambridge school acknowledged that k might also depend on factors like interest and wealth, but the main focus was on transaction. Finally, (2.3) restates the well-known quantity theory of money, although its derivation started with a microeconomic perspective.

In terms of the money demand analysis to follow, the neoclassical approach provides the insight, that the exogeneity of income with respect to real money may not hold. This however, has implications for the appropriate choice of estimation technique. In particular it has to be made sure that a feedback relationship between shocks to real money and income is allowed for.

Second, the notion of k being fixed in the short-run and the hypothesis of a short-run real balance effect imply the need for distinguishing between short and long-term horizons. Therefore, the econometric tools should also cope with this distinction.

Liquidity Demand for Money

When launching his criticism on the prevailing economic convictions of his time, Keynes did not spare monetary economics (Keynes, 1930; Keynes, 1936).

Rejecting the predominantly static, general equilibrium views, he suggested to partly abolish the classical dichotomy. In the current context, the most important step forward he made, was to include the speculative motive in the set of reasons why to hold money. Doing so, the dichotomy disappears because interest rates now affect both investment decisions (the real side) and the stock of money (the nominal side) willingly held by the public. The implications are straightforward. Increasing the supply of money, lowers the interest rate level and thereby triggers investment and real activity (liquidity effect).

Keynes (1936) did not assume the public agents to suffer from money illusion. Their demand decisions always rest on real values. That means that the classical dichotomy has not been overthrown by ignoring price adjustments. Second, for the purpose at hand, the role of the interest rate has to be kept in mind. An increase in the interest rate, which is equivalent to a rise in the return on non-monetary assets, will ceteris paribus lead to a decrease in money holdings. This is because investment in those non-monetary assets becomes more attractive. A direct consequence of these considerations is the importance of expectations about interest rates for the demand for money because they guide today's decision.

In the light of equation (2.1) the following adjustments have to be made. The income velocity, v is not considered fixed any longer. Instead, it is convenient to view v as a function of the interest rate (i) which leads to the following relationship

$$M/P = f(Q, v(i)) \tag{2.4}$$

when money illusion is ruled out. Equation (2.4) yields an interpretation as a demand for money function where the dependent variable (real money stock) is explained by the transaction demand for money and the speculative as well as precautionary money holding.

The Monetarist Approach

Friedman (1956) in a seminal paper of the monetarist school recovered the quantity theory while shifting the emphasis to money as being an asset and part of the broader consumption portfolio. This leads to the conclusion that the demand for money would depend on the price of money. This price is defined as interest. Therefore income, interest, and the price of any other relevant asset has to enter the demand for money function.

However, based on observations of income and money in the very long run, Friedman (1956), Friedmann and Schwartz (1982) contradict the prominent role assigned by the Keynesians to the interest rate in the demand for money function. They argue that the stock of money is what matters most for determining economic activity and inflation in particular. Friedman (1956) for example states that the relation between income and money stock provides the potential for "isolating the numerical 'constants' of monetary behaviour" (op. cit. p. 336). The explanation for disequilibrium situations such as unemployment rests on costs for gathering information, and costs of adjusting to changing economic conditions. In essence, deviations from the equilibrium relation in (2.4) are of a strictly temporary nature and eventually lead to an adjustment of the price level.

In addition to the transaction demand for money, the monetarist framework points out the importance of expected changes in the price level (inflation). If increases in the price level due to positive money supply shocks are expected, creditors will demand higher nominal interest rates immediately. Although income might rise in the short-run, the larger income and rising prices will reverse and even override the initial downward turn of the interest rate (income and price effect). As a consequence, the liquidity effect identified by Keynes diminishes, or is short-lived at best. The nominal interest rate will increase only as long as shocks to money supply continue to raise inflation expectations.

Other Approaches

Most of the later work on money demand focusses on one or two of its determinants. There are for example the Baumol-Tobin inventory models equating the transaction demand for money with the forgone interest earnings. It is interesting to note that this is in striking contrast to the Keynesian transaction demand which is totally independent of interest rates. However, this distinction matters less for empirical implementation. One of the most famous hypotheses of that theory poses the income elasticity of the demand for money to be equal one half.

Furthermore, cash-in-advance models have been put forth that emphasize that money is needed before the actual transaction takes place (Clower, 1967). A significant improvement of the cash-in-advance approach can be found in Svensson (1985), for example. The relaxation of the assumption that future expenses are known with certainty leads from the inventory models to precautionary demand for money models (see e.g. Dornbusch and Fischer (1990)).

Finally, a consumer demand theory approach proposed e.g. by Barnett (1980) should be mentioned. According to it money is demanded quite like any ordinary consumer good. Following this approach leads to an increase in the number of variables which yield opportunity costs of holding money instead of these assets.

2.2.2 Economic Theory and Implications for Empirical Applications

Despite the seemingly large variety in money demand theories, the implications for empirical investigations are very much the same. In fact, as Meltzer (1963) already noticed, most of the models can be summed up in a very general formulation with each of the variants representing a special case of the general framework.

The reason for that is the common ground on which all models build. First, the choice of independent, that is explanatory, variables always requires some income or transaction variable. The more sophisticated models also consider at least one interest rate as an opportunity cost measure. But the broader the monetary aggregate under investigation the larger becomes the set of interest rates to be considered. For the very broad aggregates such as M3, modern approaches to money demand e.g. in the consumer goods framework postulate monetary assets themselves to bear interest. Thus, not only interest on alternative assets has to be accounted for but also interest on money. Further explanatory variables like wealth and inflation rate can be included in the empirical model and removed later on if they turn out to be statistically insignificant.

Second, while the very early money demand theories treat all variables except the price level as exogenous variables, this need not be assumed in the empirical investigation. Instead, all variables can be treated endogenous as for instance in the multiple time series framework. Starting with all variables being endogenous is a big advantage because it provides the opportunity to statistically conjecture which variables are exogenous rather than having to impose that property from the beginning. To illustrate the need for that, let us reconsider the real balance effect: It predicts that disequilibrium situations on the money market may lead to real adjustments in output. Thus, assuming output to be exogenous with respect to the demand for money would certainly lead to invalid results because the feedback between the money market and the goods market would remain disregarded. Eventually, the real balance effect could not be discovered at all. On the other hand, allowing for such a feedback relationship does no harm, even if it does not exist.

The third common feature is the distinction between the short-run and the long-run. While all models postulate long-run equilibrium on the money market, the majority also allows for deviations therefrom. In fact, the adjustment back to equilibrium often defines the distinguishing features which are relevant for policy recommendations. Later on, it will be argued that the vector error correction model ($VECM$) with possibly non-stationary variables is the appropriate choice. Although this framework allows for vectors of endogenous variables, dynamic interaction, and - above all - to set apart the long-run from the short-run, it has to be acknowledged that it tells nothing about the short-run dynamics. However, it helps to identify those endogenous variables which adjust to disequilibrium situations.

To conclude the survey, although the various demand for money models take different points of view and occasionally end up with opposite policy advice, there exists a common ground for estimating the demand for money function. The following paragraphs will suggest a standardized procedure for conducting empirical money demand analysis.

2.3 System Analysis of Money Demand Functions

This section outlines how a system analysis of money demand can be applied to systematically recover the features of the demand for money function. The main idea is to use the so-called vector error correction modelling approach which generally results in better representations of the data generating process (DGP) if compared to earlier approaches.[1]

The following aspects will be discussed briefly: the choice of variables and their statistical properties, representation of the DGP, auxiliary economic relations, efficient estimation and weak exogeneity, identification of the demand for money functions, and finally, interpretation of the results.

2.3.1 Choice of Variables

As a natural starting point, the choice of the monetary aggregate needs to be discussed. Originally rather narrow aggregates like notes and coins in circulation and sight deposits had been modelled before the focus shifted to broader

[1] A number of reasons for using *VECMs* are surveyed e.g. in Arize and Shwiff (1993).

aggregates like M3 which, in Germany for example, also comprises time deposits up to four years to maturity. The main reason for this augmentation lies in the increased 'moneyness' of financial tools like short-term credits. This phenomenon can largely be attributed to technical innovations like automatic teller machines and to financial deregulation, both of which gave rise to easier maturity transformations, new means of payment and lower transaction costs. In the wake of these changes, researchers realized difficulties in deriving stable relationships between the narrow aggregates and traditional determinants of money demand.[2] In the 1980s the German Bundesbank for example, acknowledging these difficulties, dropped targeting the narrow central bank money aggregate in favour of the broader aggregate M3. Consequently, most empirical studies model the demand for broad monetary aggregates. As a side effect, the dynamics within the broad aggregate are often ignored. In sum, based on the aforementioned arguments a broad monetary aggregate, namely M3 is favoured.

The second variable in the investigation portfolio is the transaction variable. Here again, feasibility of the empirical exercise often guides the choice. Usually, real gross domestic product (GDP) or real gross national product (GNP) are employed. The difference for the actual transaction is obvious and thus, interpretation of the respective coefficient has to be in terms of income elasticity of money holding rather than transaction demand of which income is an approximation only. Moreover, sometimes GNP and GDP differ considerably, and the researcher might base the actual choice on how strongly the demand for money is likely to be related to either of these. Occasionally, even industrial production serves as the income measure. Due to its steadily dimin-

[2] The instabilities in the demand for M1 in the U.S.A. have been widely discussed (Laidler, 1993). An empirical approach of modelling these instabilities is provided by Lütkepohl (1993b). See also Ericsson, Hendry and Prestwich (1998) on the U.K. demand for high powered and broad money, 1878-1993. The authors account for financial innovations by augmenting the set of explanatory variables.

ishing share of the national product, this does not seem appealing, however. All in all, GDP will be used in this thesis.

The remaining variables have to account for opportunity costs of holding money as well as measures for the gains of holding money if applicable. To begin with, opportunity costs are in principle an open set, which will also differ depending on the national particularities. For small and open economies the impact of foreign interest rates may play a role while for large, nearly closed economies, foreign conditions certainly matter less. Nevertheless, three variables can be identified which need to be included in a money demand analysis.

The first among them is a long-term interest rate which has to refer to an asset not included in the monetary aggregate. Ideally, such an asset involves as much risk as holding money itself. Otherwise, it would not suffice to observe the interest rate level, but an indicator for the difference in risks as well. The implication for the variable choice is straightforward: Treasury bill rates are generally preferable to bond rates, and government bond rates dominate private sector bond rates. This said, exceptions to this rule frequently have to be allowed for. Appropriate treasury bills might simply not be relevant due to low trading volume for instance. The additional risk involved in government bonds on the other hand, might not count that much. In fact, estimation exercises employing government bonds, often deliver satisfactory results, despite the theoretical hassles. One possible explanation is that government debts usually rank very low in terms of default risk. Therefore and because of it being readily available, the government bond rate will be used in the analysis.

A further opportunity cost measure is the inflation rate as it evaluates the costs of holding money instead of real goods. The faster the rise in the price level, the more expensive goods will be in the future. Therefore, those who postpone the purchase will forgo some goods altogether. The role of the inflation rate has already been highlighted by Cannan (1921). The relation between inflation and the demand for money is hypothesized a negative one.

Finally, the inflation indicator often is either a consumer price index or the implicit GDP/GNP price deflator.

As a third category, some variables should represent the financial gains of holding money. The interest rate of choice ought to refer to a component within the monetary aggregate. Ideally, it is also closely linked to all interest rates for all assets included. The repurchasing rate, money market or three months credit rates are often picked. Unfortunately, the consequences of preferring either of them over the other are not yet well understood.

In case the empirical investigation also aims at deriving conclusions about the impact of monetary policy on say, inflation, then it has to made sure that a policy rate or a close substitute is included in a system analysis.

To complete and conclude the discussion, various further variables might be considered depending on specific circumstances. In studies e.g. by Eitrheim (1999) on Norway, by Juselius and Gennari (1998) on Italy, and by Lütkepohl and Wolters (1998) on Germany, import prices, exchange rates, oil exports, government expenditure, wealth measures, and foreign interest rates have been used.

The next paragraphs turn to the technical issues of estimation.

2.3.2 The Statistical Model, the Long- and Short-run

It has become good empirical practice to base economic reasoning on corresponding econometric evidence. The tools for the empirical exercise should reasonably fulfill the criteria defined before. In particular, they must allow for multiple dependencies between the variables and for distinguishing between short-run and long-run. Apart from that, the estimation has to be feasible and deliver reliable results. For all that, the vector error correction model has proven a popular and adequate means in the money demand context and its setup is therefore discussed. Reference to this general discussion is made throughout the remainder of the thesis.

The starting point is the distinction between long-run and short-run analysis. This seems to be necessary because many observable data series feature properties that can loosely be described as stochastic trending. The concept can be denoted as follows

$$a(L)x_t = e_t \tag{2.5}$$

where x_t represents the values of a stochastic variable over $t = 1, 2, \ldots,$ consecutive periods, $a(L)$ is a polynomial in the lag operator L with $L^i x_t = x_{t-i}$ such that $a(L) = 1 - a_1 L - a_2 L^2 \cdots - a_p L^p$, $i = \ldots - 1, 0, 1, \ldots p$, and a_i is scalar. The term e_t signifies a series of independent random shocks with expectation zero and finite variance. Deterministic terms will be introduced later. The properties of x_t crucially depend on the polynomial $a(L)$. Here, we consider two basic cases. First, stationary time series will be called those series for which a representation similar to (2.5) exists and whose solutions of the equation $a(z) = 1 - a_1 z - a_2 z^2 \cdots - a_p z^p = 0$ do not lie in or on the unit circle. The second class of time series is supposed to have exactly one of its roots on the unit circle. These two situations are denoted $I(0)$ and $I(1)$ respectively.[3]

If time series are I(1), this has far reaching consequences. The most important for the analysis to follow is that shocks occurring will have an impact on the series that will be felt in all future periods. In such a case, the time series is said to be driven by a stochastic trend. Equivalently, they are said to be integrated of order one, which in turn has severe consequences for regression analysis involving more than one series. This is because standard regression techniques become useless with respect to significance analysis; the t-values do not follow a t-distribution and the regression fit cannot be assessed by the usual R^2 coefficient, for example. Obviously, it is very important to know whether a series is $I(0)$ or $I(1)$. A large number of tests exists in order to find this out. The next chapter will discuss two of these approaches.

[3] Two roots on the unit circle are associated with the notation $I(2)$.

One easy way of dealing with $I(1)$ variables is to take first differences of the variables. This means applying the difference operator $\Delta_j^i = (1 - L^j)^i$ with $i, j = 1$ to the series.[4] Doing so would filter the single non-stationary root out of the series. However, as Engle and Granger (1987) noted, regressing the difference series could again produce misleading results if the series involved are driven by some stochastic trend they share. This is opposite to the series being driven by independent stochastic trends. If there are shared or, equivalently, common stochastic trends, then the series are said to be cointegrated. This concept has been further extended and generalized to the multiple time series case by e.g. Johansen (1988), Johansen and Juselius (1990), Johansen (1995a) where a more formal definition of cointegration can also be found. As a technical matter we should also mention processes being integrated of second or even larger order. Those processes do have two or more unit roots as solutions to the polynomial $a(z)$. There too, taking differences reduces the degree of integration and various kinds of cointegration possibilities exist.[5]

For the purpose of this thesis, the distinction between long-run and short-run properties of the time series is important. This distinction is implicit in the multi-variate analysis of non-stationary time series and can be used to identify long-run relationships between the variables of interest. Consider therefore the following general statistical model

$$X_t = A_1 X_{t-1} + A_2 X_{t-1} + \cdots A_p X_{t-p} + \varepsilon_t. \tag{2.6}$$

In (2.6) the A_i are matrices of dimension $(n \times n)$, ε_t is an n-dimensional vector of disturbances which are not autocorrelated, have expected value zero and variance-covariance matrix Ξ. $X_t = [x_{1,t}, \ldots, x_{n,t}]'$ is a $(n \times 1)$ vector. We assume all components of X_t to be integrated of order one at most such that $\Delta x_{i,t} \sim I(0)$. If one or more of the components are non-stationary, but linear combinations thereof exist which are stationary, then these linear

[4] If i or j is not explicitly given, it is set to unity.

[5] See e.g. Johansen (1992), Johansen (1997) on higher order (multi-variate) integrated processes.

combinations are called cointegration relations. The model (2.6) can then be re-written in the so-called error correction (EC) form

$$\Delta X_t = \Pi X_{t-1} + \sum_{i=1}^{p-1} \Gamma_i \Delta X_{t-i} + \varepsilon_t. \tag{2.7}$$

See e.g. Lütkepohl (1993a) on the derivation of (2.7). Depending on the properties of the $(n \times n)$ matrix Π, the process X_t can be considered non-stationary ($\Pi = 0$), non-stationary, but cointegrated ($0 < rank(\Pi) < n$) or stationary altogether ($rank(\Pi) = n$). We can now add deterministic components such as trend and constant to find a general setup for estimation. Here and throughout we denote the n-dimensional vector of endogenous variables by Y_t. It collects a number of variables $Y_t = [y_{1,t}\ y_{2,t} \cdots y_{n,t}]'$ and is subject to the data generating process

$$Y_t = \mu_0 + \mu_1 t + X_t \tag{2.8}$$

with X_t being the process given in (2.6). It should be pointed out that the framework of (2.8) rules out those cases in which the non-stationarity feature generates a quadratic trend in the levels of the series. Moreover, combining (2.7) and (2.8) we obtain the following general EC representation

$$\Delta Y_t = \nu_0 + \nu_1 t + \Pi Y_{t-1} + \sum_{j=1}^{p-1} \Gamma_j \Delta Y_{t-j} + \varepsilon_t, \quad t = p+1, p+2, \ldots \tag{2.9}$$

with $\nu_0 = -\Pi\mu_0 + (\sum_{j=1}^{p} jA_j)\mu_1$, $\nu_1 = -\Pi\mu_1$. The model (2.9) will serve as a reference for testing purposes. A closer look at the matter reveals that Π can be decomposed into the product of two $(n \times r)$ matrices of full column rank r, denoted α and β' respectively. The aforementioned stationary linear relationships between the variables are defined by the matrix β' while α informs about the extent to which the components of ΔY_t adjust to deviations from the long-run equilibrium values given by $\beta' Y_{t-1}$. Thus, there will be r stationary relationships and the whole system is driven by $(n - r)$ common stochastic trends.

As it will be argued below, some of the variables playing a role in the theoretical money demand relation also feature in some of the economically meaningful auxiliary relations. That is why the system approach seems to be most appropriate for investigating the full set of information provided by the data in accordance with economic theory. There is a plain statistical argument for considering the complete system too. It basically goes back to Engle, Hendry and Richard (1983), Ericsson, Hendry and Mizon (1998), Ericsson (1998) who note, that excluding a variable by mistake from the list of endogenous variables in the system while it is not driven by an independent stochastic trend, renders the estimation procedure inefficient. In any case, if a model like (2.9) is used for more detailed macroeconomic modelling, it seems reasonable to include more than just one equation in order to come closer to the structural models usually encountered in macroeconomic theory. Doing so, enables the researcher to recover some richer structure from the otherwise rather purely descriptive character of model (2.6). Alternatively, one would always have to condition on the remaining economic relationships to exist without being able to test whether or not they are present jointly.

The following lines will formulate general hypotheses about the time series properties of the variables in the standard set for money demand analysis. They all are assumed to possess a valid AR representation.

Money. The monetary aggregate is supposed to include a time trend which is separated from the non-stationary part of the series.[6] It is often assumed that nominal money is integrated of order 2, but cointegrating with the price level (see below) which is also I(2) to a I(1) variable.

Real income. The output variable is possibly integrated of order one and also driven by a time trend which is set apart from the non-stationary part.

Interest rates. Long and short-term interest rates are considered not to be subject to deterministic trending behaviour while being I(1). Therefore, the AR representation only includes a constant term being separated from the unit root part of the process.

Inflation. The inflation rate is defined as the growth rate of prices and as-

[6] See also chapter 3 for univariate AR representation of time series.

sumed not to be affected by a deterministic trend. It may well have stochastic trending behaviour. Similar to the monetary aggregate, prices are often regarded as I(2) variables featuring a deterministic trend.

As has been mentioned before, empirical applications usually work with the so called real money, which is defined as the stock of money divided by the price level. This procedure is justified by the assumption of linear homogeneity of prices in the demand for money relation. That implies the real monetary aggregate to be integrated of order one, if the two series it is made of cointegrate to an I(1) series. We will follow that method being aware of the fact, however, that the more general case would also allow for I(2) variables in the system.[7]

2.3.3 Economic Relationships & Cointegration Hypotheses

The more complex models of the demand for money theories not only consider a relationship between money, income, interest rates and inflation but also between subsets of these variables. This section states the cointegration hypotheses implied by the money demand theories. In addition to that, some of potential further relationships will be discussed together with their implications for cointegration hypotheses.

As a technical matter, income ($y_t = log(Q_t)$), prices ($p_t = log(P_t)$) and money ($m_t = log(M_t)$) are expressed as the log values of their levels whereas interest rates and inflation enter in levels. Throughout the thesis, the general idea is to define economically sensible relations which should hold in the long run. Deviations from the thereby defined long-run levels should be of limited duration. This implies that the corresponding residual terms (denoted $ec._{,t}$ below) of the relationships are to be stationary.

We use the following general notation for the cointegration relations defined by $\beta' Y_t$:

[7] See e.g. Juselius (1999) for a discussion of the various implications of the order of integration of prices and money for money demand and monetary policy.

$$\beta' Y_t = \begin{pmatrix} \beta_1 \\ \beta_2 \\ \vdots \\ \beta_r \end{pmatrix} Y_t$$

$$= \begin{pmatrix} \beta_{1,1} & \beta_{2,1} & \cdots & \beta_{5,1} \\ \vdots & & & \vdots \\ \beta_{1,r} & \cdots & \cdots & \beta_{5,r} \end{pmatrix} \begin{pmatrix} (m-p) \\ y \\ i^l \\ i^s \\ \pi \end{pmatrix}_t \tag{2.10}$$

Each row of β' represents a linear combination of the endogenous variables which is stationary. In the next paragraphs various candidates for cointegration relations will be introduced and discussed in terms of this general outset.

Money Demand

The money demand hypothesis can be written as

$$(m-p)_t = \beta_{2,j} y_t - \beta_{3,j} i^l_t + \beta_{4,j} i^s_t - \beta_{5,j} \pi_t,$$

or,

$$ec_{m,t} = (m-p)_t - \beta_{2,j} y_t + \beta_{3,j} i^l_t - \beta_{4,j} i^s_t + \beta_{5,j} \pi_t \tag{2.11}$$

where all coefficients $\beta_{.,j}$ should be greater than zero.[8] The $ec_{m,t}$ is called error correction term and has to be stationary for money demand to be existing. Special cases are those where $\beta_{3,j}$, $\beta_{4,j}$, $\beta_{5,j}$, all are zero, implying stationarity of a relation between income and money only. In such a case there is no demand for money in the sense that money is a commodity whose price and

[8] The second position in the subscripts is saved for indicating the number of the cointegrating vector ($j = 1, 2, \ldots, r$). We use $\pi_t = 4\Delta p_t$ to approximate the annual inflation rate on the basis of the quarterly changes in order to match its periodicity with the interest rates.

quantity is determined by market forces. Another special case is $\beta_{2,j} = 1$, where the income elasticity of the demand for money is said to be unity and we have a stationary income velocity of money. Note that no deterministic trend enters the demand for money equation.

The Fisher Relation

Fisher (1930) introduced the notion of a real interest rate to distinguish between the nominal, observable return on a credit contract and the net return. The difference occurs mainly due to inflation. Therefore, while one would assume the real interest rate to be comparatively stable and driven by some exogenous forces like real economic growth, the nominal interest rate is a result of both real and monetary (inflationary) effects. As a consequence, individuals lending money (buying domestic bonds) would ask for higher nominal interest the more they expect the currency to devaluate during the time to maturity. Empirically, this idea is cast in the following way. First, to keep out other sources of interest rate determination, such as risk of credit failure, government bond yields are considered. Second, the difference between the nominal interest rate and the inflation rate is tested for stationarity. This procedure is consistent with rational expectation formation and perfectly harmonizes e.g. with the frequent empirical finding of non-stationary interest rates. In the trivial case of a random walk for example, each consecutive future value is the sum of the current value and an unpredictable random shock. Therefore, if the Fisher effect holds, then the difference between the current nominal interest rate and the current inflation rate should show up stationary. Generally speaking, if agents really demand higher nominal returns when they expect prices to rise, then the difference between the interest rate and inflation should contain information about the inflation expectations.

For estimation purposes the Fisher relation can be written as

$$ec_{F,t} = i_t^l + \beta_{5,j}\pi_t, \;\; \beta_{5,j} = -1.$$

The Interest Rate Spread

The hypothesis of financial markets being efficient provides another, possibly statistically important link between two variables of the larger system. This relationship is often referred to as the interest rate spread and builds on the idea that financial markets rule out the possibility of sustaining risk free arbitrage opportunity. The spread is defined as the difference between two interest rates. In that difference, the subtrahend relates to an asset with a longer time to maturity than the minuend. In a world without risk, an investor might observe a difference between interest rates for credit contracts of different maturities, for example. Then it might be more profitable to invest and re-invest in short-term bonds again and again. This is the case if this strategy yields a larger return in sum than the gain from an engagement in a single contract covering the same period of time. Even if risk is introduced (e.g. due to inflation and possibility of credit failure), and if one assumes that it increases with the time horizon, the result changes very little. Time dependent risk implies that the single contract strategy yields higher nominal interest, and that the corresponding difference approaches some stationary threshold value (risk premium) which makes up for the risk involved.

In short, making similar assumptions about expectation formation as for the Fisher hypothesis, the difference between current observations of interest rates referring to different credit maturities should turn out stationary. If the short-term rates are too high and the spread is too small, then the error correction mechanism is provided by the opportunity to raise profits. Sure profits could be made, say, by switching from short-term bonds to long-term bonds thereby lowering the price of the first and pushing up the price of the latter or vice versa. As a matter of terminology it should be mentioned that this mechanism is called the expectation hypothesis of the term structure, abbreviated EHTS.[9]

[9] See e.g. Hassler and Wolters (1999) and Nautz and Wolters (1999) for recent applications.

Following Wolters and Hassler (1998), causality is implied by the expectation hypothesis. In monetary modelling, the short-term rate is often considered controllable by the authorities. Therefore, the spread should explain the changes in the short-term rates since future changes in the short-term rate should be expected and thus be reflected in the level of current long-term interest rates.[10] On the other hand, it is often argued that the bond rates are determined on the international capital markets limiting the scope for central bank influence. Consequently, the short rates would adjust to the long rates and the spread would help to explicate changes in the long-rate. If both these rates are exogenous with respect to each other however, there will be no stationary spread. Thus, the final decision about causality is a matter of empirical investigation.

Similar to the Fisher relation, the EHTS can be expressed as

$$ec_{eh,t} = i_t^l + \beta_{4,j} i_t^s$$

with $\beta_{4,j} = -1$ and $ec_{eh,t}$ stationary.[11]

A final remark with respect to the Fisher hypothesis and the hypothesis about the term structure has to be made. Disregard for a moment the term structure hypothesis and consider two nominal interest rates referring to bonds of different maturities which are driven by inflation expectations only. Then we would immediately conclude that the difference between these two interest rates would have to be stationary too, if the Fisher hypothesis holds. The reason simply is, that if the inflation rate is integrated of order one, the difference in the inflation expectations (regarding different time horizons) has to be stationary. Looking from this angle, the interest rate spread should therefore also contain information about future inflation. Empirically, it should not only help to explain the path the short-term interest rate moves along, but also the changes in the inflation rate. Of course, the information content depends on

[10] For support of this view see e.g. European Central Bank (2000).

[11] Stationarity of $ec_{eh,t}$ is not compelling evidence for the EHTS to hold. It is merely regarded as a necessary condition.

the time to maturity of the bonds involved. On the contrary, if the spread is not found stationary while the real interest rate computed on the basis of the long rate is, systematic substitution between long-term and short-term credit contracts cannot be observed.

Phillips Curve

Phillips (1958) in an empirical work observed a link between nominal wages and economic activity. Meanwhile, existence of this link has largely been dismissed. Nevertheless, e.g. Juselius (1996) argues that there might be a similar relationship between the *deviations* of real income from the time trend and the inflation rate instead of wages. She indeed finds the trend adjusted output to be non-stationary yet cointegrated with the inflation rate.

Juselius (1996) suggests to cast the Phillips curve hypothesis as

$$ec_{P,t} = y_t + \beta_{5,j}\pi_t + \beta_{6,j}t$$

with $\beta_{5,j} < 0$, $\beta_{6,j} < 0$ in support of that hypothesis. Here it is only included in the list for completeness, because the evidence found so far is rather weak. In the mentioned paper, the results are more in favour of this Phillips curve relation to be a mis-specified money demand relationship where the trend could well be replaced by the monetary aggregate. The real money allegedly shares the deterministic trend with the output measure. Nevertheless, this idea provides a starting point to capture the long-run properties of the dynamics of income growth.

Other Mechanisms

The remaining transmission mechanisms (as well as the Phillips curve) will not play a role in the empirical part of this thesis. They will therefore be mentioned briefly to provide some reasons why monetary policy should have the suggested effects on money holding.[12] First, there is the credit channel which is supposed to work if a certain degree of financial market imperfections limits the access to the capital market for small and medium sized firms. These firms would have to rely on commercial banks as lenders and thus be dependent on the interest rates offered. At the same time, the commercial banks would basically pass on the interest rate set by the central bank , even if they themselves could borrow at lower rates on the international capital markets. As a consequence, if the considers it necessary to raise the re-financing rates, smaller firms' financing costs would rise, and economic activity be dampened. This in turn limits pressure on the prices, which is the ultimate goal of the CB's policy. Empirical tests for the credit channel to work would require more specialized data.

The last channel to be mentioned is the portfolio cost channel. There we assume that economic agents have a whole bundle of assets in their portfolio. If there is an increase in the price of one of them, say, the bond this would raise the value of the sum of all. Increased wealth, however, can be expected to lead to higher demand for money (wealth effect). Thus, an increase in the bond rate which goes along with lower bond prices, should invoke a tendency for lower money holdings. It is interesting to note that at the same time, rising returns on bonds will increase the demand for money (income effect) and provide incentives to buy bonds (substitution effect). The latter is equivalent to decreasing demand for money, leaving the net effect to be determined empirically.[13]

2.3.4 Efficient Estimation and Weak Exogeneity

The previous section stressed the interrelatedness of the various economic hypotheses. This feature has a statistical correspondence known as the concept of

[12] Consider e.g. Meltzer (1995) and Bernanke and Gertler (1995) for an overview of the theory and empirical evidence for the credit channel and portfolio cost channel.

[13] See e.g. Meltzer (1995), Bernanke and Gertler (1995) and the references therein.

efficient estimation. Related concepts are weak, strong, and super exogeneity. This will be reviewed briefly.

The main point of efficient estimation is to exploit all information which is contained in a specific information set. For the purpose at hand, the information set is defined by the series of real money stock, real income, interest rates, and inflation while the focus for efficient estimation is on the long-run parameters β. In other words, the β are the parameters of interest which are to be estimated efficiently. Engle et al. (1983) develop the concept of weak exogeneity providing a concise treatment of efficient estimation. This has been adopted to the cointegration framework by e.g. Ericsson (1998) and Hendry and Mizon (1999). In a nutshell, efficient estimation of the β parameters is only feasible if all those variables are explicitly modelled, whose DGP includes some multiple of $\beta' Y_{t-1}$ as explanatory variables, where we assume the vector Y_t to consist of the series real money stock, real income, interest rates and inflation in our case. As an extreme case, the stationary linear combinations $\beta' Y_{t-1}$ may enter one single equation only. Then, according to e.g. Ericsson (1998) efficient estimation of β can also be conducted in a dynamic single equation error correction framework. In such a situation, all variables except money are called weakly exogenous with respect to the long-run money demand parameters. A possible implication for money demand analysis is to start with a system analysis, and to test whether or not weak exogeneity can be justified for some of the variables. If for example $\beta' Y_t$ does not enter the interest rate equation, interest rates would be called weakly exogenous. In a second step, the long-run money demand relationship could be estimated in a subsystem where the interest rate is not modelled. However, the more cointegration relations are present in a system, losing information about some of the long-run parameters becomes more likely when variables are excluded from the list of endogenous variables.

Strong exogeneity indicates the possibility to forecast a subset Z_t of $Y_t = [V_t' \, Z_t']'$ without having to forecast the strongly exogenous subset V_t of Y_t

simultaneously. The variables in Y_t can then be forecasted conditional on the forecasts for Z_t. Ericsson, Hendry and Mizon (1998), p. 372 definition 3 provide a detailed discussion.

For the current purpose, super exogeneity is more important than strong exogeneity, because it helps to correctly interpret estimation results. Super exogeneity is also defined with respect to some parameters of interest. As before, these are the β coefficients in our case. Super exogeneity of the subset Z_t with respect to β requires weak exogeneity and invariance. Loosely speaking, invariance is a property of the parameters of the conditional model that is the partial, or conditional, model for V_t. If these parameters are invariant to a class of interventions affecting Z_t, then they are regarded as invariant (see again Ericsson, Hendry and Mizon (1998), p. 373 for details). Adding weak exogeneity to the invariance property leads to super exogeneity.

Unfortunately, the class of interventions is not well defined. In a money demand analysis Ericsson, Hendry and Prestwich (1998), for example consider intervention dummies in the interest rate equation and conjecture invariance from the fact that they are irrelevant for the estimates of the long-run money demand relationship.

The super exogeneity concept can be regarded as an econometric implementation of the request for a stable money demand function expressed by Meltzer (1963). In particular, he asks for a money demand function which "can be shown to have existed under differing institutional arrangements, changes in the social and political environment . . ." (op. cit. p. 222).

For the EMU experiment, the Lucas critique (Lucas, 1976) certainly is the most important. Its basic message is the impossibility to use an econometric model for policy analysis, if implementing the policy would change the structure the model was attempting to capture (Ericsson, Hendry and Mizon, 1998). Thus, if agents chose V_t on grounds of expectations about Z_t, then the model parameters for V_t (λ_1) will depend on the parameter set for the marginal model for Z_t, denoted λ_2. In contrast, super exogeneity of Z_t

with respect to the parameter of interest (λ_1 in this case) interrupts this link. Hence, shocks or interventions affecting λ_2 would not spill over to the set λ_1.

Out of the two ways Ericsson, Hendry and Mizon (1998) suggest to test for super exogeneity, the second will be of some relevance for chapter 4 and is therefore re-stated here. The instruction reads (emphasis as in the original):

> Develop the marginal model until its parameters are empirically constant. For instance model the way in which λ_2 varies over time [by adding dummies, C.M.] . . . Then, test for the significance of those dummies . . . Their insignificance in the *conditional* model demonstrates the invariance of λ_1 to the modelled interventions, whereas their significance shows the dependence of λ_1 on λ_2. (op. cit. p. 376)

In chapter 4 (on France) we compare two fully specified models with one of them modelling the change of the presumable policy variables. This comparison will reveal strong dependence of the long-run parameters of interest on the changes occurring in the policy variables. Interestingly, the alleged shift in the economic environment corresponds to one of the examples Ericsson, Hendry and Mizon (1998) give, where the Lucas critique is likely to apply. They presume changes in the exchange rate regime to violate pre-existing exogeneity conditions. This is exactly what can be observed in France around 1986/87.

Next, inversion of an econometric equation should be mentioned. Inversion means, that although the demand for money is derived from the income, price and transaction or income velocity, macro-modellers often turn around the equation and thereby, conditioning on the money stock, derive expressions for the price level. If, however, the coefficients of this inverted equation are calculated on the basis of estimators for the original causal ordering, then the derived coefficients may be badly biased. Again, this bias occurs, if the determinants of the demand for money are not super exogenous with respect to the coefficients of the demand for money function.[14]

This condition has interesting implications. As for example Juselius (1999) notes, weak exogeneity of the inflation rate with respect to the demand for money "generally flaws" the claim that excess money holdings spur inflation (op. cit. p. 34). Inflation is considered not weakly exogenous w.r.t. the parameters of the demand for money function, if the respective error correction term enters the inflation equation. Thus, while there might be a desire to extract the long-run demand for money function in order to conduct empirical macro-modelling experiments, this idea is likely to go astray if another popular conviction finds support. This conviction is excess money being responsible for future inflation.

To sum up, even though super exogeneity seems difficult to establish, a convenient tool exists to establish when it does not apply. This concept is weak exogeneity. Therefore, focussing on weak exogeneity yields interesting insights even if the more complex concepts cannot be employed.

2.3.5 Identification Issues

Foreshadowing some of the results of the study on France, a few remarks are in order with respect to identification of demand functions. Ever since the comments by Working (1927) the issue of statistically identifying demand or supply curves has been discussed extensively. By now, a summary thereof can be found in standard economic textbooks such as Mankiw (1994).

A basic difficulty underlying the identification problem in the more recent literature is that supply as well as demand usually depend on the same set of parameters like price and quantity. Early approaches only knew of long-term interest rate (and income) as money demand determinants. At the same time

[14] For a formal treatment of this issue see Hendry (1985), Ericsson (1992), Engle and Hendry (1993), Ericsson, Hendry and Mizon (1998), Ericsson (1998).

money supply would not hinge on long-term interest rates, and hence identification becomes straightforward. That situation has changed, and without further assumptions about the characteristics of demand and supply, all observations are likely to be found evenly spread around the intersection of supply and demand curves. In that case, the observations will be non-informative for both demand and supply functions.

The framework of money demand analysis usually holds that the supply of money is under control of the central bank and hence potentially orthogonal to the determinants of the demand for money function. If however, this assumption is invalid, the question of what relation dominates becomes an open issue again. To see this point, re-consider the arguments in the demand for money function. There are the interest rates and inflation. Commercial banks will have an incentive to expand their lending activities if they can charge higher interest rates.[15] This of course, is opposite to the incentives the interest rate provides for the agents demanding money. Therefore, looking at the money or credit supply of commercial banks the same set of variables which supposedly describes the demand for money, potentially yields information on the supply of money function. Moreover, as Bofinger et al. (1998) show, the actual policy of the central bank can determine what relationship is more stable, demand or supply. Naturally, the more robust a functional relationship with respect to shocks, the more frequently the corresponding observations will be found close to this relation. In particular, the distinction between monetary targeting and interest rate targeting is important. In the case of France, it will be argued that the central bank conducted a policy best understood as a form of interest rate targeting. As a result, no stable money demand will be found, but a stable supply of money function instead.

A vector β_i that yields a stationary combination of the variables real money, real income and at least one out of the variables interest rates and

[15] See e.g. Bofinger, Reischle and Schächter (1998) and Nautz (2000) on the supply side of the money market.

inflation can only be regarded as a long-run demand for money function if two conditions are fulfilled. The first of them is embodied in the parameter properties discussed in the context of equation (2.11). Thus, the signs on these coefficients will tell whether the respective relationship may yield an interpretation as a money demand function. The second condition requires at least one of the equations for the variables entering the money demand function to show a significant adjustment to the lagged long-run error ($ec_{m,t-1}$). This is, because the demand for money should be sensitive to deviations of the actual stock of money from its long-run equilibrium value.

A similar requirement also holds with respect to the other potential cointegration relationships. According to the Granger representation theorem, at least one of the variables involved has to feature error correcting behaviour in order to qualify the combination in question for a long-run equilibrium relation. As a counter example one might consider Brand and Cassola (2000) who claim to have found a stationary interest rate spread but are unable to establish that either of the interest rates systematically adjusts to the long-run error which becomes apparent from their Table 7 where they test for weak exogeneity.

A Few Remarks Concerning Rank Determination

In empirical applications, the rank of β cannot be told beforehand. The decision concerning that has naturally to rest on statistical evidence. This invokes some preliminary considerations regarding the setup of the model. It has to be decided how many lagged endogenous variables enter the model, and what deterministic parts are included. The latter decision will affect both power of the test and the distribution of the test statistic. The former is likely to have implications for the power of the tests too.

To see these points, first consider equation (2.6) again. We would have to include a vector of constants in the DGP not only to guarantee that the innovations ε_t will indeed be zero on average, but also to make sure that the trending behaviour of income and real money can be accounted for. For these two variables one usually assumes that the constant term can enter the non-stationary part of the DGP. It may thereby generate a linear time trend, while this should not be the case for inflation and interest rates. As pointed out before, the test statistics depend on the choice of deterministic parts in the model, and so do the power properties of the tests. Knowing e.g. that no trend term is present, is useful information one would like to take into account when testing hypotheses. Unfortunately the standard system tests do not allow for different definitions of the constant terms in different equations. Therefore, it is worthwhile to consider also a subsystem made of these three variables only and to impose the appropriate restrictions on the constant term.

The same conclusion can be drawn from another fact, namely that there is a general tendency to end up with reduced power of cointegration tests the more parameters the model requires to be estimated. There are two basic sources of parameters. The first is the number of variables in the system (dimension) and the second is the number of lagged endogenous variables (order) needed to yield satisfactory residual properties. Here too, it might be helpful to consider subsystems of the full model. This reduces the dimension of the model and palliates the curse of dimensionality. The reduction in dimension could go as far as considering uni-variate time series. If for example one would like to test the non-stationarity hypothesis of the interest rate spread, subject to the condition that $\beta_{4,l} = -1$, the error correction term $ec_{eh,t}$ could be calculated directly and a standard unit root test performed.

In essence, the considerations outlined above provide a blueprint for system cointegration analysis of the demand for money function. The following chapters will apply this framework together with appropriate adjustments due to the special problems dealt with there.

2.4 Summary: Econometric Analysis and Economic Interpretation

In section 2.3.3 we have named a set of four, possibly stationary relations, but since we refrain from investigating cointegration relationships having a deterministic linear trend term, the list reduces to three entries.[16] Before turning to testing strategies, in the light of the hypothesized individual cointegration relationships the matrix β needs to be scrutinized.

The rank of the matrix has been said to be r, where $0 \leq r \leq 4$ if all five series individually are found I(1). The primary task is to identify the corresponding r linearly independent relationships. The previous paragraph suggested three of them. Provided that the demand for money function exists, we will look at the implications for the demand for money if all or one of the others are also present. The first insight is provided by the fact that linear combinations of cointegrating relationships will again yield cointegrating relationships. Therefore, if e.g. both interest rates individually do cointegrate with the inflation rate, then there must also be a cointegrating relationship between the interest rates. We are going to distinguish four cases. In each of them money demand is supposed to exist:

(i) no further cointegrating relationship can be found.
(ii) one interest rate (usually the long-term) cointegrates with inflation
(iii) the interest rate spread is stationary
(iv) the real interest rates (as well as the spread) are stationary.

The starting point for the following argumentation is that in the system context we add a further requirement to the definition of a demand for money

[16] Some might argue this to be too restrictive, yet in empirical praxis the more general approach tends to produce curious and nonsense results if a trend in the cointegrating relationship is allowed for. In Juselius (1996) for example, there is no statistical hint provided to distinguish between the Phillips relation and a possibly mis-specified money demand relation. Thus, more thorough investigations of this feature would be desirable.

function. This function has not only to yield an interpretation as a demand for money function, but it also has to be unique. Thus, equation (2.11) will not be considered an identified money demand function, if the Fisher hypothesis holds (case (ii)). The reason is that it could likewise be expressed as the linear combination $(m-p)_t = \beta_{2,1}y_t + \beta_{3,1}i_t^l + \beta_{4,1}i_t^s + e_{m^*,t}$ (the true long-run money demand) and $i_t^l - \beta_{5,2}\pi_t = ec_{F,t}$. In other words, some of the effects we might observe inflation and the bond rate to have on real money growth cannot be considered direct upshots of money market disequilibria.

The case (i) corresponds to the standard situation one faces in single equation money demand analyses. In the system analysis, it implies the rank of β to be one. The estimates will say something about the significance of individual variables for the money demand equation, thereby validating the hypothesis itself.

If (ii) holds, then the money demand relation reduces by one variable because two of the arguments do form a stationary linear relationship themselves. That means, one would observe the general money demand function as of (2.11) to be a linear combination of two independent relationships, namely the combination of the real interest rate and the true long-run money demand. Therefore, either the interest rate or inflation would have to be dropped to ensure uniqueness of the money demand representation. It is interesting to note that econometrically, it would not matter what variable to drop although from an economists' point of view, there might be a preference for removing the inflation rate.

The situation (iii) similarly requires to either disregard the long-term or the short-term interest rate in equation (2.11) to yield a valid representation of the money demand equation. In addition, due to the lack of the Fisher relation one would have to acknowledge, that the future path of the long-term interest rate would be based on the expectation about the development of the short-term interest rate. In other words, it would be determined by the CB policy in the long-run.

For the case (iv) not only one but two variables would have to be dropped from (2.11). Only that way allows to separate the impacts of different long-run relations on the money growth path. Consistent economic reasoning would lead to the conclusion that both long-term and short-term interest rates are driven by the expectation about future inflation rates. Thus, the short-term rate in particular would not be determined by the CB policy.

To sum up the above discussion, system analysis ensures that the money demand function can be clearly separated from other likewise important economic relationships. These serve as complementary items for the whole picture characterizing the long-run interactions of the variables and thus the whole monetary system of policy transmission.

3

Unit Root Tests for Time Series with a Structural Break

3.1 Introduction

Economists usually take the view that innovations with certain characteristics push the variables along the path which is laid out for them. Occasionally, exogenous events which are not member of the usual class of innovations hit the economy and change some basic features like the mean of the process.

In the context of European monetary policy analysis there are two basic situations in which there is clearly a scope for considering breaks in the series. The first is institutional changes made in preparation for the Euro currency in each country.[1] Amongst those is the tie of the national currencies to the European Currency Unit (ECU) ending the nominal adjustment to real imbalances between countries. An example thereof is dealt with in chapter 4, where the expected depreciation of the French Franc versus the Deutschmark is subjected to a unit root analysis. The second situation is EMU itself, which despite all convergence efforts might cause abrupt adjustments by economic agents and might therefore cause shifts in variables under investigation. This latter situation would probably become more relevant after some time how-

[1] See e.g. Juselius (1998) who claims that there was a structural shift in economic time series across Europe due to liberalization of capital markets, which too can be viewed as an outcome of the harmonization process. See also Candelon and Lütkepohl (2000) opposed to that hypothesis.

ever, because the empirical analysis requires some information after the event to become feasible.

As another example let us consider the east European countries after the introduction of the market economy. After an initial shock some of them entered a long lasting process of recovery. That is why a smooth transition to the new mean might be a good description of the underlying data generating process. Despite such hassles the researcher might still wish to test for unit roots in a time series without splitting the sample and performing separate tests on the sub-samples before and after the break point. It can be hoped that exploiting all information jointly leads to more powerful tests.

This chapter considers two models designed for coping with the problems arising when testing for unit roots under these circumstances. A shift in the mean is assumed to occur at a known point in time and is clearly separated from the possibly non-stationary part of the process. The common feature of both models is that they also allow for smooth, even nonlinear transition functions to the new mean.

The testing strategy to be pursued here, is to estimate all deterministic components (intercept, trend, seasonal dummies, the shift) first and then to apply a Dickey-Fuller (ADF) type test to the residual series.

This chapter of the thesis draws on Lütkepohl, Müller and Saikkonen (2001), henceforth LMS, where the second of the two models described in the following has been proposed. There is a shift of focus towards computational issues, model checking and examples, however. Therefore, no formal proof is provided for the properties of the estimators and the distribution of the test statistics. However, they can be found in LMS. In line with LMS it is generally assumed that the break point is known. Knowledge of the timing is generally seen as useful information that should be taken into account when testing for unit roots. Later on a few remarks will touch upon a situation where this is not the case. The reader is encouraged to apply the tests her- or himself by making use of the *GAUSS* procedures available at the KOF web page.[2] The capability of these programs and procedures is described in some detail. Therefore this chapter might be useful for all those who want to apply the tests in practice.

The structure of this study is as follows. In the next section the general setup is presented and in section 3.3 the tests are considered. Extensions of the original problem are discussed in section 3.4, some examples are presented in section 3.5 and finally, conclusions are drawn in section 3.6.

3.2 Models for Time Series with Level Shifts

In the following, two models are considered that allow for a shift in the mean of the DGP. The first has been proposed by Saikkonen and Lütkepohl (2001) (S&L in the following) and the second goes back to LMS. In order to point out that both models work with various shift functions the general framework is provided first, and only afterwards will three specific examples of possible shift functions be introduced.

Model 1 (the S&L DGP)

$$y_t = \mu_0 + \mu_1 t + f_t(\vartheta)'\gamma + x_t, \quad t = 1, 2, ... \tag{3.1}$$

In model 1 the scalars μ_0 and μ_1, the $(m \times 1)$ vector ϑ and the $(k \times 1)$ vector γ are unknown parameters and $f_t(\vartheta)$ is a $(k \times 1)$ vector of deterministic sequences depending on ϑ. The x_t is a sequence of unobservable stochastic variables which is assumed to have finite order autoregressive (AR) representation

$$a(L)x_t = \varepsilon_t \tag{3.2}$$

where $a(L) = 1 - a_1 L - \cdots - a_{p+1}L^{p+1}$ is a polynomial in the lag operator L with $x_t L^j = x_{t-j}$. Moreover for the innovations sequence ε_t it holds $\varepsilon_t \sim$

[2] KOF: Konjunkturforschungsstelle (Institute for Business Cycle Research at the Federal Technical University Zürich, Switzerland) `http://www.kof.ch/~cmueller/GAUSSprocs/unitroot`.

$iid(0, \sigma^2)$. For simplicity it is assumed that a suitable number of pre-sample values of the observed series y_t is available. Obviously, if the DGP of x_t has a unit root, the same is true for y_t. To cast the unit root hypothesis in a more convenient way, S&L rewrite (3.2) as

$$(1 - \rho L)b(L)x_t = \varepsilon_t \tag{3.3}$$

with $b(L) = 1 - b_1 L - \cdots - b_p L^p$ having all its roots outside the unit circle. The test now focuses on the value of $|\rho|$ which has to be smaller than 1 if y_t was indeed stationary. In this model the shape of $f_t(\vartheta)$ defines the shift of y_t to its new mean level. This shift could be a once-off change (step) in the constant term μ_0 or a more general, maybe nonlinear function. Two of the latter kind are suggested in section 3.4.2.

The second model accommodates smooth transition to a new level even if the initial shift is an abrupt one.

Model 2 (the LMS DGP)

$$b(L)y_t = \mu_0 + \mu_1 t + f_t(\vartheta)'\gamma + \nu_t, \quad t = 1, 2, ... \tag{3.4}$$

Here, the error term ν_t is assumed to be an AR process of order 1

$$\nu_t = \rho \nu_{t-1} + \varepsilon_t \tag{3.5}$$

with $-1 < \rho \leq 1$ and ε_t as before. If $\rho = 1$ the series y_t has a unit root. In this model the move to the new mean level is given by $b(L)^{-1} f_t(\vartheta)'\gamma$ which will generate a smooth transition even for 'steep' shapes of $f_t(\vartheta)$. Introducing the superscript i to denote a particular shift function, we let for example[3]

$$f_t^{(1)}(\vartheta) = d_t := \begin{cases} 0, & t < T_1 \\ 1, & t \geq T_1 \end{cases}$$

and define $b(L)^{-1} = 1 + \sum_{i=1}^{\infty} \alpha_i L^i$, then for $t \geq T_1$ one obtains

$$b(L)^{-1} f_t^{(1)}(\vartheta) = 1 + \sum_{i=1}^{t-T_1} \alpha_i.$$

[3] Other examples of possible shift functions are given in the formulas on page 48.

Thus, depending on the parameter values of $b(L)$, the initial jump from zero to one in period T_1 will spread out over the following periods resulting in a gradual adjustment of the mean level of y_t. Figure 3.10 on page 80 illustrates this feature. There, the left hand columns plot the rather steep realizations of $f_t^{(\cdot)}(\vartheta)'\gamma$ while the panels to the right demonstrate how these shifts are smoothed. The corresponding values of ϑ are listed in Table 3.6 (group 3, UA Money). Even more flexibility can be accomplished by appropriate definitions of $f_t(\vartheta)$. A further advantage of this model is that its estimation is quite simple even for nonlinear shift functions because it results in a least squares problem.

Finally, the shift function entering the processes has to be continuous in ϑ and must approach a limiting value when the number of observations increases. In particular, they must not generate a trend. These assumptions are needed for the test statistics reported below to be valid. A formal set of assumptions and discussion thereof can be obtained from S&L and LMS.

3.2.1 Estimation of Nuisance Parameters

In the preceding section it has been argued that the unit root hypothesis is equivalent to the hypothesis $\rho = 1$ against the alternative $|\rho| < 1$. The basic idea is to estimate all nuisance parameters under a situation close to the null hypothesis (local alternative) or under the null, and then to perform a test on the parameter ρ. This approach is similar to that in Elliott, Rothenberg and Stock (1996) and Hwang and Schmidt (1996) who do not necessarily assume validity of the null hypothesis but work with appropriate local alternatives to be specified by the analyst. Thus, suppose that the process y_t is nearly integrated, so that

$$\rho = \bar{\rho}_T = 1 + \frac{c}{T} \tag{3.6}$$

where $c \leq 0$ is a fixed real number, and T the number of observations, then for **model 1** one finds from (3.3)

$$x_t = \bar{\rho}_T x_{t-1} + b(L)^{-1}\varepsilon_t$$

and for **model 2** from (3.5)

$$\nu_t = \bar{\rho}_T \nu_{t-1} + \varepsilon_t.$$

For estimating the model parameters an appropriate empirical counterpart of c, $\bar{c}$, is chosen to yield a $\bar{\rho}_T$, and the filter $(1-\bar{\rho}_T L)$ is applied to the model.[4]

Defining the matrices

$$\begin{aligned}
Y_t &= [y_1 \ (y_2 - \bar{\rho}_T y_1) \ \cdots \ (y_T - \bar{\rho}_T y_{T-1})]' \\
Z_{1,t} &= [1 \ (2-\bar{\rho}_T) \ \cdots \ (T-\bar{\rho}_T)]' \\
Z_{2,t}(\vartheta) &= \begin{bmatrix} 1 & 1-\bar{\rho}_T & \cdots & 1-\bar{\rho}_T \\ f_1(\vartheta) & f_2(\vartheta) - \bar{\rho}_T f_1(\vartheta) & \cdots & f_T(\vartheta) - \bar{\rho}_T f_{T-1}(\vartheta) \end{bmatrix}' \\
Z_t(\vartheta) &= [Z_{1,t} \ Z_{2,t}(\vartheta)] \\
V_t &= [Y_t L \ \cdots \ Y_t L^p]' \\
W_t(\vartheta) &= [V_t \ Z_t(\vartheta)]
\end{aligned}$$

model 1 can be re-written as

$$Y_t = Z_t(\vartheta)\Phi + U_t \tag{3.7}$$

and **model 2** amounts to

$$Y_t = W_t(\vartheta)\beta + \mathcal{E}_t. \tag{3.8}$$

The parameter vectors are $\Phi' = [\mu_1, \mu_0, \gamma']$ and $\beta' = [b', \mu_1, \mu_0, \gamma']$, while $U_t = [u_1, u_2, \cdots, u_T]'$ and $\mathcal{E}_t = [\varepsilon_1, \varepsilon_2, \cdots, \varepsilon_T]'$ are vectors of error terms. Moreover for u_t one finds

$$u_t = x_t - \bar{\rho}_T x_{t-1} \tag{3.9}$$

[4] The *GAUSS* programs work with the default $\bar{c} = 0$. Though not being recommended, this value can be altered to accomplish point optimal tests in the spirit of Elliott et al. (1996) who discuss some possible choices of $\bar{c}$. The estimation approach is therefore presented for the more general case.

which is asymptotically equivalent to $u_t = b(L)^{-1}\varepsilon_t$. The error term in (3.8), $\mathcal{E}_t = [\varepsilon_1, \ldots, \varepsilon_T]'$ is given by

$$\varepsilon_t = \nu_t - \bar{\rho}_T \nu_{t-1}.$$

Finally, estimation of the parameters Φ and β is done by first guessing a value for ϑ from the admissible parameter space and then applying OLS to (3.8). The first model is computationally more challenging. In S&L a GLS procedure is described. For the following examples a *GAUSS* procedure is used that iteratively estimates Φ and b jointly.

The parameter estimates are then used to calculate the following objective functions. In the case of **model 1** it is given by

$$Q(\Phi, \vartheta, b) = (Y_t - Z_t(\vartheta)\Phi)' \, \Sigma(b)^{-1} \, (Y_t - Z_t(\vartheta)\Phi)' \tag{3.10}$$

where $\sigma^2 \Sigma(b) = Cov\left(b(L)^{-1}\varepsilon_t\right)$ is the variance-covariance matrix of U_t. It is used as a weighting matrix which should account for the autocorrelation in u_t. For **model 2** the objective function is given by

$$S(\beta, \vartheta) = (Y_t - W_t(\vartheta)\beta)' \, (Y_t - W_t(\vartheta)\beta) \tag{3.11}$$

with $\tilde{\beta} = (W_t(\vartheta)'W_t(\vartheta))^{-1} \, W_t(\vartheta)'Y_t$ being the solution to the minimization problem.

In the next step, another value of ϑ is chosen and the procedure is repeated until the objective functions are minimized. In the examples grid search over a wide range of possible ϑ values and hill climbing are applied to find the minimal Q and S. The corresponding values of ϑ serve as estimates. For seasonal data, seasonal dummies can be included in the matrix Z after applying the filter $(1 - \bar{\rho}_T L)$ as before.

To learn more about the properties of the procedures the reader is referred to L&S and LMS.

3.3 The Test Statistics

Turning to the actual tests of the unit root hypotheses, adjustment for the estimated nuisance parameters will be made first in order to remove from y_t all deterministic components (μ_0, $\mu_1 t$, $f_t(\vartheta)'\gamma$, seasonal dummies) of the DGP. The resulting residual series will then be used for testing for a unit root in a Dickey-Fuller test manner.

For **Model 1** we thus obtain

$$\hat{x}_t = y_t - \hat{\mu}_0 - \hat{\mu}_1 t - f_t(\hat{\vartheta})'\hat{\gamma} \tag{3.12}$$

and for **Model 2**

$$\tilde{\nu}_t = \tilde{b}(L)y_t - \tilde{\mu}_0 - \tilde{\mu}_1 t - f_t(\tilde{\vartheta})'\tilde{\gamma} \tag{3.13}$$

which will be plugged into auxiliary regression models

$$\hat{x}_t = \rho_{SL}\hat{x}_{t-1} + u_t^* \tag{3.14}$$

and similarly,

$$\tilde{\nu}_t = \rho_{alt}\tilde{\nu}_{t-1} + \varepsilon_t^* \tag{3.15}$$

where $\hat{x}_0 = \tilde{\nu}_0 = 0$. From (3.9) one knows that if $\hat{x}_t$ is replaced by x_t in (3.14) the covariance matrix of the errors is $\sigma^2\Sigma(b)$. Thus, letting $\hat{X}_t = [\hat{x}_1, \hat{x}_2, \cdots, \hat{x}_T]'$, $\hat{X}_{t-1} = [\hat{x}_0, \hat{x}_1, \cdots, \hat{x}_{T-1}]'$, $\underline{\tilde{\nu}}_t = [\tilde{\nu}_1, \tilde{\nu}_2, \cdots, \tilde{\nu}_T]'$ and $\underline{\tilde{\nu}}_{t-1} = [\tilde{\nu}_0, \tilde{\nu}_1, \cdots, \tilde{\nu}_{T-1}]'$ the resulting estimates become, for

Model 1

$$\hat{\rho}_{SL} = \left(\hat{X}_{t-1}'\Sigma(\hat{b})^{-1}\hat{X}_{t-1}\right)^{-1}\hat{X}_{t-1}'\Sigma(\hat{b})^{-1}\hat{X}_t$$

with error variance estimate

$$\hat{\sigma}_u^2 = T^{-1}\left(\hat{X}_t - \hat{\rho}_{SL}\hat{X}_{t-1}\right)'\Sigma(\hat{b})^{-1}\left(\hat{X}_t - \hat{\rho}_{SL}\hat{X}_{t-1}\right)$$

and for **Model 2**

$$\tilde{\rho}_{alt} = \left(\underline{\tilde{\nu}}_{t-1}'\underline{\tilde{\nu}}_{t-1}\right)^{-1}\underline{\tilde{\nu}}_{t-1}'\underline{\tilde{\nu}}_t$$

with error variance estimate

$$\tilde{\sigma}_e^2 = T^{-1}\left(\underline{\tilde{\nu}}_t - \tilde{\rho}_{alt}\underline{\tilde{\nu}}_{t-1}\right)'\left(\underline{\tilde{\nu}}_t - \tilde{\rho}_{alt}\underline{\tilde{\nu}}_{t-1}\right).$$

Finally, the 't-test' like test statistics are derived for

Model 1 as

$$\hat{\tau}_{SL} = \left(\hat{X}_{t-1}'\Sigma(\hat{b})^{-1}\hat{X}_{t-1}\right)^{\frac{1}{2}}\left(\hat{\rho}_{SL} - 1\right)/\hat{\sigma}_u$$

and for **Model 2** as

$$\tilde{\tau}_{alt} = \left(\underline{\tilde{\nu}}_{t-1}'\underline{\tilde{\nu}}_{t-1}\right)^{\frac{1}{2}}\left(\tilde{\rho}_{alt} - 1\right)/\tilde{\sigma}_e.$$

The limiting distributions are given in S&L and in LMS. In addition, Lanne, Lütkepohl and Saikkonen (1999) (LLS in the following) provide critical values which are also used in Tables 3.3 to 3.5 below.[5]

The limiting distribution is the same not only for these two test statistics, but it is also the same as Elliott et al. (1996) obtained for their t-statistic in a model whose deterministic part contains a mean value and linear trend terms only. The limiting null distribution, obtained by setting $c = 0$ is free of unknown nuisance parameters but depends on the quantity $\bar{c}$. Following LLS, we chose $\bar{c} = 0$ because only for this case, their simulations indicated that the nominal and empirical levels of significance coincide satisfactorily.

Finally, note that if we want to impose the restriction that there is no linear trend term, so that $\mu_1 = 0$, the above tests remain essentially the same except for the limiting distribution which then is the same as in a model without any deterministic terms. The trend term is not included in the regression model in this case.

[5] The critical values are reported in LLS, Table 2, rows 16 to 20 with and rows 1 to 5 without a trend entering the DGP.

3.4 Flexible Shifts, Computational Issues and Extensions

It has been mentioned before that the second model would result in rather smooth shifts even if the shock occurs in one period only and is zero afterwards. Nevertheless, the investigator might be interested in allowing for even more flexible transitions. In any case, the question which model to use has to be answered empirically. In the *GAUSS* routines provided, three types of shifts are considered.

$$\text{Type 1} \qquad f_t^{(1)}(\vartheta) = d_t$$

$$\text{Type 2} \qquad f_t^{(2)}(\vartheta) = \begin{cases} 0 & t < T_1, \\ 1 - exp\{-\vartheta(t - T_1 + 1)\} & t \geq T_1, \end{cases} \qquad 0 < \vartheta$$

$$\text{Type 3} \qquad f_t^{(3)}(\vartheta) = \left[\frac{d_t}{1 - \vartheta L}, \frac{d_{t-1}}{1 - \vartheta L}\right]', \quad \vartheta \neq 0, \ |\vartheta| < 1 \qquad (3.16)$$

For each type it is assumed that $\vartheta \in \Theta$. These functions are the same as suggested by S&L and will alternatively be labelled simple shift, exponential, and rational shifts or jumps.

Choosing the right model for a time series to be investigated involves a number of problems. First, the definitions of the shift functions provided below are chosen such that the first impact is visible in the same period it is supposed to occur, that is in T_1. Previous results sometimes found that a model that involves type 3 shift functions exhibits a better fit (measured in terms of the objective function), when T_1 is set to the period just before the period of intervention. This outcome is owed to the two-dimensional shift where one of the columns takes care of the stochastic shock of the previous period. It is then up to the researcher to decide upon the correct choice of T_1. A wide range of specification checks will be discussed below.

Secondly, the choice of the parameter space requires some attention. For Type 2 it is obvious that values larger than zero can be considered only. Theoretically, on the other hand, infinite values are even possible too. Figure 3.1 depicts the exponential and rational shift functions with two values for ϑ

each, which give an impression of what transitions might be captured. The values are chosen to come close to the limits of the parameter space which are relevant for empirical purposes. It becomes clear that values of ϑ in the neighbourhood of zero are suitable for modelling simple shift functions with the type 3 shift functions while this is the case for large values for the type 2 functions. Rather slow adjustment to the new level occurs when $|\vartheta|$ is around one (type 3) or around zero (type 2).

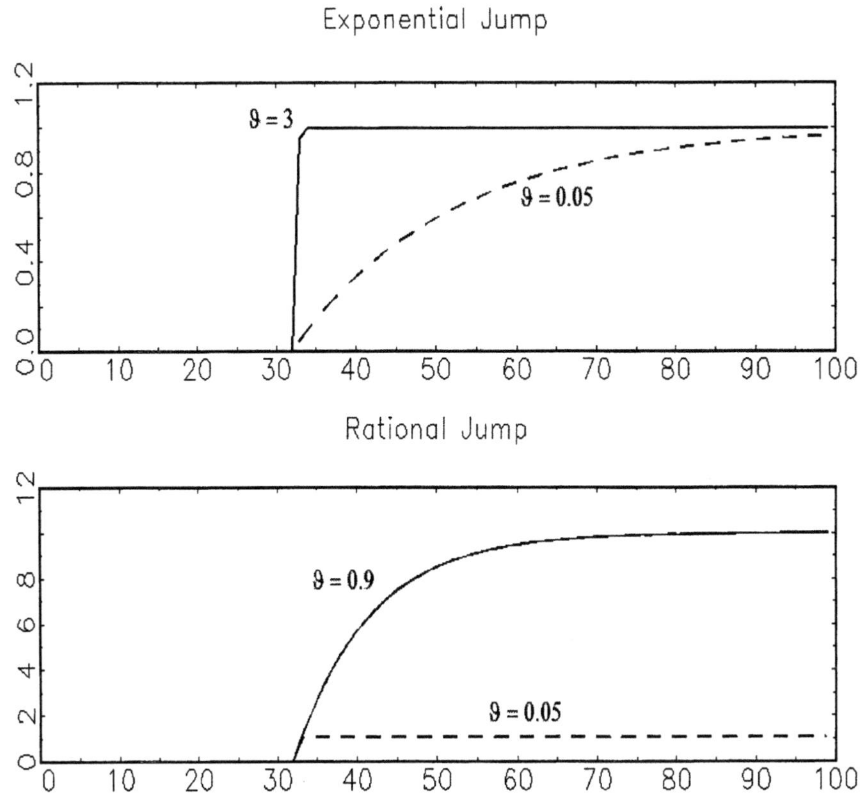

Lower panel: The graph displays the values for $\gamma' f_t^{(3)}(\vartheta)$ with $\gamma' = [1\ 0]$.

Figure 3.1. Examples of Shift Functions

Since we have $\lim_{\vartheta \to \infty} f_t^{(2)}(\vartheta) = \lim_{\vartheta \to 0} \left([1 \;\; 0] f_t^{(3)}(\vartheta) \right) = f_t^{(1)}$, for estimation, certain restrictions on the parameter space appear appropriate. The researcher should keep in mind the assumption that the shift to be considered must not increase without limit. Although each shift function proposed complies with this restriction for $(t - T_1) \to \infty$, in limited samples this is not necessarily the case. If so, care has to be taken, because the estimated shift might translate into a trend, which might not be desirable.

With respect to the type 3 jump a further note should be made with respect to the parameter space covering zero to minus one. It is generally recommended not to consider values smaller than zero, because there is a chance to pick up seasonal patterns which is not necessarily a feature of a shift.

Finally, the precision of the grid is to be decided upon, too. Occasionally there will be situations where too rough a grid does not give satisfactory results. In most cases the capability of the computer will set the limit. This is particularly true for model 1 which involves some estimation effort. To obtain results very fast another optimization algorithm is offered. Such a situation might arise when the minimum of the objective functions is looked for not only over the grid of possible ϑ at some T_1 but also over a range of prospective T_1.[6]

To sum up, depending on the data under investigation, there might be reasons to limit the admissible parameter space of ϑ and to use other optimization procedures than grid search. The program's default values are $\vartheta^{(2)}_{min} = 0.05$, $\vartheta^{(2)}_{max} = 6$, step length: 0.05, $\vartheta^{(3)}_{min} = 0.05$, $\vartheta^{(3)}_{max} = 0.995$, step length: 0.002 and can be altered by the researcher.[7] If the hill climbing pro-

[6] see Saikkonen and Lütkepohl (2001) and the discussion below. Sometimes, the time saved may amount to several minutes.

[7] The *GAUSS* code implemented in *JMulTi1.0beta* optimizes over $\vartheta^{(2)}_{min} = 0.05$, $\vartheta^{(2)}_{max} = 3$, step length: 0.01, $\vartheta^{(3)}_{min} = 0.00$, $\vartheta^{(3)}_{max} = 0.8$, step length: 0.01 and cannot be adjusted as yet.

cedure is applied, the initial step lengths are the 1/100 multiple of the step lengths for the grid search.

3.4.1 Model Checking

Having fitted the model, one might wonder if the model choice was a good one. This question involves a number of factors. There is the range of ϑ, the number of lags (p), the timing of the jump (which is in this case assumed to be known), the type of the shift and, of course, the kind of model (either 1 or 2).

We suggest to proceed in the following way.[8] First, the appropriate lag length should be determined. In principle, the program is capable of looking for the optimal ϑ over a large range of possible lag lengths.[9] The typical outcome is the maximal p allowed for because there is no penalty for overparametrisation in the objective functions (3.10) and (3.11). The graphical output provides a rough measure of the properties of the estimated error terms $\hat{\varepsilon}_t, \hat{u}_t^*, \hat{\varepsilon}_t^*$ for **model 1** and of the estimated errors $\tilde{\varepsilon}_t, \tilde{\varepsilon}_t^*$ for **model 2**. In addition to their values, the estimated autocorrelation functions together with the $\pm 2/\sqrt{T}$ confidence bands are plotted. From what has been said before, it should be apparent that absence of autocorrelation in the $\hat{\varepsilon}_t$ and $\tilde{\varepsilon}_t$ residuals should indicate a good fit of model 1 and 2 respectively while the same properties for the error terms $\hat{\varepsilon}_t^*, \tilde{\varepsilon}_t^*$ imply a good fit of the auxiliary regression on which the test statistic is based.[10] The presence of autocorrelation can be assumed if the confidence bands are crossed too often. Of course, more formal tests could be used to confirm this evaluation. An alternative approach to model selection is the application of lag order selection criteria.

[8] All of the following suggestions are implemented in the program.

[9] However, it is not possible to omit lags.

[10] To check the relevant derivation see that $\hat{u}_t^*$ is the residual of (3.14), $\hat{\varepsilon}_t^*$ is obtained by filtering $\hat{u}_t^*$ with $\hat{b}(L)^{-1}$. The $\hat{\varepsilon}_t$ are obtained in the same way, starting with the series $\hat{u}_t$ of (3.7) to be filtered. In case of model 2, $\tilde{\varepsilon}_t$ and $\tilde{\varepsilon}_t^*$ corresponds to (3.8) and (3.15) respectively.

The user might also wish to know to what extent the choice of ϑ influences the value of the test statistic. This question can be addressed in two ways. First, when choosing the grid search optimization method, the ϑ corresponding to either the maximal or minimal test statistic can be computed instead of minimizing the objective function. Using the grid search option, a plot of all values of the objective function as well as the related test statistic depending on ϑ over the grid is provided. These graphs can be used to assess whether or not the test outcome is robust against neighbouring values of ϑ. This could be especially informative if it turns out, that the objective function is minimal for implausible values of ϑ. Moreover, there have been found examples where the objective function takes extreme values in either direction, particularly close to the boundaries of the parameter space. Under these circumstances it might be desirable to re-estimate the model with restricted parameters in order to arrive at a satisfactory model specification. An example is given in Figure 3.12 on page 82.

Finally, the transition functions implied by the choice of ϑ and γ are displayed together with the time series they correspond to. This provides an informal tool for checking the adequacy of the chosen model both in terms of size of the shift and its shape. For model 2 this is given by $b(L)^{-1} f_t^{(\cdot)}(\vartheta)'\gamma$ in order to provide a realistic picture of the overall impact which is not visible from $f_t^{(\cdot)}(\vartheta)'\gamma$ alone.

3.4.2 Extensions

The testing problem at hand is extended in three directions. At first, it provides a test statistic for a model without deterministic shifts. The program also copes with the problem of possibly uncertain or unknown dates of the shift, and finally, refined test statistics are provided.

With respect to the first point, these tests and corresponding model checking are supplied for reference purposes only. The second point is a natural supplement for the initial problem. The theory thereof is dealt with thoroughly in Lanne, Lütkepohl and Saikkonen (2001) and some interesting examples are presented below. The general idea is to go through estimation and testing for many possible break points. Applying the same minimization principle, the result is an estimate for T_1 and ϑ jointly. Thus, the break point estimated is the one for which the gain in desirable model properties is the biggest when allowing for a level shift. The flaw in this approach is however, that there will always be an estimate for T_1, irrespective of whether there really was a break in the series. Therefore, this tool should be used with care.

Thirdly, LLS note that there might be considerable gains in terms of reliability of the test statistics in small samples, not only when the choice $\bar{c} = 0$ is made, but also if the auxiliary regression is improved. They propose to consider for **model 1**

$$\hat{\omega}_t = \delta_0 + \rho_{int}^{+}\hat{\omega}_{t-1} + \left[\hat{b}(L)\Delta f_t^{(\cdot)}(\hat{\vartheta})'\right]\delta_1 + \left[\hat{b}(L)\Delta F_t^{(\cdot)}(\hat{\vartheta})'\right]\delta_2 + \sum_{j=1}^{p}\varphi_j\Delta\hat{x}_{t-j} + r_t^{+}, \quad t = p+2,\ldots,T \tag{3.17}$$

instead of (3.14), where

$$\hat{\omega}_t = \hat{b}(L)\hat{x}_t$$

and

$$F_t^{(1)} = 0$$

$$F_t^{(2)} = \begin{cases} 0 & t < T_1 - 1 \\ (t - T_1 + 1)exp\{-\vartheta(t - T_1 + 1)\} & t \geq T_1 - 1 \end{cases}$$

$$F_t^{(3)} = \begin{bmatrix} \frac{d_{1,t-1}}{(1-\vartheta L)^2} \\ \frac{d_{1,t-2}}{(1-\vartheta L)^2} \end{bmatrix}$$

are the first derivatives w. r. t. ϑ of the respective shift functions, ι is a constant term and r_t^{+} is a disturbance.

Likewise, instead of (3.15), for **model 2** the following regression is run

$$\tilde{\nu}_t = \delta_0 + \rho_{int}\tilde{\nu}_{t-1} + \Delta f_t^{(\cdot)}(\tilde{\vartheta})'\delta_1 + F_t^{(\cdot)}(\tilde{\vartheta})'\delta_2 + \tilde{q}_t\delta_3 + \varepsilon_t^{+}, \quad t = 2,\ldots,T \tag{3.18}$$

with

$$\tilde{q}_t = [(\Delta y_{t-1} - \tilde{\mu}_*), \cdots, (\Delta y_{t-p} - \tilde{\mu}_*)]$$
$$\tilde{\mu}_* = \tilde{\mu}_1 / \tilde{b}(1).$$

The test statistics are derived as t-statistics for the hypotheses $\rho_{int} = 1$ and $\rho^+_{int} = 1$ respectively. They are calculated without further weighting and will be occasionally referred to as refined statistics to distinguish them from the standard statistics τ_{SL} and τ_{alt}. For these two refined test statistics which will be denoted τ^+_{int} and t_{int} respectively, LLS derive the limiting distribution.[11] Again, it varies if the a priori restriction can be made that no trend enters the data generating process.[12]

As for the previous statistics the full set of specification checking is available. In these cases the fit of test regressions is evaluated with the help of $\hat{r}^+_t$ and $\tilde{\varepsilon}^+_t$. In the following examples, all four statistics are provided together with the common augmented Dickey-Fuller test statistic as well as the version of the new tests without allowing for a shift.

3.5 Examples

This section is to highlight many of the points raised in the last paragraphs. We investigate data series for which the break point is known without doubt and also time series, for which it cannot a priori be decided, where the break point is. A comprehensive approach will be used for all series (with few exceptions) and the results of each step of the analysis are reported. These steps are the following

- brief description of the data series,
- estimation of the break point allowing for a maximum of $p = 6$ (for model 1) and $p = 8$ (for model 2) lags in each series,

[11] The critical values are listed in LLS, Table 2, last 5 rows.

[12] These values are to be found in LLS, Table 2, rows 11 to 15.

- reducing the lag length to the smallest possible in order to avoid overparametrisation or extending the lag length up to $p = 16$ and repeating the previous step[13],
- graphical analysis of model fit,
- report of the test statistic and decision.

3.5.1 Data Description

The example data are grouped into three categories. The first consists of series where there is no doubt whatsoever about the time of the break point. These breaks occurred due to well known historic events like German unification in October 1990 or the introduction of the market economy in Poland ("Big Bang") in the second half of 1989 when the then communist government was replaced in the aftermath of the May 27 elections. The second group consists of data series where the event is well known, yet the point of time at which the economies were hit is not. Examples thereof are the Finnish economy which suffered considerably when the Soviet economy struggled as a result of the market reforms having been introduced in the late 1980s and early 1990s. A large share of Finland's exports went east at the time, therefore the country had to recover once this market broke down. As a second example of this kind the French case dealt with in chapter 4 is looked at. As outlined there, the last devaluation of the French Franc versus the Deutschmark took place in 1987. If economic agents believed this to be the last devaluation, the corresponding (implicit) expected depreciation rate of the French Franc versus the Deutschmark should exhibit a downward move of the mean value to the new central rate. This move will be modelled as a shift in the mean of the process. In addition, due to differing inflation rates in Germany and France pressure remained high on the Franc however, until real economic adjustments re-established equilibrium between real and nominal exchange

[13] To this end, Lanne et al. (2001) suggest to use lag order selection criteria or to include lags up to the largest significant according to standard t-tests.

rates. The economic effect is straightforward: a run out of the Franc into the Deutschmark implying an increase in the income velocity of money in France.

Thirdly, the popular Nelson-Plosser data (Nelson and Plosser, 1982) is analyzed which raises both questions at the same time, presence of a unit root and timing of the break point.[14] These annual macroeconomic data refer to the United States of America and cover a period usually commencing in the late 19th century and finishing in the 80s of the past century. This data set enjoys widespread use among time series analysts because they cover a very long period and allow comparison of the results with those of other researchers. Among others Kleibergen and Hoek (2000) investigate possible *ARMA* feature of the underlying DGP.

Table 3.1 provides an overview of the data definitions and their origin.

3.5.2 Estimation of the Break Points

If there is any need to estimate the break point (groups 2 and 3) the search of the break point will be restricted to a period close to the visually estimated point, which can become fairly large in the Nelson-Plosser data sets.[15] The Polish data series is somewhat special because although the timing of the break point is clear from the political events, the effect on the economy seems to occur with some delay. The first remarkable blow to the industrial production seems to have occurred in the third quarter of 1989. The two models pick the fist quarter of 1990 however, when allowed to chose the break point that removes as much nuisance as possible. Nevertheless, the statistics below refer to the exogenously chosen break point which is 1989/3.

Table 3.2 reports the estimates of the break points. For these examples and model 1 the estimate of the break point considerably depends on the

[14] Here, the extended data sets are employed. I am indebted to Frank Kleibergen who kindly provided them (see Kleibergen and Hoek (2000)).

[15] Visual estimation is picking a break point according to judgement based on visual inspection of the data.

Table 3.1. Data Description and Sources

Code	Description[a]	Source
Group 1 (Germany and Poland)		
D GDP	quarterly, non seasonally adjusted data of West German real Gross Domestic Product (GDP) 1975(1) - 1990(2), 1990(3)-1996(4) GDP of whole Germany	German Institute for Economic Research, System of National Accounts
D M1	quarterly, non seasonally adjusted data, 1960(1) - 1990(1) West German monetary aggregate M1, 1990(2) - 1997(1) all of Germany[b]	OECD
D M3	quarterly, non seasonally adjusted data, 1972(1) - 1990(2) West German monetary aggregate M3, 1990(3) - 1996(1) all of Germany	Bundesbank, Monthly Report
PL IP	quarterly, non seasonally adjusted data of Polish Industrial Production Index 1982(1) - 1995(4)	International Monetary Fund (IMF)
Group 2 (Finland and France)		
Fin Cons	quarterly, non seasonally adjusted data of Finnish Private Consumption deflated by the Consumer Price index (base: 1995) 1970(1) - 1998(4)	IMF
Fin IP	quarterly, seasonally adjusted data of Finnish Industrial Production Index 1961(1) - 1998(4)	IMF
Fin GDP	quarterly, non seasonally adjusted data of Finnish GDP 1970(1) - 1998(4)	IMF
F Velocity	quarterly, seasonally adjusted data of French velocity of money 1983(1) - 1997(4): GDP/M3	IMF
F exp. depr.	expected depreciation of the French Franc against the Deutschmark over three months, monthly data 1983(01) - 1998(05), see chap. 4	Deutsche Bundesbank
Group 3 (Nelson-Plosser data)		
UA Money	annual data of U.S. Money 1889 - 1988	From F. Kleibergen (see Kleibergen and Hoek (2000))
UA IP	annual data of U.S. Industrial Production Index 1860 - 1988	See UA Money.
UA GNP	annual data of U.S. real GNP 1909 - 1988	See UA Money.

[a] All data are in natural logarithms.

[b] In the OECD data series German Monetary Union shows up one quarter too early.

choice of the lag order. Assuming very many ($6 < p \leq 16$) as well as very few lags ($p < 6$) leads to different conclusions. The initial lag order $p = 6$ turned out to deliver the most robust results in that reduction of p after fixing the estimated break point did not as much alter the estimate of T_1, if T_1 was re-estimated using the shorter lag length. At the same time, $p = 6$ seemed to be sufficient for capturing the residual correlation. As to model 2, the lag order hardly affected the estimate of T_1 at all. However, this model very often failed to account for the autocorrelation of the residuals properly.

It should be noticed that especially in the data series of the last group, due to the large time span covered, a number of breaks could be possible. Therefore, the estimation can be interpreted as weighting one nuisance removal scheme against another, e.g. the "Great Crash" against the World Wars against the oil crises. As it turns out, the 1929/1930 events appear to have the largest effect, or could be captured best by the models. Generally speaking, the problems encountered when estimating the time of the break once again underline the value added of knowing the break point beforehand.

3.5.3 Graphical Analysis

In the following, the graphical tools for analyzing the model fit and test statistics are described. Most of the features will be demonstrated with the German M3 series (D M3). An inflation adjusted version of this data series has been analysed e.g. by Hubrich (2001) and Lütkepohl and Wolters (1998) in the context of German money demand analysis. The reason for taking these data as a tutorial example is that this is one of the few cases, where both model 1 and 2 resulted in an equally good fit. The only drawback is that the corresponding functions $Q(\vartheta)$ and $S(\vartheta)$ are not exciting, therefore reference is made to the series of the expected depreciation rate and U.S. real GDP (see Figures 3.8 and 3.12 on pages 78, 82 respectively).

The output for the D M3 series is obtained by either grid search or hill climbing optimization procedure. In case of grid search optimization, the es-

Table 3.2. Estimating Time of Break

Data Series	shift function	$\hat{T}_1$ visual inspection	$min(Q)$	$min(S)$
Group 1				
D GDP[a]	all	1990/3		
D M1[a]	all	1990/2		
D M3[a]	all	1990/3		
PL IP	all	1989/3	1990/1	
Group 2				
	$f_t^{(1)}$		1988/2	1991/1
Fin Cons.	$f_t^{(2)}$	1991/1	1989/4	1990/4
	$f_t^{(3)}$		1989/3	1991/4
Fin IP	all	1992/2	1991/1	
	$f_t^{(1)}$		1989/2	1987/4
Fin GDP	$f_t^{(2)}$	1992/1	1990/2	1990/2
	$f_t^{(3)}$		1990/2	1990/2
F Velocity	all	1988/1	1988/2	
	$f_t^{(1)}$		1986/05	1987/10
F exp. depr.	$f_t^{(2)}$	1987/01	1986/05	1987/10
	$f_t^{(3)}$		1987/10	1987/10
Group 3				
	$f_t^{(1)}$		1921	1932
UA Money	$f_t^{(2)}$	1921	1921	1932
	$f_t^{(3)}$		1932	1931
	$f_t^{(1)}$		1932	1932
UA IP	$f_t^{(2)}$	1930	1930	1930
	$f_t^{(3)}$		1932	1931
	$f_t^{(1)}$		1932	1932
UA GNP	$f_t^{(2)}$	1930	1939	1930
	$f_t^{(3)}$		1932	1930

[a]No estimation performed, because break points are known by definition.

timates of $Q(\vartheta)$ and $S(\vartheta)$ are plotted together with the corresponding values of the test statistic.

The graphs provide three types of information. First, they give an impression as to how the shift functions can cope with the disturbances encountered. Second, the residuals of the regressions are plotted and an eye-proof test of remaining autocorrelation is provided for all models and all possible shifts including a model without any allowance for a break in the series. This no-shift will be denoted $f_t^{(0)}$. Finally the test statistic together with the values of the objective functions are plotted as functions of ϑ.

Consider Figure 3.2. It refers to model 1 and displays the data series as well as the shapes and sizes of the estimated shift functions in the left hand column. The panels of the second column report the series after removal of all deterministic components according to (3.12). They also hint at how good the three shifts capture the break in the series which is apparently not the case when there is no shift allowed for like in the top middle panel. These residuals $(\hat{x}_t)$ are supposed to contain information about the unit root hypothesis. The extent to which all the deterministic components of the DGP capture the series' characteristics is visible in the last column.[16] All panels in Figure 3.2 can be read row-wise from left to right except for the first row, where the data series is featured instead of the estimated shift function. However, the middle and right hand columns correspond to each other completely. From top to bottom the picture is organized along the four break removal schemes including $f_t^{(0)}$.

The next graphical tool inspects the estimated error terms at the various stages of the analysis in Figures 3.3, 3.4 and 3.7. In particular, the first row depicts the estimated residuals and the second the corresponding estimates of the autocorrelations together with the $\pm 2/\sqrt{T}$ standard errors. They all vary not only due to the different shifts considered but also according to the models and auxiliary regressions encountered. For model 1 and the statistic τ_{SL} the

[16] Here as in the following the superscripts allude to the type of shift functions.

two left hand columns report $\hat{x}_t$ and $\hat{\varepsilon}_t$ which can be calculated from (3.7) in conjunction with (3.2).[17] The latter indicates how good the proposed data generating process mimics the data. The third column refers to the residuals of the auxiliary regression model (3.14) where the parameter ρ is estimated on which the test statistic τ_{SL} is based. It is supposed to contain some remaining autocorrelation structure. The last column plots the values of $\hat{\varepsilon}_t$ implied by (3.14) and (3.9). The less autocorrelation is left there, the more reasonable is the weighting scheme for calculating the standard error of ρ and therefore the more reliable the test statistic should be. The superscript * is added to distinguish between the two derivations of ε_t in columns two and four.

To save space, only the residual analysis of the τ_{SL} test with functions $f_t^{(0)}(\vartheta)$ and $f_t^{(3)}(\vartheta)$ is reported for model 1 (Figures 3.3, 3.4 respectively) as well as the results for $f_t^{(3)}(\vartheta)$ of model 2, τ_{alt} (Figure 3.7). Similar pictures are available for the other shift functions and test statistics. In Figure 3.3 the shift in the level is visible as a huge spike in the residual series. Obviously, an outlier cannot be found in Figure 3.4 or 3.7. With respect to τ_{alt} and t_{int} of model 2, the residuals of (3.8) have to be free of autocorrelation for this model to fit well.

In some instances the differences between the residuals of the auxiliary regression within the same model and the same underlying shift are considerable, and thus highlight the significance of the refinements of the test statistics made in LLS. For D M3 this is not the case. All residual plots are organized such that the last column informs about the properties of the auxiliary regression on which the test statistics are based. Thus, a quick and easy (and incomplete) way to get an idea of the quality of the test results is to focus on this last column.

For model 2 the analysis of the model fit is similar to that of model 1. Figure 3.5, first column displays the data series and the final shape and size

[17] Strictly speaking, for the $\hat{x}_t$ this information is not really useful as such. It is provided as a first informal check of the null hypothesis.

of the shift which is given by $\tilde{b}(L)^{-1} f_t^{(\cdot)'}(\tilde{\vartheta})\tilde{\gamma}$ as outlined above. The remaining two columns yield interpretations quite like in the model 1 case. The difference is the treatment of the polynomial $b(L)$. A comparison to the estimated shifts without accounting for the autoregressive parameters can be made in Figure 3.6. If these parameters were such that $\tilde{b}(L)$ had some of its roots not too far away from the unit circle (so there was some memory), the shapes of $\tilde{b}(L)^{-1} f_t^{(\cdot)}(\tilde{\vartheta})$ and $f_t^{(\cdot)}(\tilde{\vartheta})$ would be distinct. This is not the case for D M3. Therefore Figure 3.10 provides an example where it happens to be.

When applying the grid search method, pictures like 3.8 and 3.12 are available. They graph the objective functions $Q(f_t^{(i)}, \vartheta)$, $i = 2, 3$ for model 1 and accordingly $S(f_t^{(i)}, \vartheta)$, $i = 2, 3$ for model 2 together with the respective test statistics in the lower row. They allow to find out whether or not the test statistic is sensitive with respect to (neighbouring ϑ, that means too small) changes in the shape of the functions. These examples have been chosen because they show two things. First, as in picture 3.8, the test statistic features extreme values very close to the boundary of the parameter space of ϑ (left hand column). In both these cases the test results very much depend on the actual values of ϑ. While the null hypothesis cannot be rejected over most of the possible parameter range, close to the lower (upper) bound, the test statistics drop below the 5% critical value which is -2.99. In one of these instances the smaller test statistic also corresponds to the minimum of the objective function (right hand column, type 3 shift).[18]

The second reason for choosing these examples is visible in the upper panel of Figure 3.12. The objective function to the right (referring to $f_t^{(3)}(\vartheta)$) displays two minima over the range of ϑ. While the minimum corresponding to $\vartheta = 0.05$ yields test statistics of $\tau_{SL} = -1.62$ and $\tau_{int}^{+} = -1.34$, the test statistics corresponding to the other minimum clearly reject the null ($\tau_{SL} =$

[18] For a short-cut, Figure 3.9 may be consulted to learn about the benefits of the flexibility provided by the type 3 shift function which eventually leads to rejection of the null.

-2.82, $\tau_{int}^{+} = -3.40$).[19] The former result would be obtained, if the parameter range for ϑ would be restricted to $0 \leq \vartheta \leq .8$, for example. The graphs also reveal that it is only in a very narrow neighbourhood of the ϑ corresponding to the minimal value of $Q(f_t^{(3)}, \vartheta)$ that the null hypothesis can be rejected.[20] In general, multiple local minima have rarely been found. Exceptions to that rule became frequent when the seasonal patterns of the data had been ignored. The examples discussed here underline the necessity to carefully cross check the test results. Obtaining values of ϑ which coincide with the boundaries of the parameter space may serve as a first warning to preferably have a second look at the outcomes.

Finally, a few more pictures give insight into some of the example series. There we have a plot of the results for the U.S. real GNP in 3.13 which should highlight the benefits of allowing for rather smooth shift functions. This becomes apparent from the bottom row of that graph in comparison to the others. Second, Figures 3.9 and 3.11 account for series where no trend enters the DGP. In addition, the first of these series is also referred to in chapter 4 of the thesis. Assuming a once-off shift in the level of F velocity and F exp. depr. due to the change in exchange rate policy does not suffice to explain the unit root behaviour of these series in most cases. Note that for the expected depreciation rate neither the type 1 nor the type 2 shift of model 2 adjust for the break in a reasonable manner.

3.5.4 Test Statistics and Test Decisions

Having estimated the timing of the break point, the actual test statistics are computed. In order to avoid over-parametrisation the lag number is cut down to the lowest reasonable. To this end, the graphical analysis tools described in the previous paragraph were applied. As a general result, the model 1 does much better in most cases when it comes to removing residual autocorrelation.

---

[19] The 5% critical values are -2.62 and -3.11 respectively.

[20] For another short-cut to the complete story see Figure 3.13.

There has been found only one example (UA IP), where model 2 required a smaller lag length than model 1. Although Tables 3.3 to 3.5 in many cases reports the same value of p for both models, this does not indicate that the fit of model 2 is as good as that of model 1. It has simply been impossible to remove all remaining autocorrelation even for very many lags, so the number of lags has been limited to the number of lags in model 1. One interpretation of this result is that the break dominates the parameters of the autoregressive part. Therefore, the latter might be squeezed to zero not being able to capture the autoregressive structure.

The test statistics are summarized in Tables 3.3 to 3.5. As already mentioned, the question which model to use has to be answered empirically and indeed, model 1 and 2 rarely suit the data series equally well. Therefore, the statistics referring to both models are reported together with the ordinary ADF test result which is calculated without accounting for a break. Not surprisingly, the outcome varies with the model type and shift function applied.

While the ADF test hardly rejects the null of a unit root in any of the example series, there is some evidence against it in a number of cases when more sophisticated shift functions are employed. To see this, consider the PL IP series. There, τ_{int}^{+} and t_{int} clearly reject the null of a unit root at the 10% percent level of significance when the rational shift enters the DGP. This evidence is the more convincing because the conclusion is independent of the model employed. In this case, they both fit the data reasonably well. In contrast, none of the other shapes of the shift functions would lead to rejection of the null. A similar picture emerges for Fin GDP where rejection of the null (t_{int} statistic) is the strongest when the shift functions employed allow for a smooth transition as appears most appropriate following the economic arguments.

Table 3.3. Estimated Test Statistics and Specification Information (1)[a]

Group 1 (Germany and Poland)

	D GDP				D M1				D M3				PL IP			
shift fct.	$f_t^{(0)}$	$f_t^{(1)}$	$f_t^{(2)}$	$f_t^{(3)}$	$f_t^{(0)}$	$f_t^{(1)}$	$f_t^{(2)}$	$f_t^{(3)}$	$f_t^{(0)}$	$f_t^{(1)}$	$f_t^{(2)}$	$f_t^{(3)}$	$f_t^{(0)}$	$f_t^{(1)}$	$f_t^{(2)}$	$f_t^{(3)}$
spec.[b]	c,t,s	c,t,s	c,t,s	c,t,s	c,t,s	c,t,s	c,t,s	c,t,s	c,t,s	c,t,s	c,t,s	c,t,s	c,t,s	c,t,s	c,t,s	c,t,s
AR	5/5/5	5/5/5	5/5/5	5/5/5	5/6/4	5/6/4	5/6/4	5/6/4	4/4/4	4/4/4	4/4/4	4/4/4	2/3/2	2/3/2	2/3/2	2/3/2
τ_{SL} stat.[c]	-1.44	-.96	-.96	-1.38	-2.13	-2.33*	-1.95	-1.93	-1.14	-.90	-.90	-.92	-1.20	-1.35	-1.44	-1.43
τ_{alt} stat.[c]	-1.50	-1.23	-1.23	-1.08	-1.75	-2.27	-2.04	-2.04	-1.83	-.69	-.69	-.74	-1.09	-1.25	-1.31	-1.43
τ_{int}^{+} stat.[c]	-2.40	-1.79	-1.83	-1.39	-2.48	-2.83*	-2.74	-2.92*	-1.62	-.68	-.69	-.75	-1.18	-1.34	-1.43	**-4.92**
t_{int} stat.[c]	-1.54	-2.10	-2.09	-2.53	-2.55	-2.81	-2.34	-2.76	-2.11	-1.79	-1.79	-1.73	.87	-1.01	-1.10	-2.71*
ADF stat.[c]	-2.52				-3.19*				-2.40				-1.68			

[a]Statistics being significant at the 5 and 10 percent level are indicated by bold face, and by the superscript * respectively. AR indicates the p of the autoregressive order of the DGP. The entries refer to model 1, 2, and to the ADF test respectively.
[b] Model specification: c indicates the presence of an intercept, t of a trend, and s stands for seasonal dummies in the regression.
[c] The critical values are for τ_{SL} and τ_{alt}: -3.23(1%), -2.62(5%), -2.33(10%), for τ_{int}^{+} and τ_{int}: -3.73(1%), -3.11(5%), -2.80(10%), and for the ADF test: -3.96(1%), -3.41(5%), -3.12(10%).

Table 3.4. Estimated Test Statistics and Specification Information (2)[a]

Group 2 (Finland and France)

	Fin Cons				Fin IP				Fin GDP				F Velocity			
shift fct.	$f_t^{(0)}$	$f_t^{(1)}$	$f_t^{(2)}$	$f_t^{(3)}$	$f_t^{(0)}$	$f_t^{(1)}$	$f_t^{(2)}$	$f_t^{(3)}$	$f_t^{(0)}$	$f_t^{(1)}$	$f_t^{(2)}$	$f_t^{(3)}$	$f_t^{(0)}$	$f_t^{(1)}$	$f_t^{(2)}$	$f_t^{(3)}$
spec.[b]	c,t,s	c,t,s	c,t,s	c,t,s	c,t	c,t	c,t	c,t	c,t,s	c,t,s	c,t,s	c,t,s	c	c	c	c
AR	5/16/5	5/16/5	5/16/5	5/16/5	5/8/5	5/8/5	5/8/5	5/8/5	5/16/5	5/16/5	5/16/5	5/16/5	2/3/5	2/5/5	2/3/5	2/3/5
τ_{SL} stat.[c]	-1.66	-1.77	-1.26	-1.24	-1.33	-1.35	-1.49	-1.46	-1.88	-1.78	-1.21	-1.22	-1.03	-.60	-.27	.77
τ_{alt} stat.[c]	-1.79	-1.92	-1.48	-1.78	-1.20	-1.32	-1.58	-1.56	-1.99	-1.93	-1.36	-1.37	-.95	-.45	-.21	1.10
τ_{int}^{+} stat.[c]	-1.79	-1.87	-2.13	-2.24	-1.65	-1.60	-1.71	-1.72	-2.28	-2.14	-1.92	-2.04	-1.20	-1.26	-1.23	-.59
t_{int} stat.[c]	-2.90*	**-3.32**	**-3.63**	**-4.10**	-2.56	-2.75	-2.85*	-2.86*	-3.01*	-2.77	**-4.05**	**-3.75**	.40	-1.11	-.74	-.41
ADF[c]		-2.88				-2.26				-3.15*				-1.19		

[a]Statistics being significant at the 5 and 10 percent level are indicated by bold face, and by the superscript * respectively. AR indicates the p of the autoregressive order of the DGP. The entries refer to model 1, 2, and to the ADF test respectively.
[b] Model specification: c indicates the presence of an intercept, t of a trend, and s stands for seasonal dummies in the regression.
[c] The critical values are for τ_{SL} and τ_{alt}: -3.23(1%), -2.62(5%), -2.33(10%), for τ_{int}^{+} and τ_{int}: -3.73(1%), -3.11(5%), -2.80(10%), and for the ADF test: -3.96(1%), -3.41(5%), -3.12(10%).

Table 3.5. Estimated Test Statistics and Specification Information (3)[a]

	Group 2 (cont.)				**Group 3** (Nelson-Plosser data)											
	F exp. depr.				UA Money				UA IP				UA GNP			
shift fct.	$f_t^{(0)}$	$f_t^{(1)}$	$f_t^{(2)}$	$f_t^{(3)}$	$f_t^{(0)}$	$f_t^{(1)}$	$f_t^{(2)}$	$f_t^{(3)}$	$f_t^{(0)}$	$f_t^{(1)}$	$f_t^{(2)}$	$f_t^{(3)}$	$f_t^{(0)}$	$f_t^{(1)}$	$f_t^{(2)}$	$f_t^{(3)}$
spec.[b]	c	c	c	c	c,t	c,t	c,t	c,t	c,t	c,t	c,t	c,t	c,t	c,t	c,t	c,t
AR	5/5/5	5/5/5	5/5/5	5/5/5	2/16/2	2/16/2	2/16/2	2/16/2	6/5/5	6/5/5	6/5/5	6/5/5	6/8/8	6/8/8	6/8/8	6/8/8
τ_{SL} stat.[c]	.10	-.62	-.62	.16	-2.00	-2.18	-2.33*	-2.10	-1.50	-1.54	-1.46	-.96	-1.72	-1.77	-1.05	**-2.82**
τ_{alt} stat.[c]	-.95	-1.85*	**-2.55**	-1.58	-.95	-1.04	-1.18	-1.25	-1.83	-1.80	-1.76	-1.72	-2.15	-2.28	-1.47	-1.41
τ_{int}^{+} stat.[c]	**-3.34**	**-3.70**	**-3.76**	**-3.42**	-2.81	-3.07*	**-3.28**	-2.97*	-2.46	-2.83*	-2.50	-1.78	-2.15	-1.92	-1.72	**-3.40**
t_{int} stat.[c]	.88	-2.38	-2.15	**-3.37**	-1.84	-1.85	-1.96	-2.36	-2.38	-2.33	-2.12	-2.07	**-3.24**	-2.98*	-1.30	-1.12
ADF[c]	-2.70*				-2.51				-2.65				-2.75			

[a]Statistics being significant at the 5 and 10 percent level are indicated by bold face, and by the superscript * respectively. AR indicates the p of the autoregressive order of the DGP. The entries refer to model 1, 2, and to the ADF test respectively.
[b] Model specification: c indicates the presence of an intercept, t of a trend, and s stands for seasonal dummies in the regression.
[c] The critical values are for τ_{SL} and τ_{alt}: -3.23(1%), -2.62(5%), -2.33(10%), for τ_{int}^{+} and τ_{int}: -3.73(1%), -3.11(5%), -2.80(10%), and for the ADF test: -3.96(1%), -3.41(5%), -3.12(10%).

Looking at the D M1 series, it seems that τ_{int}^{+} provides some indication for the null to be invalid, although at the ten percent level only. In this case, even the ADF test tends to reject the null marginally. Overall, the results give no clear picture for this series.

The series F Velocity and F exp. depr. naturally are of special interest for the thesis. For the former, the test results leave no doubt whatsoever about the stochastic trending behaviour because none of the tests provide the slightest evidence against a unit root. This however, cannot be regarded as universal evidence against a cointegration relationship between income and money since implicitly, rather strict assumptions are made. One of those is that possible deterministic trends are assumed to have the same slope and that the cointegration coefficients are exactly $(1 -1)$. If either of these assumptions proves wrong, the interpretation of the testing results as evidence against cointegration is at least questionable.

With respect to the expected depreciation rate of the French Franc against the Deutschmark, the results appear somewhat cumbersome. While τ_{SL} and τ_{alt} do not even come close to the rejection region, τ_{int}^{+} rejects no matter what shift function is employed and whether or not a shift is considered at all. Against that, for the model 2, rejecting the null hypothesis can only be conjectured when the type 3 shift is considered. The corresponding break adjustments are shown in Figure 3.9 which may help to understand the differences. It is only the third row that reports a reasonable removal of the downward shift in the time series. Thus, lacking evidence against a unit root in the other cases should not come as a surprise.

The results for the Nelson-Plosser data set partly contradict the views expressed by other studies in that for example the unit-root hypothesis could be rejected for money stock (τ_{int}^{+}). Neither Zivot and Andrews (1992) and Leybourne, Newbold and Vougas (1998), nor Nelson and Plosser (1982) draw the same conclusion. Li (1995) and Perron (1989) however, do. Somewhat weaker evidence against a unit-root could also be gathered for UA IP and UA

GNP. For UA IP, Zivot and Andrews (1992), Perron (1989) and Li (1995) also reject non-stationarity while this applies to GNP for the studies by Zivot and Andrews (1992) and Perron (1989) only.

Comparing the two models, occasionally (UA GNP, Fin Cons) model 2 seems to provide even more evidence against the null hypothesis than the first model. This would be questionable however, since this model does not have a good fit in these cases. When it does so (D M3, UA IP), the unit root hypothesis cannot be rejected in any of the examples considered.

The differences between the original (τ_{SL}, τ_{alt}) and the refined test statistics (τ_{int}^{+}, t_{int}) appear somewhat counter-intuitive because, in general τ_{int}^{+} and t_{int} tend to reject the null more often than their counterparts. This is surprising because LLS recognized for the test statistics τ_{SL} and τ_{alt} too many rejections of the null when it was actually true. Therefore, given that their simulation results carry over to our examples, rejection of the null by τ_{int}^{+} and t_{int} should be taken seriously.

To give an impression of how the estimated shift functions are shaped Table 3.6 lists the estimates of ϑ. For easy interpretation one could compare them to the shapes drawn in Figure 3.1.

3.6 Conclusions

Many economic time series exhibit level shifts, a feature that should not remain disregarded when testing whether or not the process has a unit root. This chapter described two models which were designed to cope with such a situation. An expatiated discussion of the analytical steps and their assessment was provided together with an application to macroeconomic data.

Comparing the performance of the two models, it seemed that the first one did cope slightly better with the data compared to the second one. This cannot be regarded as a general result however, as some of the examples showed.

Table 3.6. Estimated Coefficients of the Shift Functions

Series	shift function	$\hat{\vartheta}$ model 1	model 2
Group 1			
D GDP	$f_t^{(2)}$	6	.324
	$f_t^{(3)}$	.994	.832
D M1	$f_t^{(2)}$	.998	.879
	$f_t^{(3)}$	.417	.403
D M3	$f_t^{(2)}$	6	6
	$f_t^{(3)}$	.574	.445
PL IP	$f_t^{(2)}$	2.274	2.337
	$f_t^{(3)}$	.833	.836
Group 2			
Fin Cons.	$f_t^{(2)}$	.081	.160
	$f_t^{(3)}$	.924	.538
Fin IP	$f_t^{(2)}$	.545	.451
	$f_t^{(3)}$	.422	.522
Fin GDP	$f_t^{(2)}$	.121	.134
	$f_t^{(3)}$	.875	.857
F Velocity	$f_t^{(2)}$	1.093	.946
	$f_t^{(3)}$	.886	.886
F exp. depr.	$f_t^{(2)}$	6.000	1.135
	$f_t^{(3)}$	.556	.905
Group 3			
UA Money	$f_t^{(2)}$	1.008	.814
	$f_t^{(3)}$	.076	.463
UA IP	$f_t^{(2)}$	.706	.444
	$f_t^{(3)}$	.886	.050
UA GNP	$f_t^{(2)}$	.453	.481
	$f_t^{(3)}$	.995	.520

As to the four test statistics, the adjustments made in LLS gave more support to the alternative hypothesis than the original tests. Due to their superiority in terms of standard statistical properties which has been found by simulations in LLS, this comes to some extent as a surprise and their application is therefore recommended.

Having to determine the break point instead of knowing the timing of the break beforehand, considerably complicates the analysis and therefore, any extra information about this issue should be used before entering the estimation procedures.

Finally, all steps reported in this chapter can be reproduced with the author's ready-to-use programs and procedures for the *GAUSS* package.

3.A Figures

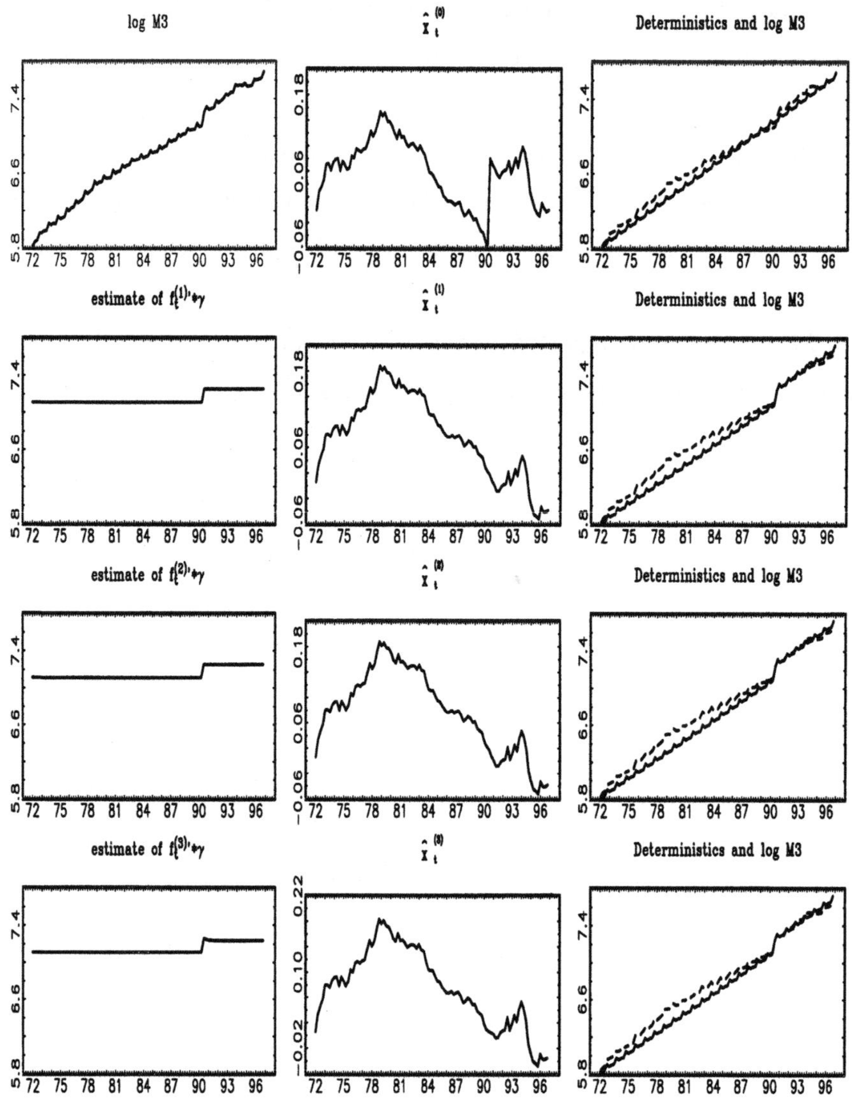

Plots of the time series (upper left panel), shift functions (remaining panels of the left hand column), adjusted series ($\hat{x}_t$ based on $p = 4$) and deterministics in relation to the data (right column).

Figure 3.2. German M3 and Model 1 DGP

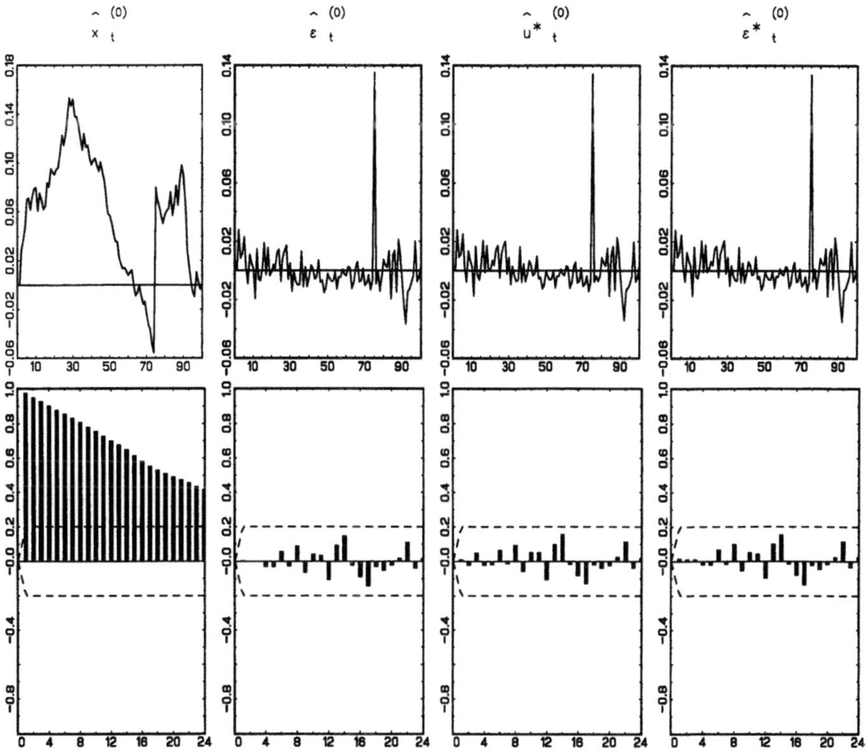

Adjusted and residual series without accounting for the shift, corresponding autocorrelation functions (lower row).

Figure 3.3. Residuals for German M3 and Model 1 DGP (1)

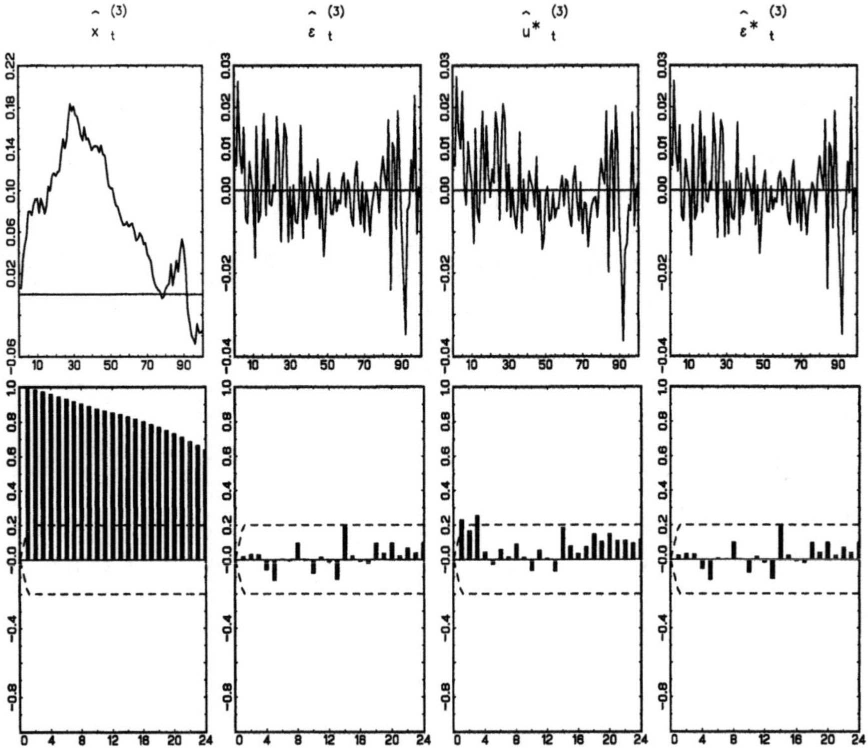

Adjusted and residual series (adjusted with shift function: $f_t^{(3)}$, τ_{SL} test regression), corresponding autocorrelation functions (lower row).

Figure 3.4. Residuals for German M3 and Model 1 DGP (2)

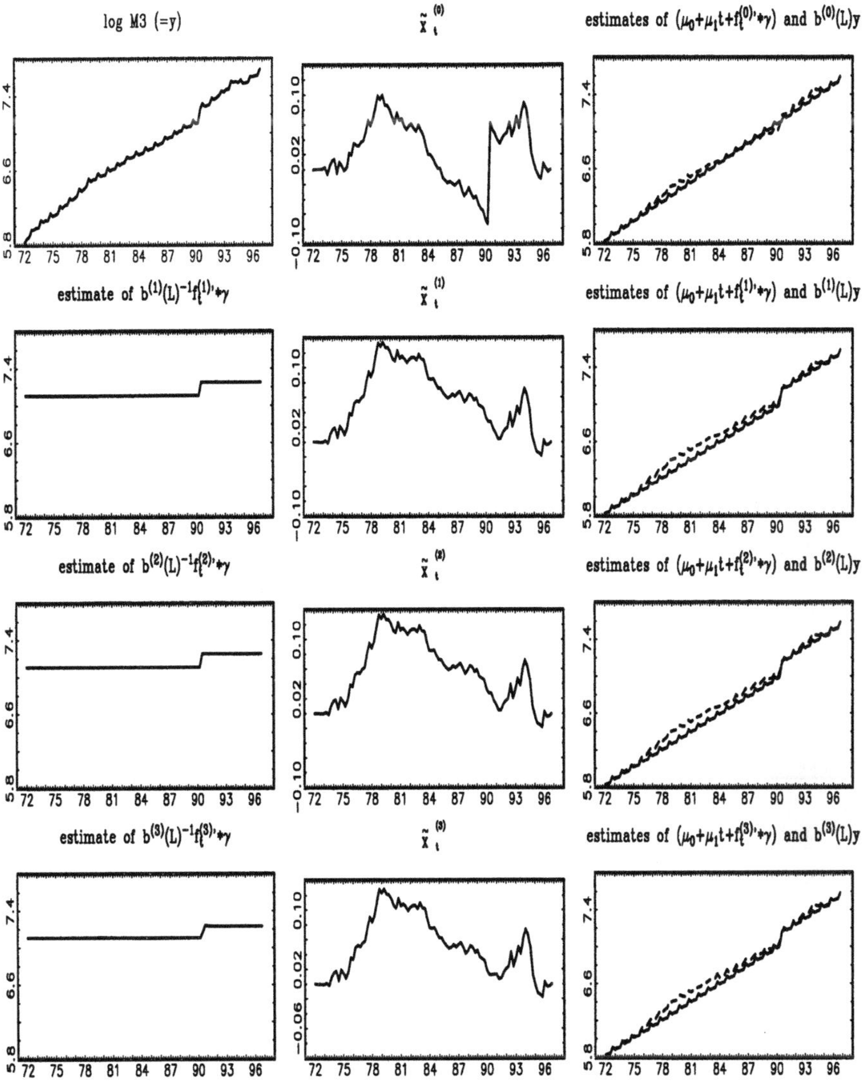

Plots of the time series (upper left panel), shift functions (remaining panels of the left hand column), adjusted series ($\hat{x}_t$ based on $p = 4$) and deterministics in relation to the data (right column).

Figure 3.5. German M3 and Model 2 DGP

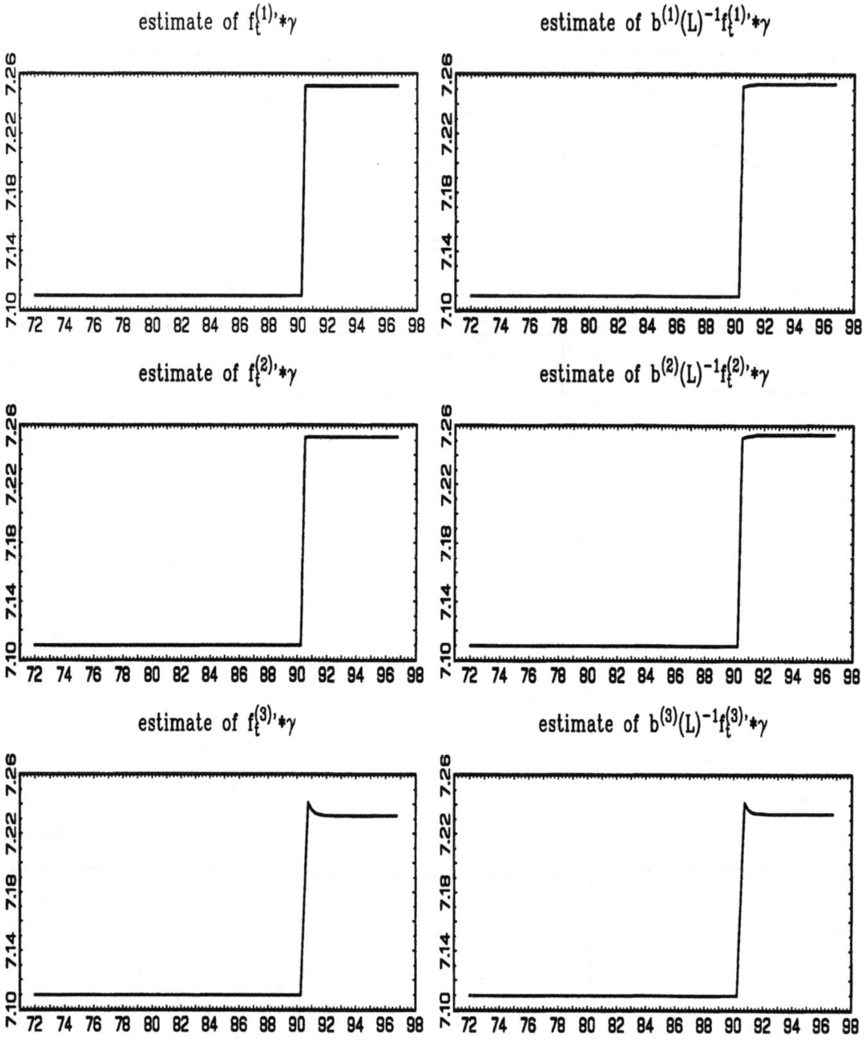

Model 2 DGP, shift functions, shapes without (left hand panels) and with accounting for the $\tilde{b}(L)^{-1}$ polynomial.

Figure 3.6. Estimated Shift Functions for German M3

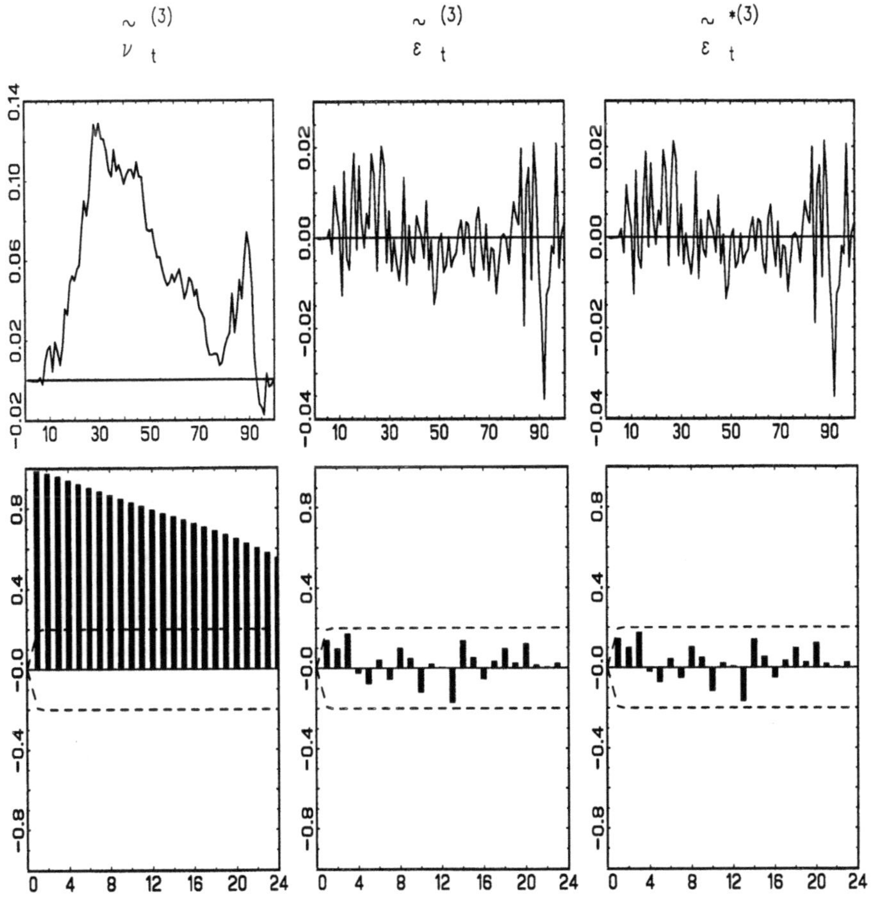

Model 2 DGP, adjusted and residual series (adjusted with shift function: $f_t^{(3)}$, τ_{alt} test regression), corresponding autocorrelation functions (lower row).

Figure 3.7. Residuals for German M3 and Model 2 DGP

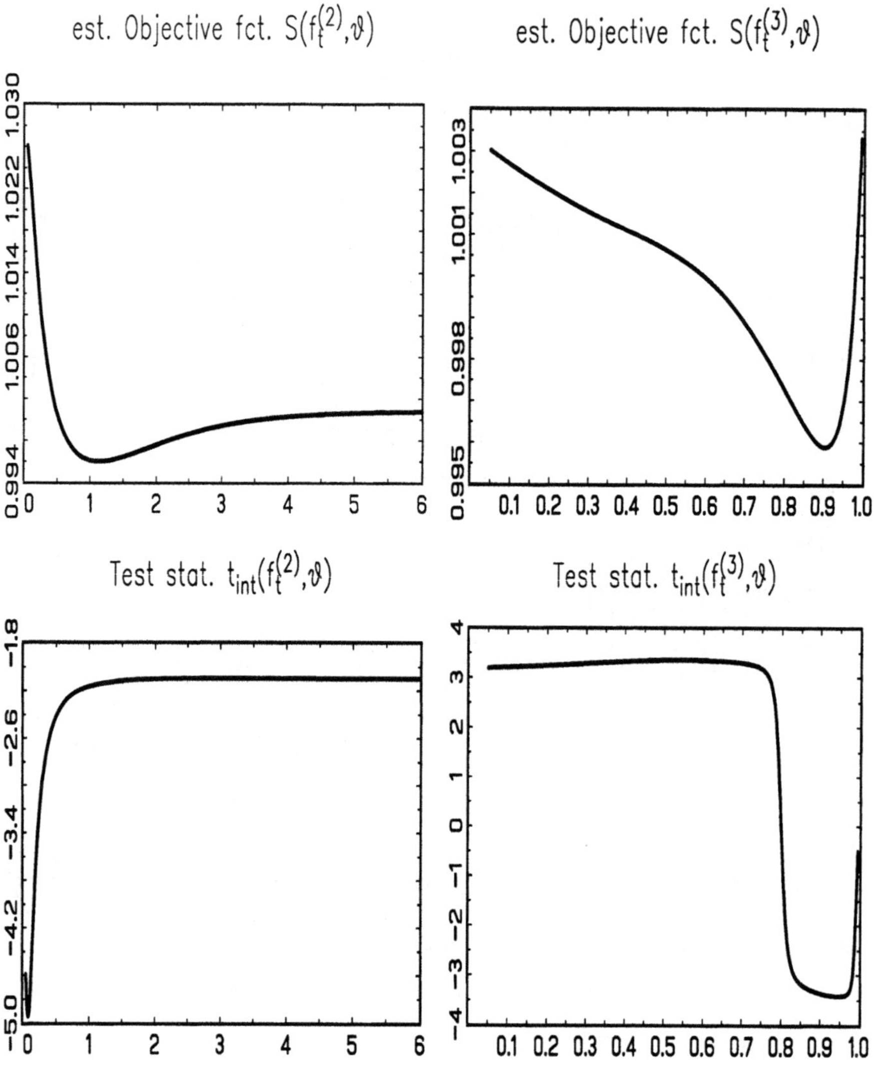

Plots of estimated objective functions (first row) of model 2 for $f_t^{(2)}$ (left column) and $f_t^{(3)}$ together with corresponding values of the test statistics as functions of ϑ.

Figure 3.8. Estimates of Objective Functions for F exp. depr.

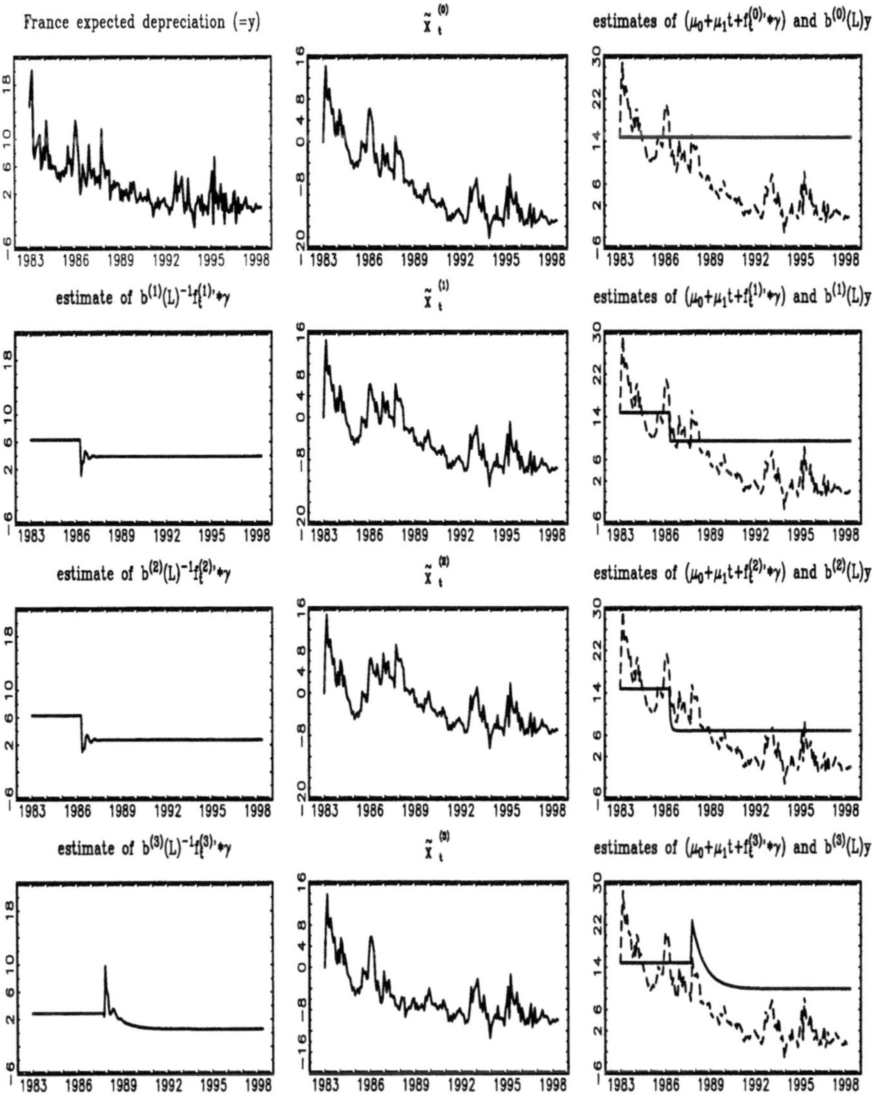

Plots of the time series (upper left panel), shift functions (remaining panels of the left hand column), adjusted series ($\hat{x}_t$ based on $p = 5$) and deterministics in relation to the data (right column).

Figure 3.9. F exp. depr. and Model 2 DGP

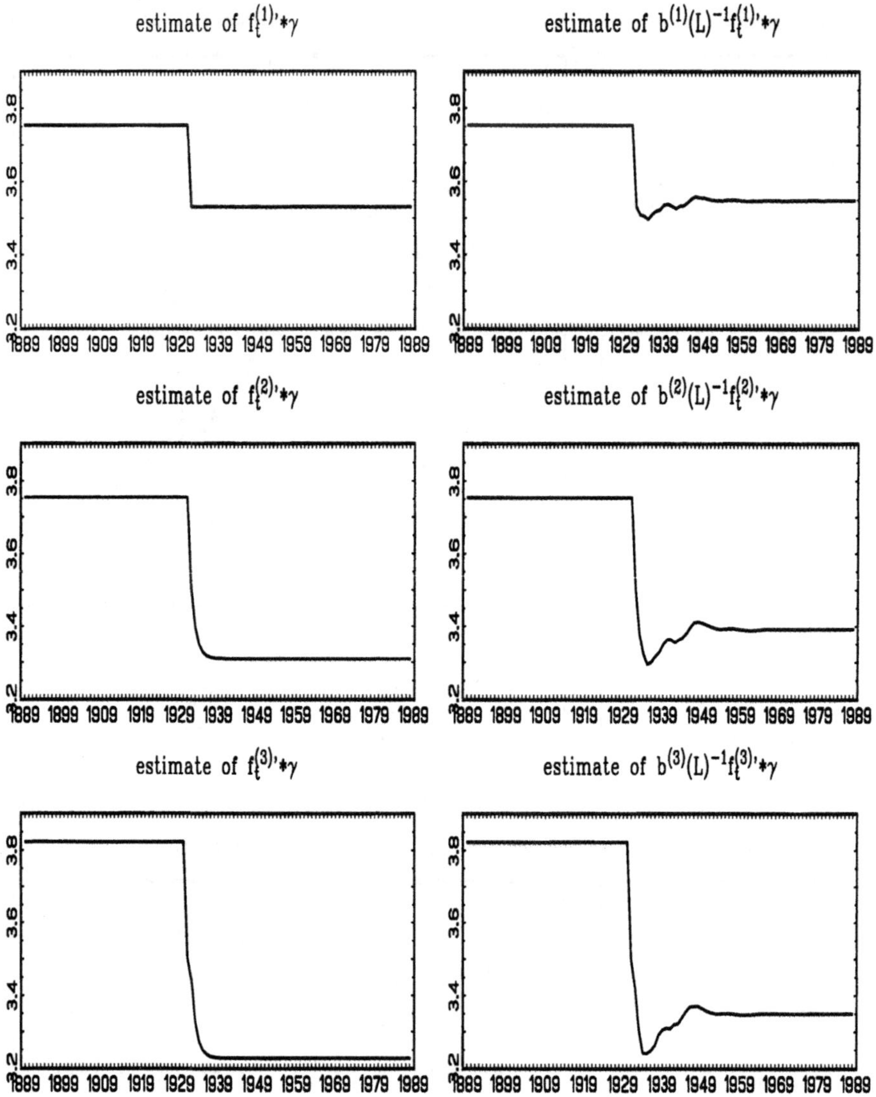

Model 2 DGP, shift functions, shapes without (left hand panels) and with accounting for the $\tilde{b}(L)^{-1}$ polynomial.

Figure 3.10. Estimated Shift Functions for UA Money

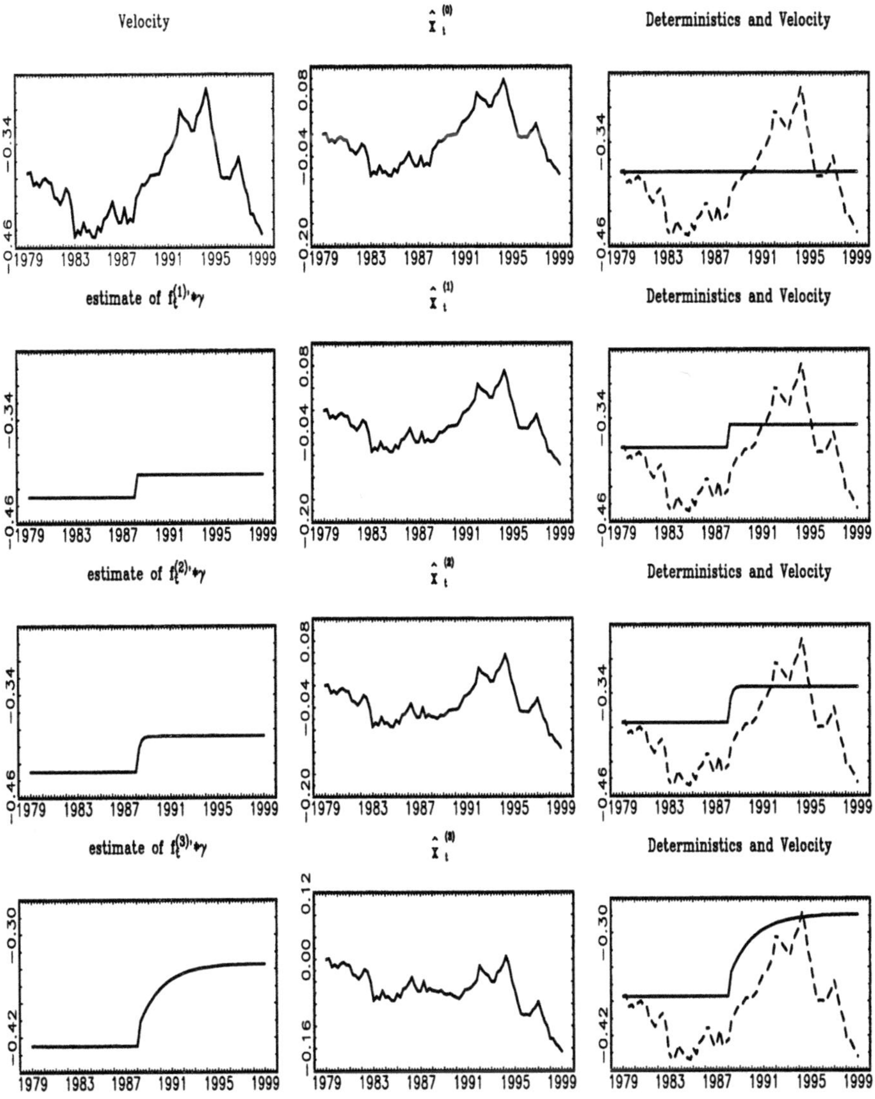

Plots of the time series (upper left panel), shift functions (remaining panels of the left hand column), adjusted series ($\hat{x}_t$ based on $p = 2$) and deterministics in relation to the data.

Figure 3.11. French Velocity of Money and Model 1 DGP

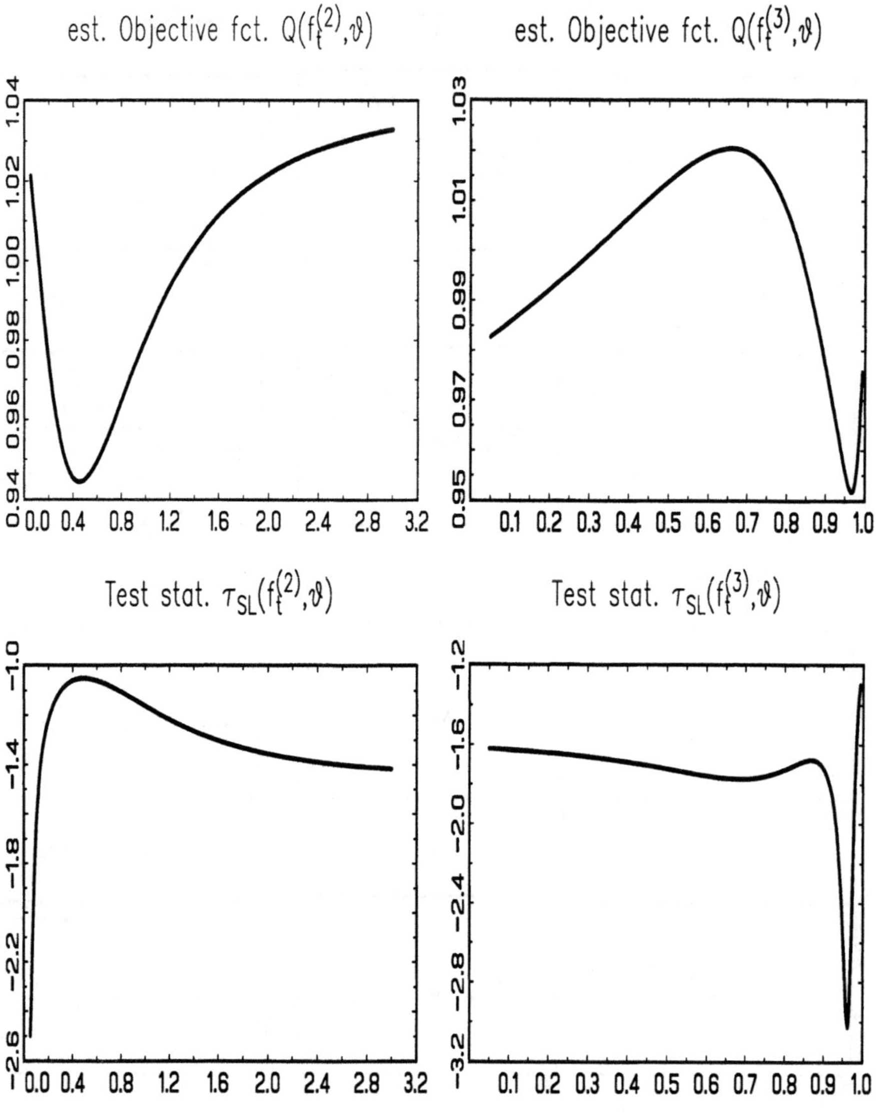

Plots of estimated objective functions (first row) of model 2 for $f_t^{(2)}$ (left column) and $f_t^{(3)}$ together with corresponding values of the test statistics as functions of ϑ.

Figure 3.12. Estimates of Objective Functions for UA GNP

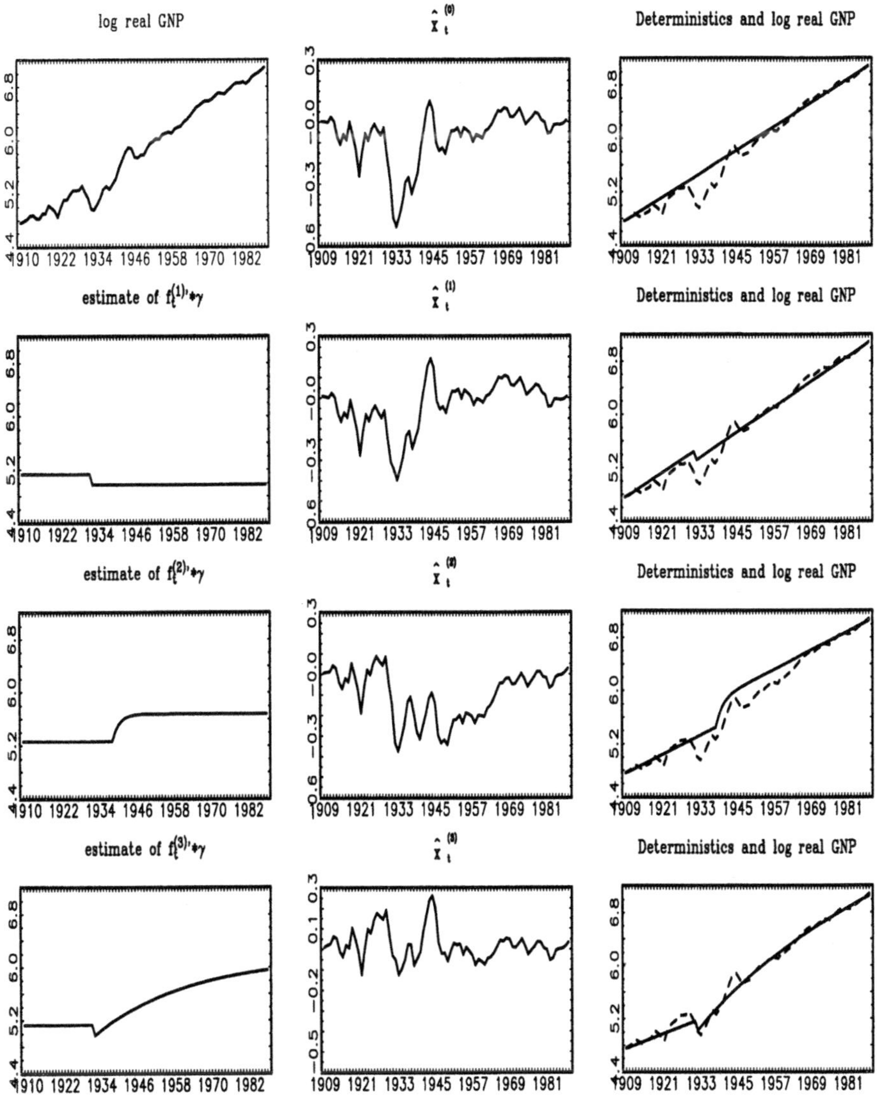

Plots of the time series (upper left panel), shift functions (remaining panels of the left hand column), adjusted series ($\hat{x}_t$ based on $p = 6$) and deterministics in relation to the data (right column).

Figure 3.13. U.S.A. Real GNP and Model 1 DGP

4

Monetary Policy in France Prior to European Monetary Union

4.1 Introduction

This chapter investigates French monetary policy during the convergence period towards European Monetary Union. Its results should form a basis for conclusions about prospects of the EMU for France.

In consideration of its size and economic power, France has so far commanded surprisingly little attention in the more recent money demand literature. Out of the few studies available, a number of slightly differing pictures emerge. Comparing the G-7 countries within a *VAR* system, Sims (1992) finds evidence for interest rate shocks to depress money stock (defined as M1) and output (approximated by industrial production). In contrast to his approach e.g. Wesche (1998) and Cassard, Lane and Masson (1995) explicitly estimate a long-run money demand relation. Their sets of variables comprise harmonized M3 (M3H), GDP and a government bond yield. In addition, Cassard et al. (1995) include an own rate of money. The contribution by Tullio, Souza and Giucca (1996) compares the money demand functions for the core EMU countries (Italy, France and Germany), but fails to find a satisfactory relationship for France.

In the following, the historic events characterizing monetary policy conditions are looked at. Their relevance for money demand investigations will be checked and finally, instead of a money demand function it will be argued that the monetary policy conditions in France can be characterized best by a stable money supply function. This result is the outcome of a preliminary investigation which aims at explaining the special economic links between Germany and France. The theoretical framework for that is the covered interest rate parity, which will be set in the context of the so-called German dominance hypothesis (see e.g. Artus and Salomon (1996) and Kirchgässner and Wolters (1996) as well as the references therein). As a centrepiece of the analysis, the impact of the realignments in 1986-1987 will be modelled. In a comparative approach it turns out that satisfactory modelling can only be conducted by accounting for these events.

The subsequent hypothesis states that a money demand investigation has to consider the history of the exchange rate regime too. Moreover, having found support for the German dominance hypothesis, economic theory implies monetary policy to be built on interest rate targeting. According to theories of money supply in Europe (Bofinger et al. (1998), Nautz (2000)) this tends to destabilize money demand functions and raises the probability of statistically identifying a stable long-run supply function. Here again, a comparison is made between estimation results obtainable with and without taking the presumed break in 1987 into account. This eventually helps to explain the disappointing results reported e.g. in Müller (1999) and Tullio et al. (1996).

Throughout the chapter, a system cointegration approach is applied to identify the relevant long-run relationships underlying the observations.

4.2 Preparing for the Euro: Implications for Money Demand Analysis

In comparison with Germany, France experienced long periods of high inflation rates up to the early 90ies of the last century. Therefore, both countries together with all other EMU candidates had to achieve a certain level of harmonization before entering the monetary union. To that aim France underwent a number of institutional changes.

These changes will be discussed and their significance with respect to money demand analysis highlighted next. A few additional econometric analyses will be pursued to corroborate some of the arguments if necessary.

4.2.1 Brief Summary of the Events

France, as most other Western European countries, let it's currency float against the US Dollar after the "break down" of the Bretton-Woods system in 1973. However, at the same time the domestic French market for capital remained regulated. Therefore, this first period culminating in 1982 in the so-called socialist experiment by the Mauroy government, with restrictions on currency trading and interest rates for commercial credits, can be characterized by regulated foreign exchange markets and the lack of a credit market. This period lasted until the end of 1982, when France abolished most of the restrictions in place.

In 1979 the European Monetary System (EMS) was founded in order to reduce the volatility of the exchange rates by, in principle, fixed rates. This meant controlled devaluations of currencies according to some macroeconomic criteria. This second period can thus be associated with working credit markets while the foreign exchange market remained subject to systematic central bank interventions. The latter aspect became even more important in the last sub-period when the French Franc (FF) for the last time was officially devaluated against the Deutschmark at the beginning of 1987 following a year of repeated adjustments of the central EMS parity.[1] Since then these two currencies have basically maintained their nominal values against each other. Figure 4.10 in the appendix depicts the nominal prices of the Deutschmark quoted in FF and a purchasing power indicator.

[1] To be more precise, this move was an appreciation of the Deutschmark against all currencies in the then ECU-basket including the French Franc.

4.2.2 An Economic Point of View

From the sequence of events and the brief characterization of the periods the economic implications are straightforward. For the first period up to the beginning of the 1980s there was no functioning domestic credit market. Therefore, there is no reason to believe a demand for money function to exist either since credits are the very basis for the creation of and the demand for money. On the other hand, the exchange rate was subject to changes due to, albeit somewhat distant, market forces. All that became different in the third phase when the FF stayed fixed against the currency basket of the EMS members. Thus, during that time, if exchange rates were credibly set by the CBs involved, market forces like purchasing power parity, should explain the evolution of the exchange rate to a lesser extent than before.

It is likewise noteworthy that nominal interest rates will become more dependent on foreign rates the tighter the links are to the foreign markets. Naturally, the less flexible the exchange rate is, the less useful it is as a tool for cushioning asymmetric shocks.

The systematic links between interest rates and exchange rate regimes is the cornerstone of the so-called covered interest rate parity (CIP) condition. In its log-linearized version it can be expressed as (4.1)[2]

$$i^s_{F,t} = \beta_{i^s_G} i^s_{G,t} + \beta_E E_t + k_t \tag{4.1}$$

$$k_t = \kappa_0 + f^{(\cdot)}(\vartheta, T_1)' z_t + a(L)\varepsilon_t \tag{4.2}$$

where $i^s_{\cdot,t}$ denote short-term interest rates at time t with the subscripts indicating the country they refer to (F for France and G for Germany), and time. E_t is the expected depreciation of the French currency against the Deutschmark.[3]

[2] See e.g. Pentecost (1993) pp. 172ff who derives the CIP hypothesis from a portfolio approach.

[3] For simplicity, the subscripts on the β coefficients as of (2.10) are replaced by the variable names. This prove efficient, because there will be found cointegrating rank one only.

We use the definition $E_t = \frac{(fx_t^{t+1} - s_t)}{s_t}$ where s_t is the spot rate, fx_t^{t+1} measures the forward rate at time t for contracts due at $t+1$. All variables are prices of the Deutschmark (DM) quoted in French Franc. The ε_t are serially uncorrelated error terms, $a(L)$ is a polynomial in the lag operator and the κ_i, $(i = 0, 1)$ are parameter vectors of appropriate dimension with $\kappa_1 = 0$ for the time being. In (4.1) the term $z_t = \tau \otimes z_t^*$ denotes a subset vector of y_t variables, z_t^*, or ones whose long-run coefficients may change according to the function $f^{(\cdot)}(\theta, T_1)$ already used in (3.16). Here, τ is a coefficient vector of dimension 2×1 in case of $f^{(3)}(\theta, T_1)$ or of dimension 1×1 for the other shift functions. In the latter situations we have $\tau = \kappa_1$. If (4.1) holds and $z_t^* = 0$, then κ_t yields an interpretation as a risk premium accounting for the possibility of imperfectly covering the investment in foreign assets by buying a forward contract. Naturally, if markets work efficiently this risk should follow a stationary process.

The CIP hypothesis in (4.1) can be analysed in the time series context by assuming all of these variables to be integrated of order one, but forming a cointegration relationship. In other words, while each of the variables may be driven by stochastic trends, at least one of these trends they should have in common to ensure that deviations from the theoretical CIP condition are short-lived. Put in a common trend representation with two stochastic trends $(\sum_{j=1}^t u_{1,j}, \sum_{j=1}^t u_{2,j}, u_{i,j} \sim i.i.d.(0, \sigma_{u_i}^2))$ dominating the system, the relationships between the variables could be described as follows

$$\begin{bmatrix} i_F^s \\ i_G^s \\ E \end{bmatrix}_t = \begin{bmatrix} b_{1,1} & b_{1,2} \\ b_{2,1} & b_{2,2} \\ b_{3,1} & b_{3,2} \end{bmatrix} \begin{bmatrix} \sum_{j=1}^t u_{1,j} \\ \sum_{j=1}^t u_{2,j} \end{bmatrix} + \text{stationary components.} \quad (4.3)$$

If there is a cointegration relationship between the interest rates and the expected depreciation rate, there must exist a linear combination of the variables which cancels the stochastic trends. In the framework of (4.1) and (4.2) this might translate into $\beta_{i_G^s} = 1$, with for example $b_{1,1} = b_{2,1}, b_{3,1} = 0, b_{1,2} - b_{2,2} - \beta_E b_{3,2} = 0$, $a(L)$ having all its roots outside the unit circle and

κ_0 being a constant larger than zero.[4] This constant measures the inevitable mean risk and the stationarity condition ensures that this risk does not grow beyond all limits.

Moreover, if the previous considerations prove true, the stochastic trend driving the French interest rate should also do the same to the German interest rate. If it can be shown however, that the adjustment back to equilibrium is the sole task of the French interest rate, it could be concluded that causality runs from the German interest rate to the French rate. Or in other words, in the long-run there is no degree of freedom for setting the French interest rate according to French preferences. The same argument cannot be applied to the expected depreciation rate however. By its forward looking nature, it appears most intuitive that it contains information about *future* movements of both the German and the French interest rate as long as agents form rational expectations and hence $b_{3,i} \neq 0, i = 1,2$. Therefore, the French and possibly also the German interest rate, but not the expected depreciation rate, should be found to adjust to past values of k_t. Thus, while weak exogeneity of the German interest rate could be interpreted as the absence of the French stochastic trend therein (e.g. $b_{2,2} = 0, b_{2,1} \neq 0$), the same could not be concluded from weak exogeneity of E_t.

Second, since in 1987 the FF was officially devaluated for the last time, it is not only the cointegration relationship which is of interest, it is also the potential changes in this relationship due to the changing exchange rate regime. To see this, the following point might be considered. As long as there is no binding commitment to fixing the exchange rate (be it within certain bands of fluctuation), the interest rates might be set by the national monetary authorities at their will. International capital trade will then ensure that no risk free arbitrage is possible by adjusting the exchange rate in a way that offsets potential differences between the interest rates. In the framework of

[4] The combination of β and $b_{i,j}$ values given is not unique. Less restrictive possibilities are presented in Table 4.1.

non-stationary time series analysis, this scenario can be described as the presence of two independent stochastic trends within the tri-variate system, where each of the trends originates from the national monetary policies. The forward rate (as well as the exchange rate) will then be driven by a combination of both these trends, while a (linear) combination of all of them has to yield a stationary relationship if arbitrage is ruled out in the long-run.

In case of interdependency between the two national interest rates, it can be assumed that either both of them adjust to each other to some extent, or that one of them will be set to account for changes of the other one. In the latter case, the interest rate in question will not only be affected by the domestic interest rate policy, but also by the foreign monetary policy decisions. In the time series context, this hypothesis can be cast as follows.[5] Define

$$\begin{aligned} Y_t &= (i^s_{F,t},\, i^s_{G,t},\, E_t)', \\ Y_t^* &= (i^s_{F,t},\, i^s_{G,t},\, E_t,\, 1,\, f_t^{(\cdot)}(\vartheta, T_1)' \otimes z_t^*)', \\ \varepsilon_t &\sim i.i.d(0, \Sigma) \end{aligned}$$

and find

$$\begin{aligned} \Delta Y_t &= \alpha\beta' Y_{t-1}^* + \sum_{i=1}^{p-1} \Gamma_i \Delta Y_{t-1} + \varepsilon_t \\ &= \begin{pmatrix} \alpha_{i^s_F} \\ \alpha_{i^s_G} \\ \alpha_E \end{pmatrix} \begin{pmatrix} 1 & -\beta_{i^s_G} & -\beta_E & -\kappa_0 & -\tau_1 \end{pmatrix} Y_{t-1}^* + \sum_{i=1}^{p-1} \Gamma_i \Delta Y_{t-1} + \varepsilon_t \end{aligned} \tag{4.4}$$

where, for the moment, z_t is zero and $f_t^{(\cdot)}(\vartheta, T_1)$ follows one of the definitions given in (3.16) on page 48. The α, β, Γ are coefficient matrices of appropriate dimension. In this setting, β defines the linear relationship representing the no-arbitrage or CIP condition, and the vector α provides information about the extent to which the endogenous variables adjust to short-run deviations from CIP. If indeed only one of the interest rates is subject to the stochastic

[5] For simplicity, only the case of a single cointegration relationship is considered.

trend of the other one, this should show up as a single significant coefficient in α in the equation for the respective endogenous variable. If however, one of the interest rates is *not* subject to the stochastic trend of the other one, the corresponding coefficient must be zero. Note also that (4.1), (4.2) can easily be related to (4.4) by noting that $E(\beta' Y_t^* - f_t^{(\cdot)}(\vartheta, T_1)' z_t) = \kappa_0$ and hence, a decrease in the inevitable risk after fixing the exchange rate can be modelled as a shift in the mean of the cointegrating vector ($\kappa_1 \neq 0$). This said, the appropriate choice of z_t would be 1 in this case.

From the foregoing discussion it follows that the subsequent analysis will focus on the derivation of the risk premium, κ_t and its properties which will provide the information necessary for drawing conclusions. Table 4.1 surveys the various hypotheses on $\Pi = \alpha\beta'$ and their economic interpretation.

Table 4.1. Hypotheses about $\alpha\beta'$ and Their Interpretation

Hypothesis	Interpretation	common trend representation,[a] see (4.3)
$\mathcal{H}_1 : rank(\Pi) = 1, \wedge \beta_{i_G^s} = 1, \wedge \beta_E \geq 0$	CIP holds	$b_{1,1} - b_{2,1} - \beta_E b_{3,1} = 0$ $b_{1,2} - b_{2,2} - \beta_E b_{3,2} = 0$
$\mathcal{H}_2 : \mathcal{H}_1 \wedge \alpha_{i_G^s} = \alpha_E = 0$	In the long-run: French interest rate policy not independent of the German but German interest rate policy independent of the French.	$b_{1,2} - \beta_E b_{3,2} = 0$ $b_{1,1} - b_{2,1} - \beta_E b_{3,1} = 0$ $(b_{3,1}\, b_{3,2})'(b_{1,1}\, b_{1,2})_\perp \neq 0$ $b_{2,2} = 0$
$\mathcal{H}_3 : \mathcal{H}_2 \wedge \kappa_1 \neq 0 \wedge T_1 \approx 1987$	Change in exchange rate regime affects CIP condition.	

[a] The subscript $\perp$ to a $(m \times 1)$ vector v signifies the $(1 \times m)$ orthogonal complement of v with $v'v_\perp = 0$ and hence, for the present case the restriction ensures that no linear combination of $(b_{3,1}\, b_{3,2})$ and $(b_{2,1}\, b_{2,2})$ exists whose outcome is zero.

Under $\mathcal{H}_2$ the common trends representation becomes

$$\begin{bmatrix} i_F^s \\ i_G^s \\ E \end{bmatrix}_t = \begin{bmatrix} b_{1,1} & b_{1,2} \\ b_{2,1} & 0 \\ \frac{1}{\beta_E}(b_{1,1} - b_{2,1}) & \frac{1}{\beta_E} b_{1,2} \end{bmatrix} \begin{bmatrix} \sum_{j=1}^t u_{1,j} \\ \sum_{j=1}^t u_{2,j} \end{bmatrix} + \begin{matrix}\text{stationary} \\ \text{components}\end{matrix}$$

which emphases the previous statement of $i^s_{G,t}$ being driven by a single stochastic trend while the French interest rate is subject to two stochastic trends one of which originating in its German counterpart. A further possibility would be to regard $b_{3,1}$ as zero which would trivially ensure that no stationary linear combination of $i^s_{F,t}$ and E_t exists. Refraining from this assumption is consistent with the view that the expected change in the exchange rate is driven by German and French stochastic trends jointly.

The last hypothesis points to a potential problem which may arise because of the change in exchange rate regime around 1987. If the agents believed the rate to be fixed from that time onwards, it would imply the expected depreciation rate to become zero on average. Put it in the time series context, no unit root behaviour should be present after 1987. For the analysis to follow, the unit root test on E_t is also performed for the sub-sample 1987-1998.

Hypotheses $\mathcal{H}_1$ to $\mathcal{H}_3$ will be investigated according to the following strategy. First, the unit-root properties of the variables in question will be investigated, second, the cointegrating rank will be established, and finally, a stability analysis performed. This stability check will very much focus on the stability of the cointegrating relationship. The aim is to identify a valid representation of the DGP according to (4.4), which provides reliable information on the structural and economically meaningful long-run relationships between the variables.

4.2.3 A Small Econometric Study

The previous discussion led to three testable and interpretable hypotheses about the relationship between the German and the French interest rates as well as the expected depreciation rate (see Table 4.1). For the econometric implementation, interest rates on credits referring to contracts over three months are considered along with the forward rate due in three months time. Thus, the maturities of the various assets are in line with each other. The data definitions and their sources are reported in the appendix, while Figure 4.1 provides a graphical impression.

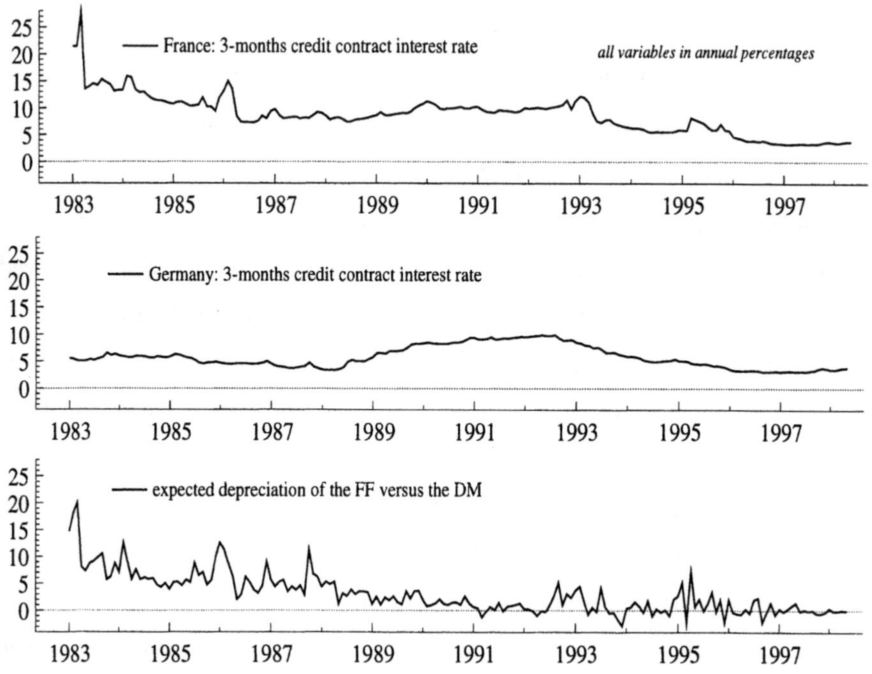

Figure 4.1. Data Input for the CIP Analysis

Time Series Properties

For investigating the time series properties, univariate as well as multi-variate analyses will be employed. Table 4.2 lists the results of various unit root tests. The hypothesis of a unit root is tested in the framework of the Augmented Dickey-Fuller test which rests on the following regression

$$\Delta y_t = \mu_0 + \mu_1 t - (1-\alpha)y_{t-1} + \sum_{i=1}^{p} \gamma_i \Delta y_{t-1} + \varepsilon_t, \quad t = -p, \ldots, 1, \ldots T$$

with $\varepsilon_t \sim i.i.d.(0, \sigma_\varepsilon^2)$ and where presence of a unit root cannot be rejected if the coefficient on y_{t-1} is found not significantly less than zero according to the Dickey-Fuller statistic. The y_t are the variables for which the unit root hypothesis is tested and μ_0, μ_1 and γ_i are scalar coefficients.

Table 4.2. CIP Analysis: Unit Root Tests

variable	setup[a]	statistic[b]	decision
Sample: 1983(Jan) - 1998(May), $T = 179$			
$i^s_{F,t}$	μ_0,3	-1.635	I(1)
$\Delta i^s_{F,t}$	μ_0,2	-12.54**	
$i^s_{G,t}$	μ_0,3	-.921	I(1)
$\Delta i^s_{G,t}$	μ_0,3	-5.199**	
E_t	μ_0,5	-2.705	I(1)
ΔE_t	μ_0,4	-10.031**	
Sample: 1987(Jan) - 1998(May), T = 135			
E_t	μ_0,1	-3.67**	I(0)

[a] μ_0: constant, the integers indicate the lags of differenced dependent variables included in the regression, no time trend is included.
[b] ADF test statistic, the MacKinnon (1991) 1%,5%,10% critical values are -3.43, -2.86, -2.57.
* Here, ** and * indicate significance at the one and five per cent level respectively.

However, the test results unanimously point to non-stationarity of all variables involved while the null hypothesis of non-stationarity could be rejected for the sub-sample 1987-1998 for the expected depreciation rate.[6] Although being in line with the events described above and thus useful information, as an auxiliary measure the stationarity feature of the E_t series for the sub-sample is ignored on grounds of lack of evidence against non-stationarity for the whole sample size. In addition, in chapter 3 on page 65 unit root tests

[6] In the ADF testing framework, the null hypothesis of a unit root is $H_0 : \alpha = 1$ against $H_1 : |\alpha| < 1$.

allowing for a nonlinear shift in the mean are considered to the effect that the null of non-stationarity cannot be rejected in most cases.

CIP System Analysis

Having found all three series non-stationary, the CIP hypothesis can be tested in the cointegration framework. To that aim, cointegration tests are performed which are designed to indicate whether or not linear combinations of the non-stationary series are stationary. Two tests will be employed. The first one is the so-called Johansen test (see Johansen (1988) and Johansen (1991)) while the second has been developed by Saikkonen and Lütkepohl (2000a) (henceforth S&L). The latter test has the advantage that it can be generalised to situations where the cointegration mean shifts without affecting the distribution of the test statistic.[7]

Table 4.3 collects the test results for various model variants. For the time being, only the first section is of interest. It reveals that the cointegrating rank in the system is at most two. The Johansen test discovers two stationary relationships at a very convenient level of significance, while according to the S&L test only one of these relationships can be found. Further investigation into the matter led to the conclusion that $rank = 1$ is indeed the correct decision, because the identification of the second relation (E_t stationary) results in a cointegration relationship with a significant trend. Thus, at this stage $\mathcal{H}_1$ already finds support.

Under the assumption of cointegrating rank one, identification of the relationship is trivial. It just requires to normalise the cointegration vector. Table 4.4 reports the various hypotheses on the cointegrating relationship for various model variants starting with the just identified relationship.

Before turning to the second and third section of Table 4.4, the standard case without changes in the cointegration mean should be scrutinized. As far

[7] See Saikkonen and Lütkepohl (2000b) and Lütkepohl, Saikkonen and Trenkler (2000) for a comparison of competing approaches.

Table 4.3. CIP Analysis: Cointegration Tests

Sample: 1983(Jan) - 1998(May), $T = 179$

Hypotheses	Johansen test statistic	5% critical value	S&L test statistic	5% critical value
$Y_t^* = (Y_t', 1)'$				
$r_0 = 0$ vs. $r_0 \geq 1$	115.92	34.8	38.97	24.08
$r_0 = 1$ vs. $r_0 \geq 2$	30.25	19.99	1.04	12.21
$r_0 = 2$ vs. $r_0 = 3$	.998	9.13	.78	4.14
$Y_t^* = (Y_t', 1, f_t^3(\vartheta = .99, 1986(Feb))')'$, (smooth shift)				
$r_0 = 0$ vs. $r_0 \geq 1$			40.27	24.08
$r_0 = 1$ vs. $r_0 \geq 2$			1.15	12.21
$r_0 = 2$ vs. $r_0 = 3$			.92	4.14
$Y_t^* = (Y_t', 1, f_t^1(1986(Feb)))'$, (step dummy)				
$r_0 = 0$ vs. $r_0 \geq 1$			40.27	24.08
$r_0 = 1$ vs. $r_0 \geq 2$			1.15	12.21
$r_0 = 2$ vs. $r_0 = 3$			.92	4.14

First section (rows 1 to 4) reports the result of the standard cointegration tests. Sections two and three are cointegration tests taking into account the results of Table 4.5 and thus aim at supporting the rank test results under the presence of structural breaks in the cointegration relationship.

as the estimation results are concerned, there does not seem to be a problem with the specification found hypothesizing H_0^2. The German interest rate and expected depreciation are weakly exogenous and the long-run coefficient $\beta_{i_G^s}$ has the correct sign and magnitude. The estimate of the mean risk measured by the CIP condition is somewhat less convincing. It is not the sign which raises suspicion rather than the estimated standard error which renders the point estimate insignificant. Thus, according to the economic interpretation provided above, no significant risk remains when hedging short run credits by forward contracts.[8]

Even more concern is raised by analysing the stability properties of the estimates according to H_0^2. The upper panel of Figure 4.13 on page 168 in

[8] The hypothesis $\kappa_0 = 0$ in conjunction with H_0^2 could not be rejected at the 14 percent level of significance.

Table 4.4. CIP Analysis: Hypotheses about the Cointegrating Relations

$$\Delta Y_t = \alpha\beta' Y^*_{t-1} + \sum_{j=1}^{p-1} \Gamma_j \Delta Y_{t-j} + \varepsilon_t,\ t = p+1, p+2, \ldots$$
$$Y'_t = (i^s_{F,t}\ i^s_{G,t}\ E_t)$$

Sample: Jan 1983 - May 1998

Hypotheses	vector	coefficient estimates on $i^s_{F,t}$	$i^s_{G,t}$	E_t	κ_0	κ_1	LR stat. [p-value][a]	d.f.[b]
1.) $Y^*_t = (Y'_t,\ 1)'$								
	$\hat{\beta}'$	1	-1.01	$-.87$	$-.12$			
			(.05)	(.03)	(.36)			
	$\hat{\alpha}$	$-.26$	.05	.45				
		(.08)	(.03)	(.23)				
H^1_0 $\beta_{i^s_G} = -1$	$\hat{\beta}'$	1	-1	$-.87$	$-.16$		.01	1
				(.04)	(.15)		[.91]	
	$\hat{\alpha}$	$-.26$	.05	.45				
		(.08)	(.03)	(.23)				
H^2_0 $H^1_0 \wedge \alpha_{i^s_G} =$ $\alpha_E = 0$	$\hat{\beta}'$	1	-1	$-.82$	$-.22$		5.25	3
				(.04)	(.17)		[.15]	
	$\hat{\alpha}$	$-.35$	0	0				
		(.07)						
2.) $Y^*_t = (Y'_t,\ 1,\ f^3_t(\vartheta = .99, 1986(Feb))')'$, (smooth shift)								
	$\hat{\beta}'$	1	$-.96$	$-.82$	-1.13	.68		
			(.03)	(.02)	(.22)	(.07)		
	$\hat{\alpha}$	$-.56$	.02	$-.05$				
		(.06)	(.03)	(.21)				
H^3_0 $\beta_{i^s_G} = -1$	$\hat{\beta}'$	1	-1	$-.83$	$-.90$	.68	1.51	1
				(.02)	(.11)	(.07)	[.22]	
	$\hat{\alpha}$	$-.55$	.02	$-.04$				
		(.06)	(.03)	(.21)				
H^4_0 $H^3_0 \wedge \alpha_{i^s_G} =$ $\alpha_E = 0$	$\hat{\beta}'$	1	-1	$-.83$	$-.91$	.69	2.34	3
				(.02)	(.11)	(.07)	[.50]	
	$\hat{\alpha}$	$-.55$	0	0				
		(.05)						

[a] likelihood ratio statistic with χ^2 distribution, except for second section. The p-value is given in brackets [].
[b] d.f. stands for degree of freedom of the χ^2 distribution.

Table 4.4 CIP Analysis: Hypotheses about the Cointegrating Relations (cont.)

$$\Delta Y_t = \alpha\beta' Y^*_{t-1} + \sum_{j=1}^{p-1} \Gamma_j \Delta Y_{t-j} + \varepsilon_t, \; t = p+1, p+2, \ldots$$
$$Y'_t = (i^s_{F,t} \; i^s_{G,t} \; E_t)$$

Sample: Jan 1983 - May 1998

Hypotheses	vector	coefficient estimates on $i^s_{F,t}$	$i^s_{G,t}$	E_t	κ_0	κ_1	LR stat. [p-value][a]	d.f.[b]
3.) $Y^*_t = (Y'_t, 1, f^1_t(1986(Feb)))'$, (step dummy)								
	$\hat{\beta}'$	1	$-.97$	$-.71$	-1.91	1.36		
			(.04)	(.04)	(.40)	(.26)		
	$\hat{\alpha}$	$-.50$	.06	$-.14$				
		(.09)	(.03)	(.26)				
H^5_0 $\beta_{i^s_G} = -1$	$\hat{\beta}'$	1	-1	$-.71$	-1.69	1.33	3.27	1
				(.04)	(.31)	(.27)	[.43]	
	$\hat{\alpha}$	$-.49$	.06	$-.12$				
		(.09)	(.03)	(.26)				
H^6_0 $H^5_0 \wedge \alpha_{i^s_G} = \alpha_E = 0$	$\hat{\beta}'$	1	-1	$-.72$	-1.64	1.29	4.10	3
				(.04)	(.32)	(.28)	[.25]	
	$\hat{\alpha}$	$-.51$	0	0				
		(.08)						

[a] likelihood ratio statistic with χ^2 distribution, except for second section. The p-value is given in brackets [].
[b] d.f. stands for degree of freedom of the χ^2 distribution.

the appendix to this chapter depicts the recursive β estimates of the same relationship starting at around 1987, adding one observation after the other and re-estimating the whole model under H^2_0. While the long-run coefficients seem to be estimated with approximately the same value over the whole sample, the uncertainty with which they are estimated appears to be rather large, especially until 1991. In fact, they cannot be regarded as significantly different from zero for almost half the sample period. This can be interpreted as a comparably bad fit of the long-run specification. Even worse results are obtained for the test statistic on the hypothesis H^2_0. Table 4.4 suggests that the hypothesis cannot be rejected at the .15 level of significance, but this does not hold for the whole sample, only for a fairly small part of it (see the lower panel in Figure 4.13).

Considering the remarks about the possible impact of the change in the exchange rate regime on the cointegration relation, the reason for the observed problems may well be that the specification of the model does not take these events into account. Therefore, in the next paragraphs the setup is extended to encompass breaks in the cointegration relationship.

Breaks in the CIP Relationship

For investigating the stability of the cointegration relationship the setup of (4.1) in conjunction with (4.2) will be used. The maximum likelihood estimation procedure by Hansen (1992) and Seo (1998) will be applied for the case that z_t is either a constant or a vector of all or of a subset of the endogenous variables. This gives rise to a number of possible changes in the cointegration relation including changes in one or more components of β and shifts in the mean of the cointegration relation. It might be interesting to note that the statistical model is not equivalent to the setup recommended by S&L in that the effects of deterministic shifts do not spread out over more than one period. This can be recognized from missing lags (of differences) of the shift variables in the regression equation provided e.g. in the header of Table 4.4.

All these possibilities will be investigated in a systematic manner. To keep the number of potential variations in the cointegration space sufficiently small, the analysis will be restricted to changes in one endogenous variable at a time or a break in the cointegrating mean. The shift functions discussed in chapter 3 serve as models for the transition to the new long-run equilibrium relationship. Albeit lacking sound theoretical grounds, the maximum likelihood estimation of the break date (T_1) and the shape parameter (ϑ) is performed by maximizing the likelihood value for the statistical model over all possible break points T_1, and over reasonable values for ϑ.This approach projects the suggestions by Saikkonen and Lütkepohl (2001) into the multi-variate case who estimate the shift parameters and T_1 by selecting those values which are associated with the maximum likelihood value of their model. The choice is made out of a set of possible values for ϑ, T_1 and the corresponding likelihood values are obtained by a grid search. In the present example, the T_1 are searched within the whole sample except for the time 12 months after start and 12 months before end of the sample period. The lag order of the *VAR* without shift has been chosen according to the Akaike Information Criterion (*AIC*) criterion and the rank decision has been based on the analysis above. It will be checked again when the break point has been identified. Table 4.5 provides the details.

The most important result of the break point search procedure is certainly the outcome that, independent of the actual variation allowed for, the optimal break point is the same. This break point coincides reasonably well with the sequence of events described before. The transition to the new long-run equilibrium starts in February 1986 which can be regarded as a good approximation of the true date of the final exchange rate peg. Second, the overall maximum of the likelihood is obtained for a shift in the long-run coefficient on E_t whose shape is determined by a rational function (type 3 shift) with the additional property that it actually consists of two parts ($f_t^{(3)}(\vartheta) = \left[\frac{d_t}{1-\vartheta L}, \frac{d_{t-1}}{1-\vartheta L}\right]'$) providing more flexibility with respect to the timing of its impact on the DGP. A graphical representation of the empirical shape is provided in Figure 4.2.

When judging on the basis of the selection criteria, the same conclusion can be drawn. It can in general be expected to generate a larger likelihood for the type 3 shift function because it involves a more flexible way of shifting. The selection criteria also take that into account when weighting the model performance against the number of estimated parameters. Thus, scrutinizing the results in that respect, it turns out that the advantage of the model with varying long-run coefficient on E_t does not do too much better than for example a type 3 shift function in the mean (see last line).

Overall, it could even be argued that the results are very similar for all variations where the largest differences occur between the types of shift function encountered rather than with the coefficients allowed to vary. Therefore,

Table 4.5. CIP Analysis 1983 Jan - 1998 May: Break Point Search

$$\Delta Y_t = \Pi Y^*_{t-1} + \sum_{j=1}^{4} \Gamma_j \Delta Y_{t-j} + \varepsilon_t,\ t = p+1, p+2, \ldots,\ rank(\Pi) = 1$$

$$Y_t = (i^s_G,\ i^s_F,\ E)'_t,\ Y^*_t = (Y'_t,\ 1,\ z_t f^{(j)}(\vartheta, T_1)')'_t,\ 12 \le T_1 \le T - 12$$

z_t	jump (j)[a]	$\hat{\vartheta}$	Loglikelihood	*AIC*	*HQ*	*SC*	$\hat{T}_1$
0	0		−479.934	−2.737	−2.398	−1.901	
i^s_G	1		−471.732	−2.853	−2.507	−1.901	1986(Feb)
	2	1.2	−472.096	−2.849	−2.503	−1.996	1986(Feb)
	3	.99	−448.150	−3.131	−2.778	−2.261	1986(Feb)
E	1		−471.960	−2.852	−2.507	−1.999	1986(Feb)
	2	1.2	−472.510	−2.846	−2.500	−1.993	1986(Feb)
	3	.99	−445.244	**-3.144**	**-2.791**	**-2.274**	1986(Feb)
i^s_F	1		−472.798	−2.835	−2.489	−1.982	1986(Feb)
	2	1.2	−473.273	−2.829	−2.483	−1.976	1986(Feb)
	3	.99	−447.624	−3.120	−2.768	−2.250	1986(Feb)
1	1		−471.875	−2.808	−2.512	−2.005	1986(Feb)
	2	1.2	−472.349	−2.852	−2.507	−2.000	1986(Feb)
	3	.99	−448.101	−3.132	−2.780	−2.262	1986(Feb)

[a] Jump indicates the shift function underlying the model. A zero stands for no shift at all, 1 for a step function, 2 for an exponential shift and 3 for a rational shift function. For the latter two, the parameter ϑ defines the shape of the functions (see (3.16) for the definition and Figure 3.1 for examples).
Bold face signifies the minimum of the selection criteria where HQ stands for the Hannan-Quinn and SC for the Schwarz Criterion.

and due to the fact that shifts in the cointegration mean have been discussed in the literature more extensively, the model to be chosen for further analysis will be the one involving a type 3 shift in the mean. A further advantage of this approach is that it can easily be interpreted as a change in the risk characterizing the investor's choice between credit contracts.

In the following, the rank decision will be checked on the basis of the S&L test mentioned before. This is done in two ways. First, the new model including the type 3 shift is tested for cointegration (see section two of Table 4.3) and second the step function is employed. This procedure may be regarded as cumbersome but since testing with smooth shift functions is not yet a standard procedure dealt with in the literature, the comparison to the simpler step dummy case serves as an indication of the reliability of the results.[9] In the current example, the results for both shifts are not only similar, they are even identical up to the forth decimal. They clearly point to the cointegrating rank of one. Thus, the analysis can be continued under the assumption of the presence of one cointegration relationship and a shift in the mean of the cointegration relationship starting in February 1986.

4.2.4 Comparison of Two Econometric Models of the CIP

The previous sections pointed out the necessity to model the cointegration relationship implied by the CIP hypothesis with time varying coefficients. It turned out that a shift in the mean of the cointegration space does almost as good as competing approaches. In this section, the properties of the model with such a shift are investigated and compared to those of the constant coefficient case estimated before.

As a first measure, Figure 4.2 shows a graphical representation of the type 3 shift now included in the model in comparison to a simple shift dummy at the same point in time. From the graph it becomes apparent that the superior performance of the type 3 shift can at least partly be attributed to the additional flexibility it allows for. Here, the final level (normalised to one) is achieved around June 1987 before which some extreme values are touched upon. It is worth mentioning that this kind of shift function could in principle

[9] Note that a shift in the coefficient of one of the endogenous variables would be even more problematic because it requires computationally expensive simulations for which no proper software is available yet (see Seo (1998)).

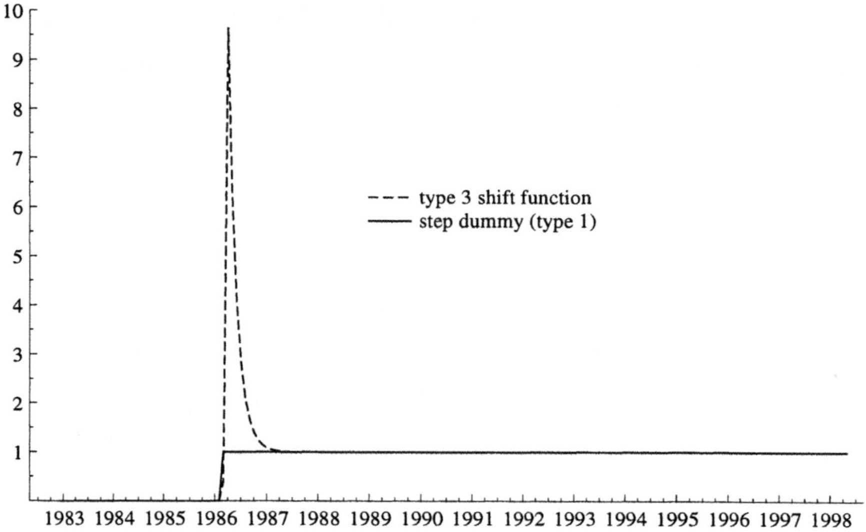

Figure 4.2. CIP Analysis: Shifts in the Cointegration Mean

also select a single data point as a shift date. This will be case when the upward shift is accompanied by a downward shift of the same magnitude, if thereby the gain in explanatory power becomes accordingly large. Thus, the spike visible in Figure 4.2 cannot be interpreted as a single outlier rather than an outlier being part of the non-linear transition to the new cointegration mean.

Estimating the CIP Relationship

Up to this point, evidence has been gathered as to what modelling approach would fit the data best. Economic theory provided the framework and the historic events eventually shaped the final decision about the econometric implementation. What is left, is a look at the actual estimates, the evaluation of the final specification and an interpretation of the results. With respect to the first point, Table 4.4, section two reports the long-run estimates under similar hypotheses as before. Again, the joint hypothesis on the parameters of β and α cannot be rejected. The marginal level of significance is .50 in the present case.

Comparison of the point estimates under H_0^4, H_0^6 in Table 4.4 to the situation with constant coefficients (H_0^2) reveals no major differences with one remarkable exception. This exception is the mean value of the cointegration relationship, which becomes significant when its value is allowed to vary over time. Furthermore, as Figure 4.13 on page 168 lower section implies, one of the arguments which led to the rejection of the hypothesis of constant coefficients cannot be applied any longer.

Two major improvements can be observed instead. First, point estimates seem to be estimated much more accurately than before, and second, the joint hypothesis (H_0^4) cannot be rejected at any point in time during the sample under consideration (see bottom right panel). For convenience, the scaling of the vertical axis is identical to the scaling in Figure 4.13 upper part. Thus, these results demonstrate the advancement achieved in the performance of the model.

It remains to assess the final specification in terms of residual analysis. To that aim, the whole model is re-estimated under H_0^2 and H_0^4 respectively with restrictions on the short-run parameters in the Γ_i matrices. These restrictions are generated by a top-down reduction strategy where the Akaike information criterion is used to decide whether or not to remove the variable in question.[10] For comparison, the constant coefficient model is treated in the same way. Table 4.6 gives an overview of the estimation outcome together with some test statistics evaluating the model performances.

As it turns out, the model with time varying cointegration mean appears superior with respect to residual standard deviation, residual autocorrelation

[10] See Lütkepohl (1993a), pp. 180 ff. The results are obtained with the software package *JMulTi1.0beta*, where a corresponding procedure is implemented. The newest version of this package is available as a free download from `http://www.jmulti.de`.

Table 4.6. CIP Analysis: Restricted Reduced Form Estimation Results

		Equation (dependent variable)[a]					
independent		time varying model			constant coefficient model		
variable	lag	$\Delta i^s_{F,t}$	$\Delta i^s_{G,t}$	ΔE_t	$\Delta i^s_{F,t}$	$\Delta i^s_{G,t}$	ΔE_t
Δi^s_F	1	.20		1.02	.11		.73
		(.06)		(.20)	(.08)		(.21)
	2		.08		−.01	.03	
			(.03)		(.07)	(.03)	
	3		.04		−.04	.02	
			(.02)		(.05)	(.02)	
	4				.02		
					(.04)		
Δi^s_G	1		.13			−.07	
			(.07)			(.07)	
	2				−.18		
					(.20)		
	4	.29	.14	1.03	.21	.16	.88
		(.16)	(.07)	(.52)	(.24)	(.07)	(.54)
ΔE_t	1	−.25	−.03	−.73		−.01	−.46
		(.04)	(.01)	(.07)		(.01)	(.07)
	2	−.18	−.05	−.49		−.03	−.29
		(.03)	(.01)	(.09)		(.01)	(.08)
	3	−.14	−.04	−.37		−.02	−.22
		(.02)	(.01)	(.07)		(.01)	(.07)
	4	−.11	−.02	−.22	−.05	−.01	−.13
		(.02)	(.01)	(.06)	(.03)	(.01)	(.06)
intercept		−.02	−.01	−.10	.17	−.01	−.07
		(.04)	(.02)	(.13)	(.06)	(.02)	(.13)
ec term	1	−.56			−.59		
		(.05)			(.04)		

[a] Sample: 1983 Jan - 1998 May. The entries report the coefficient estimates and the estimated standard errors in parentheses.

and it also features fewer ARCH effects, which in general does not come as a surprise because the data is collected from financial markets. Normality is rejected for both sets of residuals. It should be noted that, apart from the cointegration relationship, the models are not different from each other. Therefore, the differences in the model performances can solely be attributed to this sin-

Table 4.7. CIP Analysis: Restricted Reduced Form Estimation Properties

Sample: 1983 Jan - 1998 May

Residual analysis with statistics; degrees of freedom [p-value]

Test	time varying model			constant coefficient model		
	$\Delta i^s_{F,t}$	$\Delta i^s_{G,t}$	ΔE_t	$\Delta i^s_{F,t}$	$\Delta i^s_{G,t}$	ΔE_t
correlation and	**.52**	·	·	**.80**	·	·
standard	.28	**.23**	·	.30	**.24**	·
deviation[a]	.43	-.01	**1.72**	.50	.03	**1.79**
Portmanteau (16)[b]		118.15; 123 [.60]			233.75**; 122 [.00]	
Nonnormality[c]		169.61**; 6 [.00]			238.37**; 6 [.00]	
ARCH (4)[d]	8.49* [.08]	5.46 [.24]	1.43 [.84]	11.90** [.02]	8.88* [.06]	5.58 [.23]
ARCH (16)	18.09 [.32]	32.31** [.01]	11.43 [.78]	24.69* [.08]	32.58** [.01]	14.11 [.59]

[a] The diagonal elements in bold face report the standard deviations, the off-diagonal entries refer to the correlations between the residuals of the corresponding equations (vertical order = horizontal order).

*,** indicate significance at the ten and five level of significance respectively.

[b] Test for vector autocorrelation of the residuals of up to order 16 with; degree of freedom and p-value of corresponding χ^2 distribution. See Lütkepohl (1993a), pp 150 ff.

[c] Test for vector normality of the residuals. See Lütkepohl (1993a), pp 155 ff.

[d] Single equation test for autoregressive heteroscedasticity of the residuals up to order 4 and 16 with 4 and 16 degrees of freedom respectively.

gle instance of flexibility allowed for. In addition, while the coefficient on the error correction term (denoted *ec* term in the table), is almost exactly the same in the time varying model independent of the restrictions imposed on the Γ_i matrices, the same statement does not hold for the constant coefficient model, where it rises from .35 to .59 in absolute value when statistically unnecessary variables are removed. Thus, the time varying model seems to be more robust in that respect which might also be seen as an advantage over the constant coefficient model.

Finally, Figures 4.14 on page 169 in the appendix plot the residuals obtained from the specifications in Table 4.6.

4.2.5 CIP Analysis: Concluding Remarks

Interpretation

In the foregoing, the *VAR* model with time varying cointegration restriction has been shown to be a reasonable description of the data generating process. Therefore, it is sensible to base the interpretation of the data on the outcome of this econometric model. Under the hypothesis H_0^4 the following long-run equilibrium relationship has been found

$$i^s_{F,t} = i^s_{G,t} + .83E_t + .91 - .69f^3_t(.99, 1986(Feb)) + ec^1_t. \tag{4.5}$$

All its parameters have been shown to be highly significant, and they also have the signs suggested by economic theory. Here, ec^1_t stands for error correction term, which is a stationary process with mean zero. The error correction term only enters the equation for the French short-term interest rate which gives rise to the interpretation as the dependent variable in the long-run. In other words, German interest rate policy had a decisive long-run impact on the French monetary policy but not vice versa.

This dependency arose from the covered interest parity condition as reflected in (4.5). It is a relationship that underwent a transformation when the exchange rate regime was adjusted for the introduction of the Euro currency. From 1987 onwards the official parity of the currencies did not change but moved within narrow bands instead. In the long-run relationship this change is reflected in the variation of the cointegrating mean. As outlined before, the mean value of the long-run relation can be regarded as the average risk premium on cross border credits hedged by forward contracts. While this premium was approximately .91 before 1987 it decreased to a value of $(.91 - .69) = .22$ afterwards.

To sum up the results of the CIP analysis, Table 4.1 may be reconsidered. In due course, all of the hypotheses $\mathcal{H}_1$ to $\mathcal{H}_3$ have found support providing evidence for the view that French monetary policy was structurally dependent on the German interest rate policy but not vice versa. The corresponding transmission channel was the CIP condition, a link which tightened after 1987 as it is reflected in the lowering risk premium.

Implications for Money Demand Analysis

The study of French interest rates revealed a change in the structure of the determination of short-term interest rates. It turned out that, in line with economic theory, the exchange rate regime is the crucial point. Artus and Salomon (1996) quote the year 1986 as the period during which the central parity had been adjusted a number of times. When in early 1987 the Deutschmark was appreciated against the EMS basket, this marked the last change in the official exchange rate between the FF and the Deutschmark. Thus, the date January 1987 can also be seen as the end of a devaluation period rather than as a single event and the timing of the shift identified appears reasonable. Since then the exchange rate basically stayed the same within narrow bands and even sustained the speculative attacks during the early 90s. Notably, the introduction of the Euro, and hence the abolishment of the two currencies, does not alter the situation with respect to the relationship between the exchange rate and the short-term interest rate. This is because the situation of zero variations in the parity as of the time after 1998 is approximately equivalent to maintaining the central parity with very small, temporary deviations. This can be considered a first indication that a money demand analysis which certainly considers interest rates, and which is restricted to the period prior to the EMU should deliver results which might also be valid afterwards.

Against this rather optimistic interpretation, on the basis of weak exogeneity results, the analysis demonstrated that in the long-run French monetary policy, that is interest rate policy, was dependent on the German conditions.

A transmission of policy shocks in the opposite direction could not be found as far as the long-run structure is concerned. Therefore, the present results support the hypothesis of long-run German dominance referred to by several authors like for example Hagen and Fratianni (1990), Artus and Salomon (1996), Kirchgässner and Wolters (1996) (see also the references therein). As a consequence, the conditions under which the central banks in these two countries conducted their policies was quite different. While the Bundesbank was seemingly able to act like being independent of foreign monetary policy (at least independent of its largest neighbour France), this does not hold for the French central bank. The unidirectional dependence grew even stronger over the years. Consequently, while the Bundesbank was able to pursue a much more independent monetary policy according to the economic conditions of the domestic German economy, this seems to be very unlikely for the Banque de France. Thus, the claim made by Cassard et al. (1995), namely that France also applied a money targeting policy appears to be questionable.

If the latter statement was taken seriously, naturally the question arises, what the central bank did instead, and what the implications for the standard money demand analysis are likely to be. The most trivial answer to the first question is interest rate targeting, or to be more precise, exchange rate targeting by means of adjusting the central bank interest rate accordingly.

As to the second question, the answer is less straightforward. While on the one hand, the agents can be supposed to demand money as agents can generally be assumed to, it could well be that the econometric approaches discussed in the introductory chapter are less likely to discover the related behavioural function. The central argument to be put forward in that respect has already been produced by Working (1927) and is the subject of every modern macroeconomic textbook; namely the necessity to identify both supply and demand if either of these curves is subject to statistical analysis.

Usually, identification of the supply curves remains a rudimentary procedure which can be justified by the assumption of exogeneity of the money supply. The intuition is, that in the case of monetary targeting as in the standard money multiplier model the authorities would focus on a supply of money. The exact amount offered depends on the forecast for the most important argument of the money demand function, income, and an implicit target inflation rate like the approximately two percent in the ECB reference growth rate of money. This commitment in turn implies a degree of exogeneity for the money supply process which most of the time allows to conveniently identify the demand curve. This is because in such a case the CB interest rate is used to achieve the monetary target and can be linked to the exogenous money supply process. If successful, this strategy will lead to a situation where the money supply function will shift along the demand curve in accordance with the targets set by the authorities. The observations made under these circumstances will recollect points on the demand curve, and therefore identify the demand function.

The foregoing is not a priori applicable though, if the money supply process itself is subject to exogenous influence. For France this might well be the case because the short-term interest rate has been shown to be ruled by the German rate. Therefore, the interest rate can not be used as a tool for achieving a money growth target when aiming at the exchange rate at the same time. Thus, the identification of money demand and supply becomes an issue again and it is far from clear that the standard approach will necessarily disclose the features of the demand rather than the supply function. This argument is particularly relevant, since the scheme discussed in chapter 2 collected not only those variables which potentially enter the demand function but also factors being important in the money supply process. Therefore, if any of the candidate relationships (money supply or demand) dominates in the long-run, it will be identified and the actual coefficient estimates of the long-run relationship will inform about the prevailing relation.

Finally, having discovered a change in the channel transmitting foreign shocks to the French economy, it seems reasonable to assume that other relationships which are relevant for monetary policy transmission such as the Fisher relation, the expectation hypothesis on the term structure, and the money demand or supply function may change too.

4.3 Money Supply in France Prior to EMU

Chapter 2 presented a blueprint for money demand analysis in that it discussed the choice of variables, hypotheses, estimation strategies and interpretation techniques. The task is now to apply these suggestions.

The structure of the approach is the following. The literature on money demand for France is first briefly reviewed, then a few remarks on the data will precede the econometric exercise. Finally, my conclusions will be supplemented by a discussion of the implications for EMU from the French perspective.

4.3.1 On French Money Demand

In striking contrast to its size, political and economic weight within the European monetary system's member countries, France has attracted little interest in the empirical analysis of monetary policy, and money demand in particular. It was not even considered in the extensive analysis of monetary transmission mechanisms in European countries by Juselius (1998) covering Italy, Germany and Denmark. When considered, French money demand has typically been treated within a group of European countries (see e.g. Tullio et al. (1996), Wesche (1998), Fagan and Henry (1999), Clausen (1998)).

A natural drawback of such approaches is the inevitable loss of information about valuable details like stability of parameter estimates, adjustment mechanisms other than adjustments of money to the money demand relation, complementary long-run relationships and the like.

The early study of Cassard et al. (1995) also addresses some of these questions. Their initial argument is that France is pursuing monetary targeting and they find evidence not only for a money demand relationship but also for a significant reaction of money growth to the equilibrium error. Their sample covers the period from the first quarter of 1979 to the second quarter of 1990. The data features most of the properties which are also present in the current analysis. In general, their study partly complies with the demands on a money demand analysis outlined above. The framework is a system of macroeconomic variables (nominal money, real income, long-term and short-term interest rates), cointegration is tested and one of the two stationary relationships is identified. Eventually, stability of the final specification for money growth is investigated by a forecast statistic.

There are some questions left which Cassard et al. (1995) raise but refrain from answering. They acknowledge the troublesome period of capital restrictions and their subsequent abolishment starting around the mid-eighties. Likewise the change in exchange rate policy in 1987 is mentioned. They do not account for either of these incidents in their econometric experiment, nor do they explore potential impacts on the estimation outcome, however. Furthermore, the properties of the long-run money demand functions are hardly investigated in terms of significance of the parameter estimates over time, for example. The only exception in that respect is Müller (1999), a study which can be regarded as the predecessor of the current one.

The following analysis extends the previous approaches to French money demand in a number of ways. First, while the focus will also be on the money demand function, other long-run relationships which might be present will likewise be identified. Having emphasised the relevance of the adjustment parameters for policy analysis, their properties will also be looked at. Finally, in the light of the CIP analysis of the previous section, it will be assumed that a break in the cointegration relationships may have occurred around 1987. Modelling such an event will be compared to a model which does not take this extra information into account. Anticipating the outcome of this approach, allowing for a change in the cointegrating space helps to identify a long-run money supply function for France and provides an explanation for the apparent failure of preceding studies on French money demand.

4.3.2 Data and Model

Data Issues

Acknowledging the relevance of the data quality for interpretation, comparability and usefulness of the results, the data sources are thoroughly reported and possible alternatives will be discussed. For the current problem, a major difficulty is the introduction of the new European Standard for Accounting in 1995 (ESA 95). It replaces earlier methods and comparability is not universally ensured. Moreover, this new standard has been in place for a couple of years only, thus limiting the available data pool.

In addition to these fairly general, European problems, France seems to be somewhat peculiar with respect to the GDP measure. While one would usually prefer rather raw data, that is non seasonally adjusted data, it appears virtually impossible to obtain it in this case. As a consequence, the following analysis will have to build on seasonally adjusted data.

In the next sections a money demand system of the standard type discussed in the introductory chapter will be estimated. It consists of the logarithm of real money variable (M3 deflated by the harmonized index of consumer prices, hicp), log of real GDP income (y_t), government bond rates (i_t^l), call money rates (i_t^{cm}) and inflation ($4\Delta hicp_t = \pi_t$). They are all measured at a quarterly frequency. The money data series as well as the interest rates have been obtained from an International Monetary Fund (IMF) data base, while the income data is provided by the Organization for Economic Cooperation and Development (OECD) (see Table 4.22). The harmonized index of consumer prices serves as the price indicator. Out of these five variables, income is certainly the most problematic. Three data sources were employed before opting for one of them. These sources were the OECD (twice), the IMF and Eurostat. Although generally preferable, Eurostat data could not be used because it goes back to 1989 only. Instead, the data from one of the OECD sources will be used, and a graphical depiction of the differences is plotted in Figure 4.11. More details of the data are provided in the appendix including their graphical presentation in Figure 4.12.

The Model

In the following, the model is set up formally, the pre-estimation test results are reported and the estimation performed. In the light of the preliminary analysis, special attention is paid to the stability properties of the resulting relationship. To this end, formal tests will be applied and alternatives to the constant coefficient model suggested.

For modelling the complete money demand system the framework given by (2.6) in conjunction with (2.9) and $\beta'\mu_1 = 0$ will be employed

$$\Delta Y_t = \nu_0 + \Pi Y_{t-1}^* + \sum_{j=1}^{p-1} \Gamma_j \Delta Y_{t-j} + \varepsilon_t, \quad t = p+1, p+2, \dots . \tag{4.6}$$

The vector Y_t therein is defined as $Y_t = \left((m - hicp),\ y,\ i^l,\ i^{cm},\ \pi\right)_t'$ resembling the variables introduced in the foregoing, and situations where $Y_t^* \neq Y_t$ will be considered below.

It is worth emphasizing that the possibility of linear trends in the cointegration relationships is ruled out because they would put the analysis beyond the scope of the economic framework of this study. To put it more trenchantly, a money demand with a negative time trend would imply the rise of communism some day, where, according to a popular pre-vision, money would become superfluous, while a positive trend implies infinite money hoarding. However, assuming a time trend in the money demand relation may occasionally result in a preferable statistical model (see e.g. Juselius and Gennari (1998)). Therefore, the inclusion of a trend in the cointegration relation can to some extent be regarded as trading desired statistical properties against economic expression. Consequently, if there is a long-run money demand function to be found only if it also includes a deterministic time trend, it will not be considered a money demand relation at all. In this instance, the framework of (4.6) is applied where $\beta'\mu_1 = 0$ (and hence $\nu_1 = 0$) which at the same time underlines that trending behaviour of the endogenous variables is allowed for in general, since μ_1 itself might well be different from zero.

Moreover, this setup also encompasses a situation in which the monetary aggregate and income both grow with differing time trends. This is what the German central bank claims for example. It says that for Germany a deterministic decline in the income velocity of money of three percent a year has to be taken into account. In our framework this would translate into a coefficient on the income variable greater than one when normalising on real money or, to put it differently, income elasticity of money is larger than one.

The restriction $\beta'\mu_1 = 0$ also points to another modelling aspect. This is because economically, three of the five variables in the standard money demand model are usually supposed not to be ruled by a deterministic trend. These are the interest and inflation rates. The reason is that none of these should deterministically grow beyond all limits, be the slope of the time trend positive or negative. In the present setup and assuming that μ_1 consists of non-zero elements, this is very likely true if the rank of β is exactly three. If so, the rank of its orthogonal complement, denoted $\beta_\perp$ is two, and hence the constants may generate two linear trends in the remaining non-stationary directions only. These two trends could then be attributed to income and real money, although formal tests would have to confirm this assumption. On the other hand, ranks of β smaller than three do not imply automatically that either of the three non-trending variables is modelled with a time trend. This is, because it is not a-priori clear if all the components of μ_1 are non-zero. In general, the economic prior of no trends in the interest rates and inflation will be taken into account if possible, and contradictory results owed to different restrictions can be expected.

The following two subsections are dedicated to identifying the rank of the matrix Π of equation (2.9).

4.3.3 Estimation of the Long-run Parameters

Cointegration Tests

The introductory chapter already discussed the concept of cointegration for economic reasoning. Thus, the cointegrating rank will be determined before turning to the identification of the long-run relationships. This is done in two steps. First, the degree of integration of each individual data series is checked, and then cointegration tests are performed on the whole system as well as on subsystems. The latter will be done on the basis of economic considerations and aims at cross-checking the results as well as circumventing inevitable power problems owed to the limited data set.

A problem which cannot be dealt with satisfactorily is the presumed break in the cointegration relationship. The sample size is already rather small and that is why it cannot be split any further. Apart from that, the kind of break to be employed later on has not yet been coped with in the context of testing for cointegration. Instead, the cointegration rank will have to be assumed as known, what for the moment leads to the auxiliary measure of ignoring the potential change in the cointegration relation when testing the rank of Π.

Univariate Integration Tests

In a first step the unit root hypothesis is tested for all variables (Table 4.8).[11] This is done in the framework of the Augmented Dickey-Fuller test (see section 4.2.3).

Clearly, all variables $(m - hicp)_t$, y_t, i_t^l, i_t^{cm}, π_t, have a unit root. For the income variable this conclusion holds for the ten percent level of significance,

[11] All computations were performed with EViews 2.0 if not specified otherwise. Capital letters denote levels, small letters generally denote logarithms of the levels.

Table 4.8. Unit Root Tests

Sample: 1983(1) - 1998(4), $T = 64$

variable	setup[a]	ADF statistic	5% crit. val.[b]	decision
$(m - hicp)_t$	t,3	-.49	-3.48	I(1)
$\Delta(m - hicp)_t$	3	-3.29**	-2.86	
y_t	t,3	-2.12	-3.48	I(1)
Δy_t	2	-2.67*	-2.86	
π_t	3	-2.01	-2.86	I(1)
$\Delta\pi_t$	3	-9.19**	-2.86	
i_t^l	4	-1.94	-2.86	I(1)
Δi_t^l	3	-4.48**	-2.86	
i_t^{cm}	2	-1.18	-2.86	I(1)
Δi_t^{cm}	2	-4.55**	-2.86	
$(i^{cm} - i^l)_t$	1	-2.10	-2.86	I(1)
$\Delta(i^{cm} - i^l)_t$	1	-5.42**		
$(i^l - \pi)_t$	2	-2.87**	-2.86	I(0)
$(i^{cm} - \pi)_t$	3	-.90	-2.86	I(1)
$\Delta(i^{cm} - \pi)_t$	2	-8.82**	-2.86	

[a] The t signifies a trend among the regressor group, the integers indicate the lags of differenced dependent variables included in the regression and a constant is always included in the regression to ensure that the regression residual has mean zero. Order selection criteria are applied.
Small letters indicate logarithms except for i_t^l and i_t^{cm}, and $\pi_t = 4\Delta hicp_t$ with $hicp_t$ is the logarithm of the harmonized index of consumer prices in period t.
[b] MacKinnon (1991) critical values
* and ** indicate significance at the ten and five per cent level respectively.

though. There is also evidence for two of them (i_t^l and π_t) forming a cointegration relationship of the Fisher type. On the other hand, neither the spread nor the short-term interest rate minus the inflation rate can be considered stationary. Thus, there are signs for the whole system being cointegrated of order higher than zero. The next step is to test for cointegration in the multi-variate framework.

Multi-variate Tests

System cointegration testing generally requires to decide upon the *VAR* lag order first. Previous simulation studies, for example by Müller (1998) have indicated though, that the decision might severely alter the results of the tests, particularly if the sample size is limited. Second, according to e.g. Hubrich, Lütkepohl and Saikkonen (2001) and Hubrich (2001) the appropriate choice of modelling the deterministic components in the DGP is of importance for the test performance.

The first problem is dealt with by calculating test statistics for varying lag lengths in order to identify reliable patterns and not to get stuck with some results obtained only by chance. Nevertheless, lag order selection criteria are also applied in order to provide some information on the possibly correct lag length of the *VAR*. The criterion applied here is the AIC. In Tables 4.9 and 4.10 the line which corresponds to the lag length chosen by AIC is put in bold face. It is selected from *VAR* models up to order four.

Model (2.9) serves as the reference for the DGP with the additional restriction imposed that no trend enters the cointegration relationship ($\beta' \mu_1 = 0$ and hence $\nu_1 = 0$). This is because from an economic perspective long-run deterministically trending equilibrium relationships are of no interest here.[12] When

[12] Other researchers also consider trending relations like a Phillips curve including inflation, a time trend and income, see e.g. Juselius (1998), Ericsson, Hendry and Mizon (1998).

considering sub-systems, further restrictions are enforced in order to rule out trending features in the interest rates and inflation rates.

Still, the cointegration tests have to be nominated. In applied work the so called Johansen test (Johansen (1988), Johansen and Juselius (1990), Johansen (1991), Johansen (1995a)) for cointegrating ranks has become a kind of standard testing procedure. Yet alternatives exist, and in some situations seem to be more suitable. For example, Lütkepohl and Saikkonen (2000) estimate μ_0 and μ_1 in a two-step procedure under the assumptions made in the null hypothesis. Then, they subtract the estimated deterministic components from the original data and perform cointegration tests on the thereby trend adjusted series. These tests may or may not be calculated under the restriction $\beta'\mu_1 = 0$. In case they are, Saikkonen and Lütkepohl (2000a) developed another, more specific test. Here of course, the restriction is taken into account. Yet another test by Saikkonen and Lütkepohl (2000c) rests on the same principle, but uses a different method to estimate μ_0 and μ_1. This method (signified by the superscript ^{GLS}) does not allow for enforcing limitations on $\beta'\mu_1$.[13] As to the properties of all the tests, Lütkepohl and Saikkonen (2000) and Saikkonen and Lütkepohl (2000a) recommend applying more than just one test because simulation studies indicate that none of the options strictly dominates the others.[14]

Test Results

The results of the cointegration tests do provide a more or less coherent picture.[15] One should notice though, that no test except for the Johansen tests may also account for the fact that in the subsystems without income and

[13] Strictly speaking, the restriction could be enforced, but this case has not been dealt with explicitly in this article.

[14] See also Hubrich et al. (2001) and Hubrich (2001) for detailed simulation results.

[15] Computation in this section is performed with the author's *GAUSS* for NT procedures.

Table 4.9. Cointegration Test: Ranks Selected by Various Tests (1)[a]

Sample: 1983-1998

Model: $\Delta Y_t = \nu_0 + \alpha\beta' Y_{t-1} + \Sigma_{j=1}^{p-1} \Gamma_j \Delta Y_{t-j} + \varepsilon_t$

p	LR^i	LR^i_{ta}	LM^*	$LM_2^1(it)$	LR^{GLS}_{ta}
$Y_t' = ((m - hicp), y, i^l, i^{cm}, \pi)_t$, full model					
1	1	1	1	1(2)	2
2	**1**	**1**	**1**	**1**	**2**
3	1	1(2)	2	2	1
4	2	2	2	1(2)	2
$Y_t' = ((m - hicp), y, i^l, i^{cm})_t$, inflation excluded					
1	0	0(1)	1	0(1)	0
2	**0**	**0(3)**	**1(3)**	**0(1)**	**0**
3	0	3	3	0(1)	0
4	2	2(3)	3	1	1
$Y_t' = ((m - hicp), y, i^l)_t$, inflation and call money excluded					
1	0	0	0	0	0
2	0	0	0	0	0
3	0	0	0(1)	0	0
4	**1**	**0**	**2**	**1**	**1**
$Y_t' = ((m - hicp), y, i^{cm}, \pi)_t$, bond rate excluded					
1	**1**	**1**	**1**	**2**	**1**
2	1	1	1	1	2
3	1	1	1	1	0(1)
4	2	1	1	1	0

[a] Columns report the ranks selected at the 5 % level of significance and at the 10% level in parentheses if there is a difference. A sequential test procedure is applied.
LR^i and LR^* refer to Johansen (1991). Critical values are available e.g. in Johansen (1995b) Tables 15.3. (for LR^i) and 15.2. (for LR^*). Only LR^* takes into account the restriction $\mu_1 = 0$ (if imposed).
LR^i_{ta} and LM^* refer to Saikkonen and Lütkepohl (2000a), p. 381, eq. (3.12) and eq. (3.10) respectively. Lütkepohl and Saikkonen (2000) at p.186 , eq. (4.10) present $LM_2^1(it)$ with the two-step procedure for estimating μ_0 and μ_1, *it* indicates iterative variant. LR^{GLS}_{ta} can be found in Saikkonen and Lütkepohl (2000c), p. 442, eq. (4.7).
Bold face marks the results of the preferable lag order.

Table 4.10. Cointegration Test: Ranks Selected by Various Tests (2)[a]

Sample: 1983-1998 $\Delta Y_t = \nu_0 + \alpha\beta' Y_{t-1} + \Sigma_{j=1}^{p-1} \Gamma_j \Delta Y_{t-j} + \varepsilon_t$

p	LR^*	LR^i_{ta}	LM^*	$LM^1_2(it)$	LR^{GLS}_{ta}
$Y_t' = (i^l, i^{cm}, \pi)_t,\ \mu_1 = 0$, Fisher and spread					
1	0(1)	0		0	0
2	1	0		0	1
3	**0(1)**	**0**		**0**	**0**
$Y_t' = (i^l, i^{cm})_t,\ \mu_1 = 0$, spread					
1	0	0		0	0
2	**0**	**0**		**0**	**0**
3	0	0		0	0
$Y_t' = (i^l, \pi)_t,\ \mu_1 = 0$, Fisher (1)					
1	1(2)	0		0	0
2	**1**	**0**		**0**	**1**
3	1	0		0	0
$Y_t' = (i^{cm}, \pi)_t,\ \mu_1 = 0$, Fisher (2)					
1	0	0		0	0
2	0	0		0	0
3	**0**	**0**		**0**	**0**

[a] Columns report the ranks selected at the 5 % level of significance and at the 10% level in parentheses if there is a difference. A sequential test procedure is applied.
LR^i and LR^* refer to Johansen (1991). The corresponding critical values are available e.g. in Johansen (1995b) Tables 15.3. (for LR^i) and 15.2. (for LR^*). Only LR^* takes into account the restriction $\mu_1 = 0$ (if imposed).
LR^i_{ta} and LM^* refer to Saikkonen and Lütkepohl (2000a), p. 381, eq. (3.12) and eq. (3.10) respectively. Lütkepohl and Saikkonen (2000) at p.186 , eq. (4.10) present $LM^1_2(it)$ with the two-step procedure for estimating μ_0 and μ_1, *it* indicates iterative variant. LR^{GLS}_{ta} can be found in Saikkonen and Lütkepohl (2000c), p. 442, eq. (4.7).
Bold face marks the results of the preferable lag order.

real money (Table 4.10) μ_1 is set to zero. That means, these other tests are more general which could possibly lead to a loss in power, if μ_1 is indeed zero. Therefore, it seems appropriate to focus on the Johansen test when it comes to interpreting the respective results.

Finally, the sum of evidence including the univariate results will lead to a decision about what cointegration rank has to be considered the correct one.

Starting with the full system, all but one test in Table 4.9 indicate that one cointegrating relation is present. This finding is unanimously obtained for the preferred lag length, which is two in this case. A cointegrating rank of two is found by the LR_{ta}^{GLS} test at lag orders 1, 2 and 4. The same result is obtained by the other tests (LR_{ta}^{i}, LR^{i}, LM^* and $LM_2^1(it)$) when the lag order is different from two or if the level of significance is ten percent. Thus, the outcome for the complete model is at least inconclusive. One of the reasons is certainly that the different tests are affected by the power problem in different ways. Therefore, additional evidence will be gathered to decide about the cointegration properties.

As a first measure, some variables will be dropped and the tests applied to the thereby defined subset models. Doing so reveals the important part the inflation rate seems to play in the system. To see this, consider the second section in Table 4.9. Dropping the inflation rate severely reduces the evidence for cointegration to be present at all. Going one step further and also dropping the call money interest rate leaves even fewer evidence for cointegration. The results for lag length four cannot entirely be trusted because at this lag length the number of parameters to be estimated is already pretty large compared to the number of observations available.[16] In contrast, the last section consistently points to a single cointegrating relationship within the subsystem made of $(m - hicp)_t, y_t, i_t^{cm}, \pi_t$.

[16] In addition to that, the corresponding stationary relationship is given by $((m - hicp)_t + 2.68y_t + 8.10i_t^l) \sim I(0)$ which can hardly be found an interpretation for.

It has to be pointed out that a corresponding cointegration vector cannot include the stationary real long-run interest rate found by the univariate test. Therefore, in Table 4.10 some of the univariate exercises are repeated. To begin with, a three dimensional system consisting of the interest rates and the inflation rate is considered. The evidence for cointegration is the strongest for the test which can explicitly take into account the restriction of no trend to be present (LR^*). All pair wise combinations except for (i_t^l, π_t) do not provide any evidence for cointegration. Thus, the previous finding of a cointegrating relationship between the bond rate and inflation seems to be confirmed.

In the aggregate of the evidence, the system can be regarded as cointegrated of order two. The main two reasons for this conclusion are that the two subsystems defined by $Y_t = ((m - hicp), y, i^{cm}, \pi)_t'$ and $Y_t = (i^l, \pi)_t'$ are cointegrated of order one each. Because the cointegration property is independent of the exclusion of variables not entering the relation in question, it is reasonable to impose cointegrating rank two on the system.

4.3.4 Determination of the Cointegration Matrix

While there are good reasons to believe that the rank of the matrix Π in (2.9) is two, the parameters of the stationary linear relationships are not yet known. There is some information though, which can be exploited. First, uni- and multivariate cointegration analysis pointed to the stationarity of some linear relation between inflation and bond rate. Moreover, the second relationship is made up of a combination of the remaining variables if the bond rate is dropped.

All this information will be used in the following identification strategy. Starting with a set of exactly identifying restrictions, more restrictions will be added and tested. In the light of the previous analysis, care will be taken not to exclude inflation from both the cointegration relations. Ideally, the procedure terminates when interpretable relations are obtained. A number of stability tests provide information on the properties of the relationships.

Thus, the aim of the identification scheme is to derive two linearly independent cointegration relationships which prove to be valid restrictions of the unrestricted model and which can also be imposed over a range of subsets of the data sample. The latter will be called stability analysis. It is concerned with the question to what extent the cointegration relationships identified within the whole data set (1983 to 1998) would also be acceptable for sub-samples all starting in 1983 and ending in 1992, 1993, ... and so on.

Finally, an investigation of the properties of the adjustment coefficients (α estimates) will disclose some information about the interactions within the variable set.

Estimation is performed by maximising the log-likelihood of observing the sample data given the vector error correction model (2.9) with $\nu_1 = 0$. The optimisation algorithm (linear switching) is described in Doornik and Hendry (1997).[17]

Identifying Cointegration Relationships

Exact identification requires to impose $r - 1 = 2 - 1 = 1$ restrictions on each cointegrating vector plus one restriction to scale the coefficient estimates. Thus, the following structure is imposed

$$\beta' Y_t = \begin{pmatrix} \beta_1 \\ \beta_2 \end{pmatrix} Y_t = \begin{pmatrix} 1 & \times & 0 & \times & \times \\ 0 & \times & 1 & \times & \times \end{pmatrix} \begin{pmatrix} (m - hicp) \\ y \\ i^l \\ i^{cm} \\ \pi \end{pmatrix}_t \tag{4.7}$$

where $\times$ stands for a freely estimated coefficient while the positions filled with 1 and 0 serve to exactly identify the two cointegration relationships. Table 4.11 reports the initial estimates and those of the following steps.

[17] For identification and testing PcFiml 9.1 by Doornik and Hendry (1997) is used.

Table 4.11. Identifying Cointegration Relationships

$$\Delta Y_t = \nu_0 + \alpha\beta' Y_{t-1} + \Gamma_1 \Delta Y_{t-1} + \varepsilon_t$$
$$Y_t = ((m - hicp)_t \; y_t \; i_t^l \; i_t^{cm} \; \pi_t)'$$

step	*vector*	$(m-hicp)_t$	y_t	i_t^l	i_t^{cm}	π_t	*d.f.*	χ^2
1	β_1	1	−1.83	0	−4.51	2.04		
			(.23)		(.56)	(.68)		
	β_2	0	−.03	1	−.52	−.67		
			(.03)		(.10)	(.14)		
2	β_1	1	−1.63	0	−4.14	2.40	1	.22
			(.13)		(.56)	(.73)		[.64]
	β_2	0	**0**	1	−.46	−.61		
					(.08)	(.10)		
3	β_1	1	−1.59	0	−1.12	−4.08	2	10.45*
			(.13)		(.56)	(1.66)		[.01]
	β_2	0	0	1	**0**	−1.63		
						(.25)		
4	β_1	1	−1.64	0	−4.15	2.76	2	1.10
			(.13)		(.54)	(.66)		[.58]
	β_2	0	0	1	**(-1+.54)**	**-.54**		
						(.08)		

Columns 3-7: Parameters and, if estimated, their corresponding standard errors in parentheses. Column 8: Degrees of freedom of the χ^2 statistic. Column 9: χ^2 statistic and the corresponding marginal level of significance in brackets.
Where no number in parentheses is given, the corresponding coefficient value had been imposed. Bold face signifies those coefficients which are additionally restricted in the respective step.
The * indicates significance at the five percent level.

The general strategy for imposing restrictions on the cointegration matrix to achieve identification is to restrict those coefficients to zero whose absolute t-ratio is close to or smaller than two.[18] Validity of the restriction is tested by a likelihood ratio test having a standard χ^2 distribution.[19] The last column

[18] Here and throughout, the term t-ratio denotes the t-test statistic of the hypothesis $c = 0$, with c being the coefficient on the variable in question.

[19] A thorough description of this test can be found in Johansen (1995b), chapters 7 and 8.

in Table 4.11 reports this test statistic. Departing from the just identifying restriction, the coefficient on income in the second relation is set to zero. The remaining coefficients appear to be highly significant. It also applies to the call money rate in the second relationship. The respective t-ratio is 5.75. If this second relationship was the real interest rate though, it should be possible to remove the call money rate from it. Therefore, in the third step a corresponding zero restriction is imposed and tested. The outcome does not leave any doubt about the fact that this restriction is too tight. Not being able to impose this restriction is obviously in stark contrast to the previous finding of a cointegration relation made up of inflation and the bond rate alone. Despite this contradiction, the following analysis complies with this test result and continues with three variables in the second cointegrating vector.

Instead of restricting the coefficient on the short-term interest rate to zero, step four reflects a situation where it sums up to minus one when added to the coefficient on inflation. This together with the zero restriction on the income coefficient cannot be rejected at the .58 level of significance.[20]

In the following, the results of Table 4.11 are subjected to a number of further analyses, including restrictions on the adjustment coefficients (weak exogeneity analysis) and stability of the whole long-run matrix. After that, interpretations will be given.

Weak Exogeneity

Interpretation of the results also depends on the properties of the adjustment parameters. For example, the question what variables adjust to the deviations from the long-run equilibrium provides information about the economic mechanisms at work. Suppose e.g. that the inflation rate adjusts to excess money

[20] Note that the same outcome also emerges if the initial restrictions leave the coefficient on i_t^l in the first relation unrestricted. It is then found insignificant and dropped.

in the economy then the monetarist view of money being the source of price inflation might find support.

Moreover, weak exogeneity is a necessary albeit not sufficient condition for both strong and super exogeneity (see Engle et al. (1983) and Ericsson, Hendry and Mizon (1998) on details) which may have far reaching consequences for policy analysis. There are two possible approaches to derive conclusions about weak exogeneity properties. Either the possibly over-identified cointegration or the just identified cointegration vectors are considered (and over-identification follows conditioning on these results). Technically, the outcome should not depend on the approach if the over-identification restrictions are truly valid. However, in applied work it sometimes does. For the present situation it turns out that the results can be derived in either way. In the following, the weak exogeneity results are derived conditioning on the previously obtained cointegrating relationships. Again, a likelihood ratio test having a χ^2 distribution allows to test for the validity of the restrictions imposed with the degrees of freedom now being the sum of both over-identification and α restrictions (see Boswijk (1995)). Table 4.12 collects the hypotheses and test statistics.

The first section of Table 4.12 (steps 5 to 9) hypothesizes that none of the two identified cointegration relationships enter the equation for the variable given in the header of the table. This is indicated by the zeros. For the real money and the short-term interest rate the test statistic does not reject. Thus, both these variables are weakly exogenous in the current setting. In the second section, it is checked which of the relationships enter the equations for the remaining variables, before testing all restrictions jointly.

Summarizing the test results for the α and β matrices, the following long-run relations and adjustment coefficients are estimated (standard errors in parentheses).

Table 4.12. Testing for Weak Exogeneity (α restrictions)

$$\Delta Y_t = \nu_0 + \alpha\beta' Y_{t-1} + \Gamma_1 \Delta Y_{t-1} + \varepsilon_t$$

step	$(m-hicp)_t$	y_t	i_t^l	i_t^{cm}	π_t	d.f.	χ^2	p-value
5	0	x	x	x	x	4	3.48	0.48
6	x	0	x	x	x	4	18.67**	.00
7	x	x	0	x	x	4	19.15**	.00
8	x	x	x	0	x	4	2.73	.60
9	x	x	x	x	0	4	15.56**	.00
10	x	$\alpha_{2,1}=0$	x	x	x	3	9.03**	.00
11	x	$\alpha_{2,2}=0$	x	x	x	3	1.18	.76
12	x	x	$\alpha_{3,1}=0$	x	x	3	4.83	.18
13	x	x	$\alpha_{3,2}=0$	x	x	3	16.13**	.00
14	x	x	x	x	$\alpha_{5,1}=0$	3	48.71**	.00
15	x	x	x	x	$\alpha_{5,2}=0$	3	12.63**	.01
16	0	$\alpha_{2,2}=0$	$\alpha_{3,1}=0$	0	x	8	8.60	.37

The respective null hypotheses are either indicated by the zero entries or explicitly given as $\alpha_{i,j} = 0$. A zero means that none of the two identified cointegration relationships enters the equation for the variable given in the header of the column.
In the lower part of the table restrictions on single adjustment parameters are tested and the last line presents the results for a joint test of all restrictions previously accepted at the five percent level of significance.
The ** indicates significance at the one percent level.

$$\alpha\beta' Y_t = \begin{pmatrix} \alpha_1 & \alpha_2 \end{pmatrix} \begin{pmatrix} \beta_1 \\ \beta_2 \end{pmatrix} Y_t$$

$$= \begin{pmatrix} \alpha_1 & \alpha_2 \end{pmatrix} \begin{pmatrix} ec_m \\ ec_F \end{pmatrix}_t$$

$$= \begin{pmatrix} 0 & 0 \\ .05 & 0 \\ (.01) & \\ 0 & -.24 \\ & (.06) \\ 0 & 0 \\ -.08 & .86 \\ (.03) & (.19) \end{pmatrix} \begin{pmatrix} 1 & -1.82 & 0 & -4.20 & 2.35 \\ & (.16) & & (.57) & (.74) \\ 0 & 0 & 1 & -.35 & -.65 \\ & & & & (.06) \end{pmatrix} \begin{pmatrix} m-hicp \\ y \\ i^l \\ i^{cm} \\ \pi \end{pmatrix}_t$$

As stated above, all the zero entries in these matrices are accepted at the marginal significance level of .37 for the sample period 1983(1)-1998(4). In the next paragraph the robustness of the results with respect to time is investigated. The motivation behind that is the desire to find an econometric model which is likely to be useful for further analysis, e.g. one which remains valid even if the economic environment changes.

4.3.5 Stability Analysis

The stability of an econometric model has two principal aspects. One is backward looking, that is, the model should be valid for the whole sample range and not only for a part of it. The second is forward looking in the sense that the model remains valid when future information becomes available.

For each of these two aspects, a number of tests is available. Of course, the first of them is much easier to check. The standard tool is to assume validity of the model and then to re-estimate it for ever larger sample sizes until all observations are used. As a result, not only can the parameter estimates be looked at and compared for varying sample definitions, but also the tests on restrictions like the ones presented above. In addition, at each data point a forecast for the next observation can be made and then compared to the actual observation. If the difference is too large this would indicate instability of the model. This test will be called one-step forecast test.

Future stability of a model is much harder to detect. It becomes more difficult the stronger the intended statement about the model's property is. For example, for claiming that the model will also fit future observations it can be sufficient to spare some observations at the end of the whole sample and to perform out of sample forecast tests. These tests are in principle the same as the one-step forecast test described above, but the difference is that now the model underlying the forecast has been estimated without the information for which the prediction is made. If accepted, the test can be regarded as evidence for the model to be stable for observations generated by the same (true) data generating process. In contrast to that, a change in the key environmental conditions like monetary policy strategy, cannot be accounted for by this approach. If one wishes to make statements about stability of the system, or more precisely, of important parts of it under changing conditions, then a different concept has to be applied. To this end, Engle et al. (1983) and Ericsson, Hendry and Mizon (1998) among others suggest the concept of super exogeneity (see chapter 2 for details). In the present case the relevant change in the economic conditions might be the change in the exchange rate regime in 1987 as a past event and the introduction of the new currency whose effects on the economy are not known. Ideally, the estimated model can be found to sustain policy shifts in which case it will be useful to derive conclusions about the prospects of the Euro era for France.

Of course, the latter considerations have to be made operational. In the current case, the part of interest is mainly the relation of money and prices to the remaining variables while the policy variable is the call money rate. Unfortunately, the sample neither contains considerable nor numerous known policy changes which could be appropriately modelled. The only exception is the 1987 event which would imply an inconvenient split of the whole sample. Therefore, another, less ambitious check will tell us something about the relation between policy variables and agents' behaviour. Suppose that the call money rate is generated by 'unstable' policy decisions. Let us also say that for this reason the call money rate cannot be be satisfactorily modelled while at the same time its impact on the remaining variables remains constant. Then, the conclusion is that instability in the policy instruments does not affect the relations of interest.

Recursive Stability Tests

The following stability analysis is depicted in graphical form. First, the zero and cross-coefficient restrictions as of Table 4.12, step 16 on the long-run matrix Π are tested for varying sample sizes, starting at 1983-1991 and adding observations up to 1998, fourth quarter (see Figure 4.3). Usually, this recursive test is carried out with fixed α coefficients. Here, however, these coefficients (and the coefficients of Γ_j) vary too. This makes the test more sensitive. The graph reveals that after 1994 only the imposed restrictions conform with the observations. They indicate invalidity of the final representation of the long-run relationship given in (4.7) for the period prior to 1994.

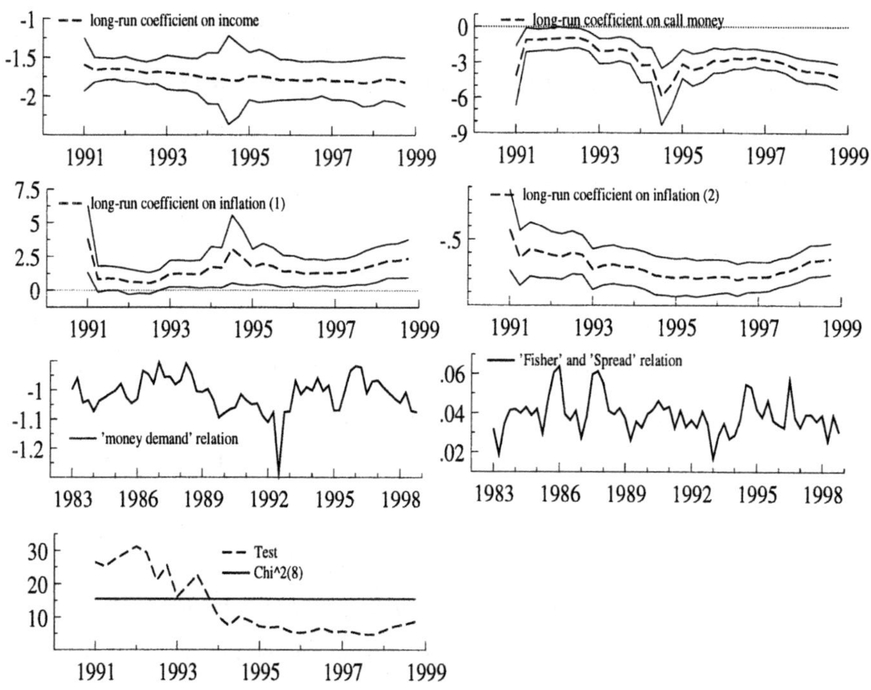

Top row and second row left: Recursive estimates of the long-run parameters (β coefficients) of the first cointegrating relation, labelled 'money demand'.
Second row right: Recursive estimate of the long-run parameters (β coefficients) of the second cointegrating relation, labelled 'Fisher' and 'Spread' relation.
Third row: Estimated cointegration relationships. The labels are provided for reference purposes only.
Bottom left: Recursive test statistic of the joint restrictions on α and β according to step 16 in Table 4.12. All components of Π are re-estimated at each quarter.

Figure 4.3. Stability of the $\alpha\beta'$ Coefficients over Time

It is worth mentioning that this conclusion depends mainly on the treatment of the adjustment coefficients (α) in the recursive analysis. As long as they are re-estimated together with the coefficients of β as in Figure 4.3, instability of the Π coefficient estimates has to be acknowledged. This applies not only to the 16th step of the identification procedure but also to the 4th step where no restrictions on α are imposed. In contrast to that, a graph depicting the situation which is equivalent to Figure 4.3 without re-estimating the coefficients on α indicates far less variations of the estimates (see Figure 4.4). Moreover, the corresponding recursive test statistic is not significant at any point in time considered.[21]

Against that rather positive view, one could argue that the seemingly higher stability is only obtained at the expense of larger estimation uncertainty as can be seen from the generally wider confidence bands around the β estimates in graph 4.4 compared to those in 4.3. All in all, further formal stability tests might be helpful in deciding about the modelling strategy in the case of truly unstable relationships.

Hansen and Seo Stability Test

One alternative possibility to test for the stability of the long-run relationship over time is the procedure suggested by Seo (1998) of which Hansen (2000b) derives a likelihood-ratio variant to be applied here. The framework these authors and Hansen (2000a) suggest is an extension of the econometric model in (4.6) and can be written as (4.8)

$$\Delta Y_t = \nu_0 + \alpha\beta(t)'Y_{t-1} + \sum_{j=1}^{p-1} \Gamma_j \Delta Y_{t-j} + \varepsilon_t, \quad t = p+1, p+2, \ldots \qquad (4.8)$$

where the ν_1 have been dropped to match the actual situation and the errors ε_t is a sequence of i.i.d. Gaussian variables with mean zero and covariance Matrix Σ. The modification to the standard model is given by

[21] This finding does not necessarily hint to unstable α parameters because the instability result arises from both α and β coefficients.

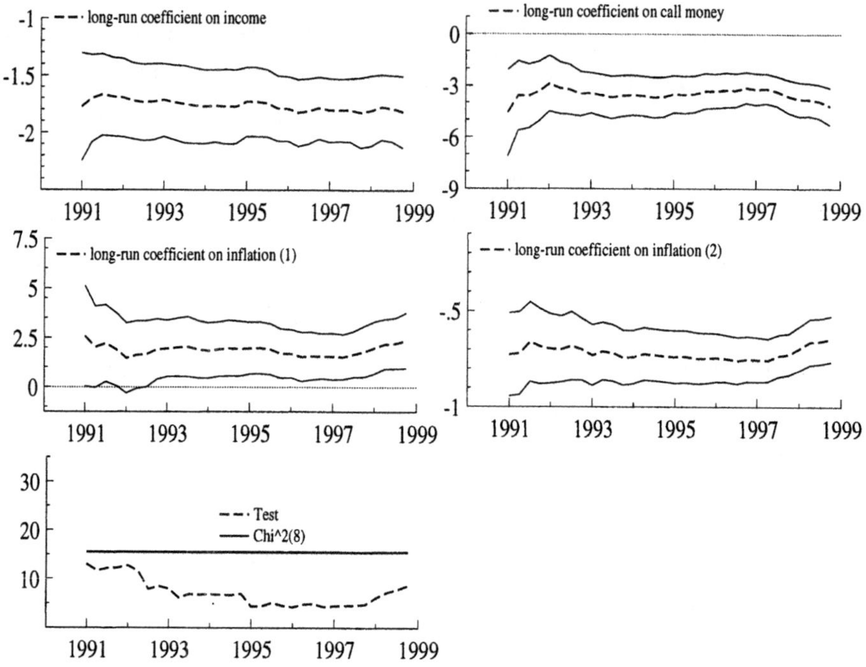

Top and second row: Recursive estimates of the long-run parameters (β coefficients) of the first cointegrating relation, labelled 'money demand'.
Bottom left: Recursive test statistic of the joint restrictions on α and β according to step 16 in Table 4.12. Only the β coefficients are re-estimated at each quarter.

Figure 4.4. Stability Analysis of the β Coefficients

$$\beta(t) = \begin{cases} \beta_1 \; t = 1, \ldots, \tau_1 \\ \beta_2 \; t = \tau_1 + 1, \ldots, \tau_2 \\ \vdots \\ \beta_q \; t = \tau_{q-1} + 1, \ldots, T. \end{cases}$$

which leaves the adjustment coefficients (α) and the remaining short-run coefficients (Γ_j) unchanged. Thus, the number of possible breaks in the cointegration relation is finite and denoted q. While Hansen (2000a) introduces a test statistic which allows to test for the significance of a potential break against a constant coefficient model if the break point is known, Seo (1998) and Hansen (2000b) suggest a testing procedure for the case $q-1=1$ and an unknown break point. Unfortunately, the latter statistic lacks a standard distribution and requires simulation of the critical value. To circumvent the latter problem, in what follows, the break point will be assumed known although it will be chosen according to some preliminary analysis.

A second look at (4.8) reveals that without further restrictions on β_j, the number of parameters to be estimated in addition to the standard case defined by equation (2.9) grows at the rate $(q-1)nr$. Considering the already given limitations in the number of observations, this seems to be too strong an increase. Therefore, the number of coefficients allowed to vary will be confined to two. Two more reasons can be put forward to support this choice. In the light of the preliminary analysis the focus is on the policy interest rate. Therefore, variations in the corresponding coefficient will be considered. In addition to that, the coefficient on the inflation rate is going to be varied. The second reason is that in contrast to the example in Hansen (2000a), the present study considers two cointegrating relations rather than just one. Thus, the identification problem would become much more difficult if all coefficients would be allowed to change.

To conclude the discussion, it has to be acknowledged that the procedures described above raise a number of questions with respect to their theoretical foundation in the present context. This implies that using these tools should be regarded as a mainly descriptive analysis.

The following steps will be taken. First, the procedure for detecting possible break points will be described. Second, based on the break point identified, the Hansen (2000b) likelihood ratio test for stability of the cointegrating relations will be applied. Finally, applying some optimality criterion, the previous constant coefficient model is going to be re-estimated. A comparison of the two empirical models will conclude the section.

Break Point Analysis

For estimating the model in (4.8), Hansen (2000b) suggests the following variation to the standard reduced rank regression proposed by Johansen (1988). Defining $\tilde{Z}_{0t} = \Delta Y_t$, $Z_{1t} = Y^*_{t-1}$, $\tilde{Z}_{2t} = (\Delta Y'_{t-1}, \dots, \Delta Y'_{t-(p-1)}, 1)'$, $\Psi = (\Gamma_1, \dots, \Gamma_{(p-1)}, \nu_0)$ model (4.8) can be re-formulated as

$$\tilde{Z}_{0t} = \alpha\beta'\tilde{Z}_{1t} + \Psi\tilde{Z}_{2t} + \varepsilon_t \tag{4.9}$$

and for $q > 1$ we define $Z_{11t} = Z_{1t}I(t \leq \tau_1), Z_{12t} = Z_{1t}I(\tau_1 + 1 \leq t \leq \tau_2), \dots Z_{1qt} = Z_{1t}I(\tau_{q-1} + 1 \leq t \leq T)$ and $\tilde{Z}_{1t} = (Z'_{11t}, \dots, Z'_{1qt})'$ which will result in a model equivalent to (4.9). In this new model, β is substituted by $B = (ß'_1, \dots, ß'_q)'$ and $\tilde{Z}_{1t}$ replaces Z_{1t}. Here, $I(t \leq \tau_1)$ are matrices which indicate what elements of the Z_{1t} matrices are active. When $\alpha\beta'$ is of reduced rank, the Johansen (1988) reduced rank regression can be straightforwardly generalised to the case of (4.9) by defining

$$\begin{aligned}
\tilde{M}_{ij} &= \frac{1}{T}\sum_{t=1}^{T} \tilde{Z}_{it}\tilde{Z}_{jt}, \quad i,j = 0,1,2 \\
\tilde{R}_{it} &= \tilde{Z}_{it} - \tilde{M}_{i2}\tilde{M}_{22}^{-1}\tilde{Z}_{2t}, \quad i = 0,1 \\
\tilde{S}_{ij} &= \frac{1}{T}\sum_{t=1}^{T} \tilde{R}_{it}\tilde{R}'_{jt}, \quad i,j = 0,1
\end{aligned}$$

which leads to the estimates

$$\begin{aligned}
\hat{B} &= (\tilde{v}_1, \dots, \tilde{v}_r) \\
\hat{\alpha} &= \tilde{S}_{01}\hat{B} \\
\hat{\Sigma} &= \tilde{S}_{00} - \hat{\alpha}\hat{\alpha}' \\
\hat{\Psi} &= \tilde{M}_{02}\tilde{M}_{22}^{-1} - \hat{\alpha}\hat{B}'\tilde{M}_{12}\tilde{M}_{22}^{-1}
\end{aligned}$$

where $(\tilde{v}_1, \dots, \tilde{v}_r)$ are the eigenvectors corresponding to the r largest eigenvalues $\tilde{\lambda}_1, \dots, \tilde{\lambda}_r$ as solutions of the eigenvalue problem

$$|\lambda\tilde{S}_{11} - \tilde{S}_{10}\tilde{S}_{00}^{-1}\tilde{S}_{01}| = 0$$

(see Johansen (1988), Hansen (2000b)). The maximum of the likelihood function is given by

$$L_{max}^{2/T}(\hat{\alpha}, \hat{\beta}, \hat{\Psi}, \hat{\Sigma}) = (2\pi e)^n |\tilde{S}_{00}| \prod_{i=1}^{r} (1 - \tilde{\lambda}_i)$$

of which a proof is available in Johansen (1988).[22]

Thus, the maximum of the likelihood has an explicit formula which simplifies computation of the estimates. These estimates are obtained for given values of q and $\tau_1, \ldots, \tau_q$. When the latter of these is not known for sure, or to be more precise if it cannot be decided beforehand, at what quarter within a limited time span the break occurred, then the likelihood value can be calculated for all likely τ_j. The estimate of the break point ($\hat{\tau}_j$) will then be the one that corresponds to the maximum of the likelihood over all τ_j scrutinized given the observations and the parameter estimates.[23]

Naturally, as q increases, the optimisation becomes more and more costly. In fact, the number of likelihood values which need to be computed is $q(T - T^{up} - T^{low})$ where T^{up} and T^{low} denote the upper and lower bounds of the break points allowed for among the T observations. For the experiment to follow, q is set to 2 and the break is assumed to occur in only two variables among the endogenous variables at a time. Therefore, the optimisation procedure can be viewed as a search for the maximum likelihood in two dimensions, one for each τ_j.

Following Boswijk (1995) pp. 10f optimisation is straightforward as long as the rank is known and no over-identifying restrictions are imposed on the cointegrating vectors. Thus, for this step of the analysis all tools are available. Table 4.13 reports the results of various attempts to maximize the log-likelihood. Apart from the preferred choice (time varying coefficients on i_t^{cm} and π_t), variations in either i_t^{cm} or π_t, in the cointegration mean alone and no

[22] In the first term on the r. h. s. e denotes Euler's constant.

[23] The same strategy has also been used by Saikkonen and Lütkepohl (2001) in a univariate setting.

variation at all is considered. As in Table 4.5 in addition to the log-likelihood values, the information criteria are given.

Table 4.13. Money Demand Analysis: Break Point Search and Model Selection

Model (4.8), $p = q = rank = 2$, $1985(1) \leq \tau_i \leq 1989(4)$, $i = 1, 2$

no.	Z_{11t}	Z_{12t}	Loglikelihood	AIC	HQ	SC	$\hat{\tau}_1$	$\hat{\tau}_2$
$\mathcal{H}_0$			284.796	−21.976	−21.360	−20.417		
$\mathcal{H}_1$	i_t^{cm}		294.536	−22.353	−21.711	−20.728	1986(4)	
$\mathcal{H}_2$	π_t		296.732	−22.420	−21.777	−20.794	1985(4)	
$\mathcal{H}_3$	1		295.792	−22.322	−21.680	−20.687	1989(3)	
$\mathcal{H}_4$	i_t^{cm}	π_t	304.333	**-22.724**	**-22.056**	**-21.032**	1986(4)	1985(4)

Bold face signifies the minimal value of the respective column.

Not surprisingly, the maximum of the log-likelihood over all possibilities is obtained for the situation where both coefficients, on i_t^{cm} and on π_t, are allowed to vary. For deciding about the appropriate model among all variants in Table 4.13, the selection criteria are certainly more informative. Here again, the model under $\mathcal{H}_4$ seems to be superior to its competitors. In case of the policy rate, the optimal break point (1986(4)) almost perfectly coincides with the previously mentioned change in exchange rate policy at 1987, first quarter. Thus, the prior knowledge about when the data generating process is likely to change, appears to be confirmed endogenously. With respect to inflation, the argument is not as straightforward. The most plausible explanation for the shift to occur in the fourth quarter of 1985 is that at about this time the inflation rate started to settle at a much lower level than before. This however, is more a valid description rather than an explanation as to *why* it became so small.

It should also be pointed out that $\mathcal{H}_4$ nests $\mathcal{H}_0$, $\mathcal{H}_1$ and $\mathcal{H}_2$ while $\mathcal{H}_0$ is part of $\mathcal{H}_1$ and $\mathcal{H}_2$, which enables us to perform likelihood ratio tests which under the assumptions of known q, $rank(\Pi)$, τ_i asymptotically have a standard χ^2 distribution with the degrees of freedom equal to the number of restrictions. The null hypothesis is validity of the more restricted model. Defining $\hat{\lambda}_i$, $i = 1, \ldots, r$ the eigenvalues of the general model, and denoting the eigenvalues of the restricted model by $\tilde{\lambda}_i$, Hansen (2000b) derives a test statistic which reads

$$LR_T(\tau) \equiv T\left[\sum_{i=1}^{r} log\left(1-\hat{\lambda}_i\right) - log\left(1-\tilde{\lambda}_i\right)\right].$$

Table 4.14 summarizes the various test statistics, degrees of freedom and the corresponding p-values.

Table 4.14. Money Demand Analysis: Testing Time Varying Models

Model (4.8)$^+$

H_1	H_0	$LR_T(\tau_i)$	d.f.	p-value
$\mathcal{H}_4$	$\mathcal{H}_0$	39.078**	4	0
	$\mathcal{H}_1$	19.593**	2	0
	$\mathcal{H}_2$	15.201**	2	0.001
$\mathcal{H}_2$	$\mathcal{H}_0$	23.873**	2	0
$\mathcal{H}_3$	$\mathcal{H}_0$	21.992**	2	0
$\mathcal{H}_1$	$\mathcal{H}_0$	19.480**	2	0

$^+$ $p = rank = 2$, q, τ_i as in Table 4.13. The ** indicate significance at the one percent level of significance when r and τ are known.

All test statistics clearly indicate the superiority of the most flexible model. Note however, that the exact critical values of the χ^2-distribution can only be used if the break point is assumed to be known.

Before turning to an evaluation of the newly derived time varying model, a few remarks with respect to the procedure are appropriate. In the light of the preliminary analysis and of chapter 3, the way in which the coefficients have been allowed to vary is a rather special one. If one is ready to accept that the transition to the new coefficient value is a general non-linear function of time, like those in (3.16), then even better models could be derived. Judging on the basis of the selection criteria, the best model is obtained when assuming the coefficients on i_t^{cm} and π_t to follow an exponential shift function. These shifts are rather smooth though, which would put the analysis beyond the theoretical framework in which testing is still feasible. This said, modelling the structural changes in the money demand system by varying the long-run coefficients should be regarded as a suggestion rather than the only possible way. Alternative modelling approaches may deliver reasonable results too. Therefore, future research in generalisations of the transitions process would be desirable.

Second, apart from the variation in the β matrix, Hansen (2000a) suggests a whole battery of possible structural changes in the cointegrated *VAR*. Among them are changes in the adjustment parameters, time dependent heteroscedasticity of the error process, changes in the cointegrating rank and various combination of the aforementioned. Of course, the more variation is allowed for, the more observations are needed to clearly distinguish between the alternatives. If the τ_i were known, then the appropriate model could be found by testing the more general models against the more restrictive ones. For the current purpose, the model has implicitly been restricted to constant rank of β, constant α coefficients, *i.i.d.* error terms and two break points only. While these restrictions might appear too strong, the technical difficulties and the preliminary analysis can be regarded as arguments in favour of starting with the prior that structural change only occurs in the coefficients of β. In particular, the uncertainty about to what quarter to assign the break point required the use of prior assumptions about the character of the structural changes within the cointegration analysis.

So far, two different models have been suggested for explaining the observed data. As in the preliminary analysis, the comparison between them will include not only the recursive estimation results but also the residual properties and related statistics. To that end, the not yet identified cointegration relationships of the time varying model will be identified, recursive estimation performed and subset models derived. In the end, the final specification serves as the basis for the residual analysis.

4.3.6 Comparing Model Alternatives

The following paragraphs repeat the exercises of the constant coefficient model in that the cointegration relationships will be identified, over-identification restrictions imposed, tested and the recursive coefficient estimates calculated.

From Hansen (2000a) it can be concluded that the standard test procedure for testing restrictions on the cointegrating vector (β) and adjustment coefficients (α) can also be applied in the present situation.[24] In addition to these tests, Table 4.16 reports the values of the model selection criteria for each step of the following identification procedure.

As before, identification is achieved by adding restrictions on the cointegrating matrices starting from the completely unrestricted but just identified model. Table 4.15 provides the details.

In conjunction with Table 4.16 it can be argued that the model corresponding to the 6th step of the identification process in Table 4.15 is a reasonable description of the data generating process.

After re-arranging, the following representation provides a summary of the long-run relationships and their impact on the endogenous variables:

[24] In the preliminary analysis (section 4.2.3) a different transition process was assumed for which it is not yet known if the standard test statistics can be applied. Therefore, the information criteria were used instead.

Table 4.15. Identifying the Time Varying Cointegration Relationships

$$\Delta Y_t = \nu_0 + \alpha\beta' Y^*_{t-1} + \Gamma_1 \Delta Y_{t-1} + \varepsilon_t$$
$$Y_t = ((m-hicp)_t,\, y_t,\, i^l_t,\, i^{cm}_t,\, \pi_t)',\;\; Y^*_t = (Y'_t,\, I_{86(4)} i^{cm}_t,\, I_{85(4)}\pi_t)'$$

step	*vector*	$(m-hicp)_t$	y_t	i^l_t	i^{cm}_t	π_t	$I_{86(4)} i^{cm}_t$	$I_{85(4)}\pi_t$	*d.f.*	χ^2
1	β_1	1	−1.17 (.07)	0	−1.24 (.25)	.72 (.25)	−.35 (.19)	−1.99 (.35)		
	β_2	0	.002 (.03)	1	−.36 (.12)	−.72 (.12)	.19 (.09)	−.65 (.16)		
2	β_1	1	−1.17 (.05)	0	−1.25 (.22)	.72 (.25)	−.35 (.16)	−2.00 (.33)	1	.003 [.96]
	β_2	0	**0**	1	−.36 (.09)	−.72 (.12)	.20 (.07)	−.66 (.14)		
3	β_1	1	−1.17 (.05)	0	−.98 (.20)	−.27 (.18)	−.38 (.17)	−.38 (.38)	2	2.39 [.30]
	β_2	0	0	1	−.20 (.06)	**-1**	.18 (.07)	.18 (.19)		
4	β_1	1	−1.18 (.05)	0	−.88 (.18)	**0**	−.35 (.17)	−2.60 (.43)	3	3.22 [.36]
	β_2	0	0	1	−.20 (.06)	−1	.19 (.07)	−.88 (.19)		
5	β_1	1	−1.18 (.05)	0	−.87 (.17)	0	−.33 (.15)	−2.64 (.41)	4	3.24 [.52]
	β_2	0	0	1	**-.20**	−1	**-.20** (.05)	−.91 (.18)		
	α'_1	−.40 (.05)	.04 (.03)	.03 (.03)	−.01 (.06)	−.01 (.08)	–	–		
	α'_2	−.43 (.10)	−.10 (.06)	−.16 (.05)	−.05 (.12)	.62 (.14)	–	–		
6	β_1	1	−1.14 (.05)	0	−.69 (.16)	0	−.47 (.14)	−2.35 (.36)	10	8.88 [.54]
	β_2	0	0	1	−.16	−1	.16 (.04)	−.79 (.16)		
	α'_1	−.43 (.05)	**0**	**0**	**0**	**0**	–	–		
	α'_2	.45 (.09)	**0**	−.12 (.04)	**0**	.65 (.11)	–	–		

Sample: 1983 - 1998
Columns 3-9: Parameter estimates and their corresponding standard errors in parentheses. Column 10: Degrees of freedom of the χ^2 statistic. Column 11: χ^2 statistic and the corresponding marginal level of significance in brackets. Where no number in parentheses is given, the corresponding coefficient value had been imposed.

Table 4.16. Model Selection Criteria

model	*K*	*log* $\mid \Sigma \mid$	*AIC*	*HQ*	*SC*
1	50	−51.33	−49.77	−49.10	−48.08
2	49	−51.33	−49.80	−49.15	−48.15
3	48	−51.29	−49.79	−49.16	−48.17
4	47	−51.28	−49.81	−49.19	−48.23
5	46	−51.28	−49.84	−49.23	−48.29
6	40	−51.19	**-49.94**	**-49.41**	**-48.59**

K is the number of freely estimated parameters, and bold face signifies the minimum of the selection criteria.
The empirical model is defined in Table 4.15. The entries in column *model* refer to the first column there.

$$\alpha\beta' Y_t^* = \begin{pmatrix} \alpha_1 & \alpha_2 \end{pmatrix} \begin{pmatrix} \beta_1 \\ \beta_2 \end{pmatrix} Y_t^*$$

$$= \begin{pmatrix} \alpha_1 & \alpha_2 \end{pmatrix} \begin{pmatrix} ec_{MS} \\ ec_f \end{pmatrix}_t$$

$$= \begin{pmatrix} -.43 & .45 \\ (.05) & (.09) \\ 0 & 0 \\ 0 & -.12 \\ & (.04) \\ 0 & 0 \\ 0 & .65 \\ & (.11) \end{pmatrix} \begin{pmatrix} 1 & -1.14 & 0 & -.69 & 0 & -.47 & -2.35 \\ & (.05) & & (.16) & & (.14) & (.36) \\ 0 & 0 & 1 & -.16 & -1 & .16 & -.80 \\ & & & (0) & & (.04) & (.16) \end{pmatrix} \begin{pmatrix} m - hicp \\ y \\ i^l \\ i^{cm} \\ \pi \\ I_{86(4)} i^{cm} \\ I_{85(4)} \pi \end{pmatrix}_t$$

It turns out that the general patterns of the time varying model remain the same as in the constant coefficient model with two remarkable differences though. The first relationship (β_1) can be given an interpretation as a money supply function where from 1985, fourth quarter, inflation enters with a positive sign. In the constant coefficient model this sign is negative:

$$(m - hicp)_t = 1.14y_t + .69i_t^{cm} + .47I_{86(4)}i_t^{cm} + 2.35I_{85(4)}\pi_t + ec_{MS,t}$$

More important however, is the highly significant coefficient for adjustments of real money growth to the long-run money supply relationship. Only the presence of adjustment in the direction of real money eventually qualifies the long-run relationship as a function describing the behaviour of the monetary aggregate rather than as any other long-run equilibrium relation determining some other, endogenous quantity. While in the constant coefficient model no adjustment at all of real money seems to take place, all other variables now appear weakly exogenous with respect to the supply of money function.

The second relation (β_2) can be regarded as a very special form of the Fisher type relationship. This can be concluded from the fact, that the coefficients on i_t^{cm} and $I_{86(2)}i_t^{cm}$ have equal magnitude but opposite signs. Therefore, after the fourth quarter of 1986, the bond rate is cointegrated with the inflation rate alone. Furthermore, this cointegration relation can be separated in two parts one of which holds until 1985 third quarter and exhibits the coefficients implied by the Fisher hypothesis $(1 \quad -1)$ while in the second sub-period the coefficients yield $(1 \quad -1.8)$.

Comparison of the Long-run Parameters

Comparing the constant coefficient model to the recent estimates, the gain in parameter stability and estimation precision appears most remarkable. This is particularly valid for the money supply relationship as can be reasoned from the comparison of the Tables 4.11 and 4.15. Figure 4.5 depicts the differences in a graphical form. To simplify comparison, the corresponding recursive estimates are plotted in the same panels. The comparison is confined to some representative β-coefficient estimates, and restricted to the situation where the adjustment coefficients are also re-estimated.

The graphs indicate that the largest gains in terms of estimation reliability and parameter stability are obtained for the first cointegrating relationship now labelled money supply. In the second relation the results are almost

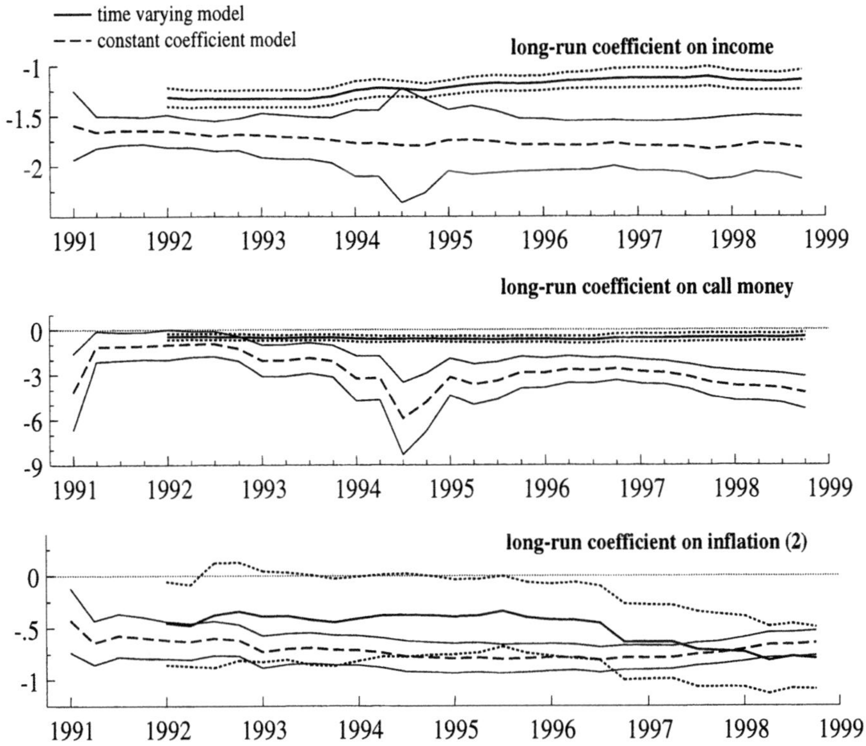

Top panel: Recursive estimates on the long-run income coefficients in the money supply relations.

Second top panel: Recursively estimated coefficients on the call money rate in the money supply relations. Note the zero line does not lay within the confidence bands of the recursive coefficients in the time varying model.

Bottom panel: Recursively estimated long-run coefficient on inflation rate in the 'Fisher' type relationship.

All estimates are obtained by estimating both α and β vectors recursively.

Figure 4.5. Comparative Stability Analysis

equivalent. In this case however, the constant coefficient model does slightly better. It should also be noticed that similar results emerge from recursive estimations of α and β without imposing zero restrictions on the adjustment parameters. Therefore, the superior performance of the time varying model cannot be related to the smaller number of coefficients allowed to vary.

A further comparison is made with respect to the cointegrating vectors. Figure 4.6 displays the cointegration relations normalised on a common mean value which reveals that the major differences occur between the long-run money supply relations ($ec_{m,t}$, $ec_{MS,t}$) while the 'Fisher' type relationships ($ec_{F,t}$, $ec_{f,t}$) look very much the same.

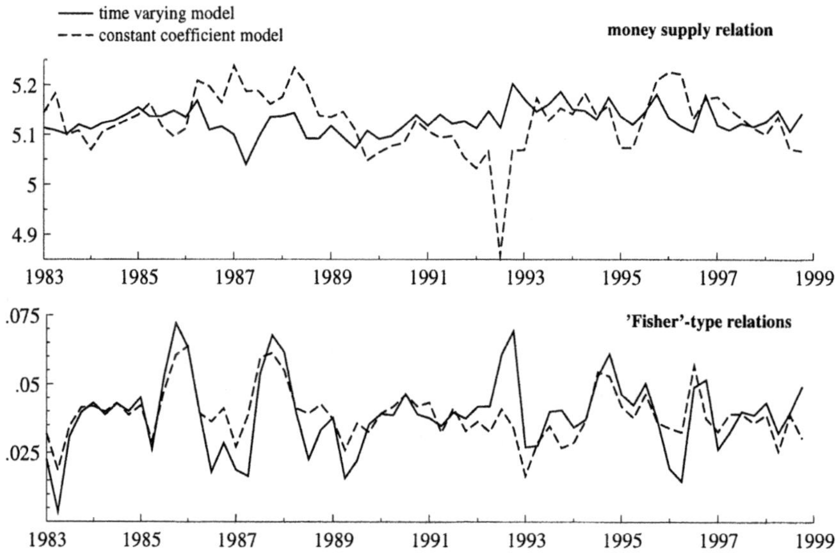

Mean adjusted cointegration relationships.

Figure 4.6. Differences and Similarities Between the Cointegrating Vectors of the Constant and Time Varying Coefficient Models

Moreover, the money supply relation now features less variance and also lacks huge spikes such as the one in 1992 in the constant coefficient model.[25]

Forecast Stabilities and Restricted Reduced Forms

So far, mainly backward looking analysis revealed stability of the new model. More insight into the properties can be gained by one-step-residual and one-step-forecast tests. But before turning to this analysis, yet another transformation of the model is applied. In addition to the restrictions on the long-run matrix, a sequential test procedure is used to identify redundant short run coefficients. To that aim, a reduction strategy is applied as suggested by Brüggemann and Lütkepohl (2001). It deletes step by step those coefficients from the model which lead to an improvement of the Akaike Information Criterion. The intercept terms and the long-run matrix were spared. The testing procedure starts from a model which has one more lag in the *VECM* representation, corresponding to a *VAR* of order three. This augmentation should ensure better residual properties as compared to a model with just one lag in the *VECM*. Table 4.23 in the appendix to this chapter provides a detailed account of the satisfactory properties of the initial models, while Tables 4.18 and 4.20 provide details of the same residual properties after the parameter reduction.

In the end, two models (one with the constant long-run coefficient and one with time varying long-run coefficients) are obtained which are supposed to be both parsimoniously specified and as congruent as possible with the data.[26] The results for these reduced form models can again be compared. Tables 4.17 and 4.19 report the coefficient estimates of the restricted reduced

[25] In another experiment this single spike has been modelled with a dummy variable. The corresponding coefficient turned out insignificant however.

[26] The restrictions are obtained by EGLS estimation implemented in *JMulTi* while the resulting model was estimated using a Full Information Maximum Likelihood estimation procedure available in PcFiml version 9.10 by Doornik and Hendry

form models and a number of specification tests all of which point to some problems especially with autocorrelation of the residuals to a varying degree depending on the model estimated and the variable under consideration. On the other hand, the vector mis-specification tests tend not to indicate any unwanted residual properties.[27]

When comparing the two models to each other, the previous conclusion of superiority of the time varying coefficient model is confirmed on a number of grounds. Among them most prominently is certainly the lower estimation uncertainty with respect to the real money equation and inflation equation, both of which naturally are the most interesting endogenous variables. In fact, the only account worth mentioning on which the constant coefficient model does better, is the income equation where the move to the time varying model inflicts a loss in explanatory power of around 18 percent in terms of the standard error while there is a gain of 37 and 15 percent for real money and inflation respectively.

All estimated residuals are plotted in Figure 4.7, where apart from a slightly downward trending behaviour of the residuals in the money equation of the constant coefficient model visual inspection reveals no major differences. Therefore, additional tools are applied to study the performance of the models.

One of these is the analysis of the forecasting power of the models. Two methods are applied. First, starting at some time before the end of the sample the estimated models are used to forecast the next value of the dependent variable. Then, the forecast is compared to the actual observation and the difference will be called one-step residual. Second, the models are estimated with the information available up to 1996(4) and these models are used for forecast-

(1997). Unfortunately, differences between these two software tools occur, partly also due to differences in rounding.

[27] In general, the hypotheses tested are formulated as H_0 : the effect is not present; where effect stands for autocorrelation, non-normality etc.

Table 4.17. Restricted Reduced Form Estimates of the Constant Coefficient Model

independent variable	lag	Equation (dependent variable) $\Delta(m-hicp)_t$	Δy_t	Δi_t^l	Δi_t^{cm}	$\Delta \pi_t$
$\Delta(m-hicp)_t$	1		.06			
			(.06)			
	2	.23		$-.05$		
		(.10)		(.04)		
Δy_t	1			.26		
				(.09)		
	2	.76		.23	.85	
		(.26)		(.10)	(.23)	
Δi_t^l	1	.47		.30		$-.66$
		(.29)		(.10)		(.34)
Δi_t^{cm}	1	.25	.32		$-.32$	
		(.13)	(.06)		(.11)	
	2	.25	.33			
		(.13)	(.05)			
$\Delta \pi_t$	1		$-.06$	$-.08$		
			(.04)	(.03)		
	2		$-.07$			
			(.03)			
intercept		.00	.07	$-.01$	$-.01$	$-.13$
		(*n.a.*)	(*n.a.*)	(*n.a.*)	(*n.a.*)	(*n.a.*)
$ec_{m,t}$	1		.06			$-.09$
			(.01)			(.02)
$ec_{F,t}$	1			$-.24$		.82
				(.05)		(.16)

ing the values of the endogenous variables in 1997(1). This procedure will be repeated until 1998(3) when a forecast is made for the last observation available. These forecasts can be considered out-of-sample forecasts, although the β coefficients are spared from being re-estimated. The corresponding predictions are called one-step forecasts and differ from the previously mentioned one-step residuals in that they are calculated without using information of those periods for which the forecast is made. Figures 4.8 and 4.9 depict the

Table 4.18. Residual Properties of the Constant Coefficient Model

Test	Statistics ;degrees of freedom [p-value] $\Delta(m-hicp)_t$	Δy_t	Δi_t^l	Δi_t^{cm}	$\Delta \pi_t$
correlation and	**.970**	·	·	·	·
	-.03	**.363**	·	·	·
standard	.16	-.02	**.367**	·	·
	.01	.02	.26	**.846**	·
deviation[a]	-.31	.08	.36	-.02	**1.255**
AR(1-5)[b]	2.26*	2.40*	3.53**	2.25*	1.18
	[.06]	[.05]	[.01]	[.07]	[.33]
Vec. AR(1-5)[b]		1.01; 125, 152 [.48]			
Nonnormality[c]	6.93**	.60	2.22	23.95**	3.41
	[.03]	[.74]	[.33]	[.00]	[.18]
Vec. Nonnormality[c]		36.89**; 10 [.00]			
ARCH (4)[d]	2.22	4.33	2.11	1.17	1.82
	[.70]	[.36]	[.72]	[.88]	[.77]
Vector ARCH (2)		485.27; 450 [.12]			

[a] The diagonal elements in bold face report 100 times the standard deviations, the off-diagonal entries refer to the correlations between the residuals of the corresponding equations (vertical order = horizontal order).
*, ** indicate significance at the ten and five percent level of significance respectively.
[b] Test for autoregressive residuals up to order 5. Single equation tests: 5 degrees of freedom; χ^2 distribution.
[c] Test for (vector) normality of the residuals based on the estimated first two moments. See Lütkepohl (1993a), pp 155 ff. Degrees of freedom equal to number of estimated moments considered (vector: 5 times 2, two else); test statistic follows χ^2 distribution.
[d] Single (and vector) equation test for autoregressive heteroscedasticity of the residuals up to order 4 (2) with 4 (450) degrees of freedom; χ^2 distribution.

respective results including the two-standard error confidence bands. Reasonable predictions are made as long as the observed values lie within these error bands (the fine solid lines around the dotted in Figures 4.8 and 4.9).

Each row in these graphs correspond to an equation, and the columns report the one-step residuals (left) and the forecast test respectively. Starting with the recursive residual analysis, in-sample stability seems to be confirmed.

Table 4.19. Restricted Reduced Form Estimates of the Time Varying Coefficient Model

independent variable	lag	Equation (dependent variable) $\Delta(m-hicp)_t$	Δy_t	Δi_t^l	Δi_t^{cm}	$\Delta \pi_t$
$\Delta(m-hicp)_t$	2			$-.06$		
				(.04)		
Δy_t	1		.27	.23		
			(.12)	(.09)		
	2	.31	.23		.82	
		(.19)	(.12)		(.22)	
Δi_t^l	1			.34		$-.56$
				(.10)		(.28)
Δi_t^{cm}	1	$-.18$			$-.36$	
		(.09)			(.11)	
$\Delta \pi_t$	1			$-.09$		.20
				(.04)		(.11)
intercept		2.05	.00	.00	$-.00$	$-.03$
		(*n.a.*)	(*n.a.*)	(*n.a.*)	(*n.a.*)	(*n.a.*)
$ec_{MS,t}$	1	$-.40$				
		(.04)				
$ec_{f,t}$	1	.44		$-.11$		.65
		(.07)		(.03)		(.09)

Apart from the call money rate, no major problems can be observed. For this variable, the one step residual is clearly outside the two-standard error bands around 1992(2) which happens to be in the midst of the EMS crisis during which unusual measures were taken by the central banks across Europe to save the currency system. This exceptional situation cannot be considered to be captured by the DGP for the remaining sample period.

When it comes to comparing the two models, a few remarks are appropriate. First, even though the constant coefficient model seems to slightly outperform the time varying model in terms of one-step forecasts it has to be kept in mind that this is partly due to the fact that the overall estimation uncertainty is larger in the constant coefficient model which is automatically

Table 4.20. Residual Properties of the Estimated Time Varying Coefficient Model

Test[a]	Statistics; degrees of freedom [p-value]				
correlation and	**.707**	·	·	·	·
	.01	**.438**	·	·	·
standard	.19	.01	**.375**	·	·
	.04	.12	.20	**.839**	·
deviation	-.30	.13	.37	.01	**1.091**
AR(1-5)	1.20 [.20]	2.63^{**} [.04]	2.29^{*} [.06]	2.50^{**} [.04]	2.84^{**} [.03]
Vec. AR(1-5)			.99; 125, 157 [.51]		
Nonnormality	1.78 [.41]	2.78 [.29]	.31 [.85]	23.02^{**} [.00]	2.26 [.33]
Vec. Nonnormality			32.69^{**}; 10 [.00]		
ARCH (4)	2.22 [.70]	4.33 [.36]	2.11 [.72]	1.17 [.88]	1.82 [.77]
Vector ARCH (2)			485.27; 450 [.12]		

[a] See explanations in table 4.18 on page 150.

reflected in wider confidence bands. Therefore, the same absolute forecast error is more likely to be outside the confidence bands in the time varying coefficient model than in its counterpart. Second, even though one might get the impression that both models do almost equally well, it should be recalled that the reasons for introducing changing coefficients have been found in the earlier part of the sample and might not be noticed so much at the end of the period.

Summing up the results of the modelling experiments one should consider the time varying coefficient model as the empirical counterpart of the true DGP. This can be concluded from a variety of model evaluation criteria among them the standard information criteria, standard errors of the estimated residuals and above all, the properties of the long-run coefficient estimates which are after all the focus of the current investigation. Therefore, the economic interpretations to be given in the next section will build on the corresponding results.

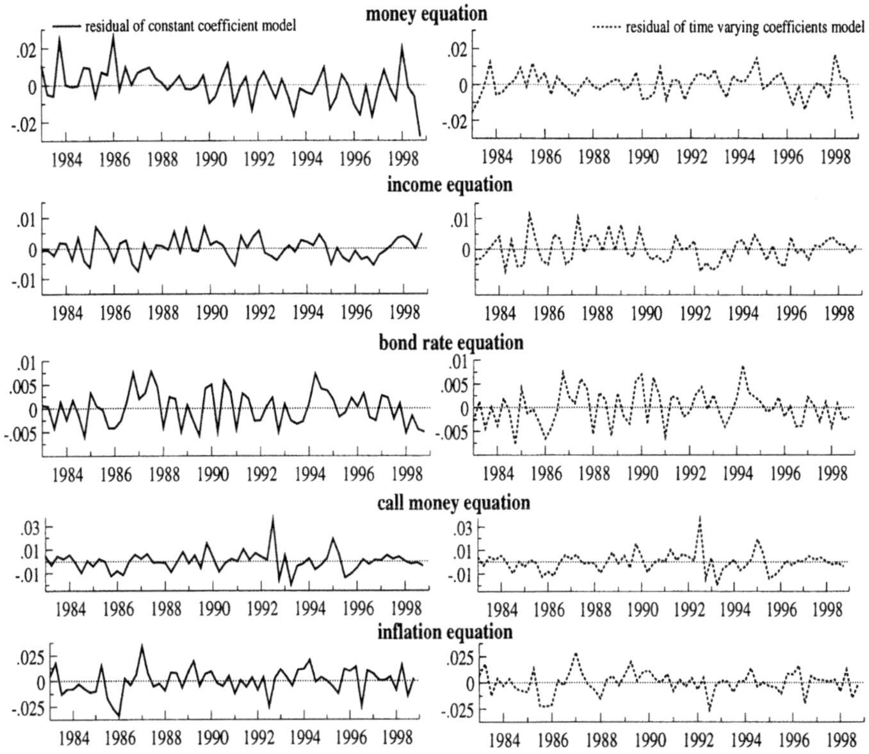

Each row corresponds to one equation. From top to bottom these are the growth rates of real money, income, bond rate, call money rate and inflation. The left hand column plots the residuals of the constant coefficient model while the right hand side displays the residuals of the time varying coefficient model.

Figure 4.7. Comparison of Econometric Models: Residual Plots

4.3.7 Economic Interpretation

Under the circumstances described above and focussing on the model with time varying cointegration coefficients, for the time after 1986(4) the following two expressions are considered valid and stable long-run relationships

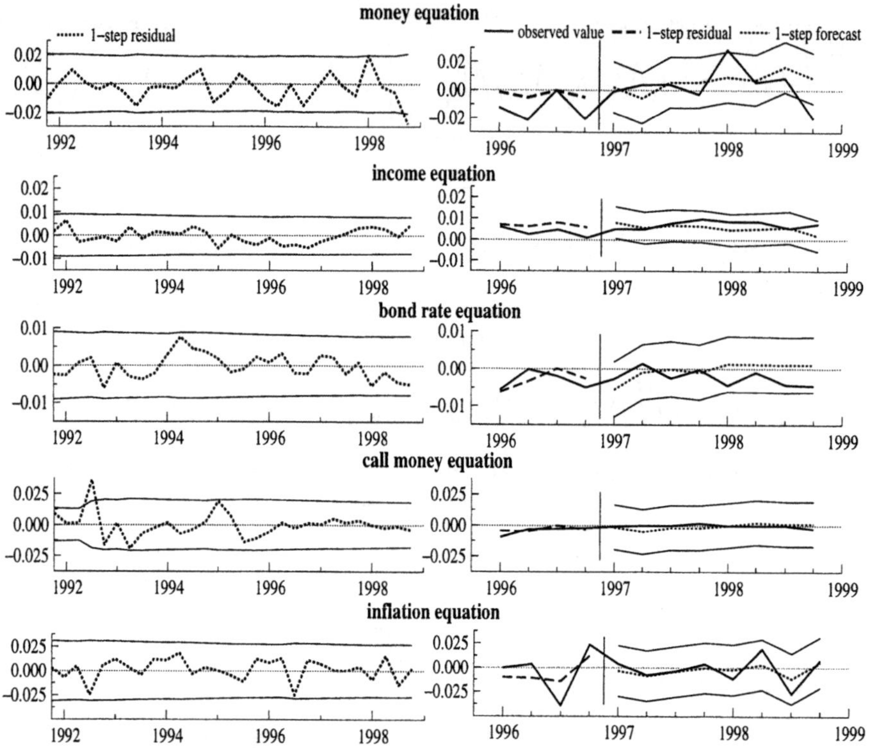

Each row corresponds to one equation. From top to bottom these are the growth rates of real money, income, bond rate, call money rate and inflation. The left hand column gives information on the recursively estimated and standardised residuals within the sample 1983(1) - 1998(4) while the panels to the right report one-step out of sample forecast point estimates (dotted lines) the corresponding two standard error bands (dashed lines), the actual observations (solid lines) and the recursive one-step residuals (long dashes).

Figure 4.8. Forecast Stability of the Constant Coefficient Model

$$(m - hicp)_t = 1.14y_t + 1.16i_t^{cm} + 2.35\pi_t + ec_{MS,t} \tag{4.10}$$

$$i_t^l = 1.8\pi_t + ec_{f,t}, \tag{4.11}$$

where the situation at the end of the estimation period is reported. The terms $ec_{MS,t}$ and $ec_{f,t}$ denote deviations from the long-run equilibrium between the remaining variables.[28]

[28] The graphical representations can be found in Figure 4.6.

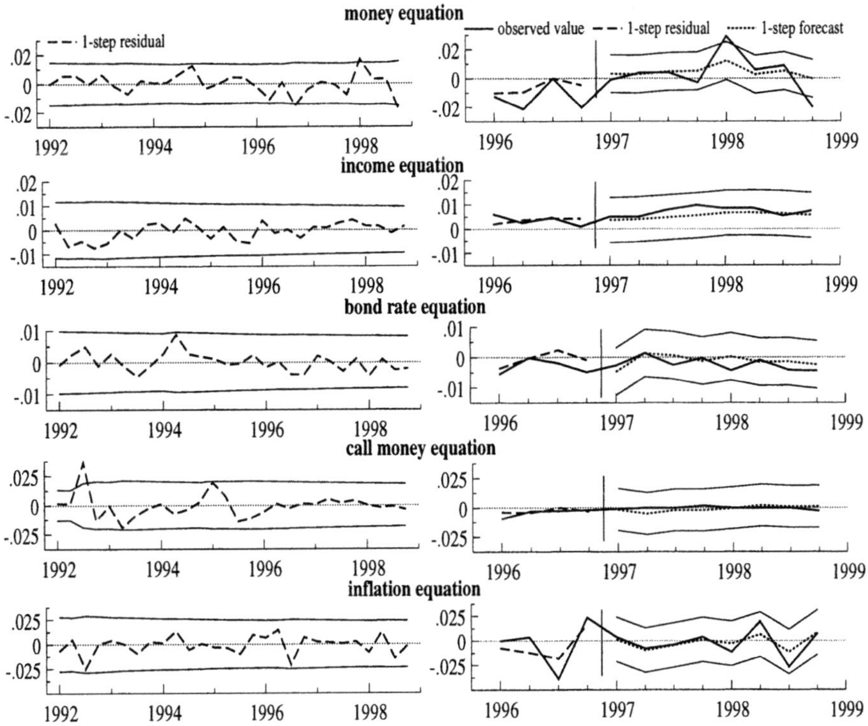

Each row corresponds to one equation. From top to bottom these are the growth rates of real money, income, bond rate, call money rate and inflation. The left hand column gives information on the recursively estimated and standardised residuals within the sample 1983(1) - 1998(4) while the panels to the right report one-step out of sample forecast point estimates (dotted line) the corresponding two standard error bands (dashed lines), the actual observations (solid line) and the recursive one-step residuals (long dashes).

Figure 4.9. Forecast Stability of the Time Varying Model

Following the outlines in the introductory chapter, the first of these two relationships cannot be called a long-run money demand relationship because the signs of the coefficients on the short-term interest rate and on inflation are at odds with the theoretically correct ones. While the income variable enters with the expected magnitude and sign, neither the bond rate nor the inflation rate seem to exercise the influence they are supposed to in the long-run. The positive sign on the call money rate cannot be considered sufficient evidence for a money demand relation to be observed. On the other hand, even though it cannot be ruled out ex ante that the demand for money should not also be positively affected by deposit rates to which the call money rate is linked. The most important argument therefore is the lack of an appropriate (opportunity) cost variable without which it is difficult to call an economic relationship a demand function. To see this point, consider the case where the standard Fisher relationship holds (stationary real bond rate). In such a case it would suffice to include the inflation rate in the demand function if the corresponding sign was negative. Then, the cointegrating relationship could be re-arranged in a way to replace the inflation rate in the money demand function by the bond rate without changing the long-run properties of the model. Here however, such a reformulation is impossible because the inflation rate has the wrong sign and because there is a positive link between the bond rate on the one hand and inflation and the short-term interest rate on the other. Before discussing potential explanations of the outcome, the second relationship should be briefly examined.

This second cointegrating vector has been labelled "Fisher type" relation because it is made of the two variables necessary for forming the standard Fisher relationship, or equivalently real bond rate. The coefficients are not the correct ones, however. In particular, while the Fisher hypothesis states that the level of the nominal interest rate can be expressed as the sum of the real rate, the expected inflation rate and a (stationary) risk premium, this does not seem to hold in the current case.

The reason for this failure might be found in either of the following considerations. The first is that the Fisher hypothesis is invalid altogether. One possible explanation is the effect of taxation. The higher the marginal tax rate, the larger the nominal return on assets requested by the investors will be. Second, as outlined in the introductory chapter, in empirical applications the expected inflation rate is very often approximated by the current inflation rate which is justified by rational expectation formation where nothing but the information about the actual price inflation enters. Thus, if the Fisher hypothesis cannot be confirmed, this could likewise be due to inferior modelling of the inflation expectations. If for example, the tremendous decrease in the inflation rate over the sample period had not been perfectly foreseen by the markets, it would be reasonable to expect a comparably conservative market rate for bonds which means a sluggish adjustment of the nominal bond rates to the ever lower inflation rates.

Considering this, the coefficient of 1.8 seems justified. The drawback of the argument certainly is that it cannot claim to hold in the very long-run because the decline in the inflation rate has to stop at some point implying an inevitable change in the coefficient on the inflation rate in this Fisher type relationship.

Returning to the first relationship, the notion of having failed to find a money demand relationship naturally raises the question why it has not been identified. One possibility is that the methodology is not suitable for identifying an according relationship. This however, is very unlikely because the same and even less advanced methods have been successfully applied by other authors for other countries. In contrast to the large number of studies considering Germany, or more recently Europe for instance, the evidence for money demand functions to exist in France appears rather meager.[29] Table 4.21 therefore reports some results available for France, of course without claiming completeness of the selection.

The typical feature of a French money demand investigation seems to be that it is conducted simultaneously within a group of countries. In the survey of Table 4.21 this is true for all studies except for Müller (1999). Therefore, it is not surprising that a thorough comparison including the stability of the estimates, weak exogeneity properties and the like appears impossible.

[29] Hubrich (2001), pp. 98ff lists about 20 studies on German money demand; a European aggregate has been analysed at least as often as that, see next chapter.

Table 4.21. Comparison of French Money Demand Function Estimates

sample	endogenous variables	coefficient estimates					reference
		y_t	i_t^{out}	i_t^{in}	π_t	$\alpha_{1,1}$	
79(1)-90(2)	real M3 (deflated by hicp), real GDP, 10 yrs gov. bond yield, 3mths inter-bank rate	1.31	−1.4	1.4	-	−0.267	Cassard et al. (1995)
73(1)-94(4)	real M3H (deflated by hicp), real GDP, gov. bond yield	1.27	−1.4	-	-	−0.07	Wesche (1998)
79(1)-96(4)	real M1 (deflated by implicit GDP deflator), real GDP, gov. bond yield, short rate	−.05	−1.22	-	-	n.a.	Clausen (1998)
81(1)-94(4)	real M3H (deflated by implicit GDP deflator)	1.7	.19	-	-	n.a.	Fagan and Henry (1999)
83(1)-97(4)	real M3 (deflated by implicit GDP deflator), real GDP, long-term bond yield call money rate, GDP inflation	1.23	-	2.88	−2.88	0	Müller (1999)
83(1)-98(4)	real M3 (deflated by *hicp*), real GDP, bond rate, call money rate, *hicp* inflation	1.14	-	1.16	2.35	−.41	this study

Wesche (1998) and Fagan and Henry (1999) both indicate existence of a second long-run relationship which remains unidentified, however. The coefficient estimate on the long-term interest rate in Fagan and Henry (1999) has a t-ratio of .4.
The long-run coefficient estimates in the Clausen (1998) investigation are all insignificant, the estimates on the short-term interest rate are not reported.

As an example, Fagan and Henry (1999) and Wesche (1998) solely focus on the existence of the money demand relation and derive feasibility of monetary targeting from its parameters and weak exogeneity of money (Wesche, 1998). They both do not thoroughly investigate the properties of their estimates, however. Therefore, it is neither known whether their estimation results are stable over time, nor what the short-run dynamics' impact is. In contrast, Tullio et al. (1996) simply state that they "were unable to estimate satisfactory dynamic versions of the demand for money functions" (see page 318). Sims (1992) on the other hand, uses an unrestricted *VAR* in levels disregarding possible cointegration features and obtains partly odd results when reporting a significant influence of France's monetary conditions on the world commodity price index.

In sum, accepting the reported estimates' face values, overall an income elasticity larger than one seems to be a consistent finding. With respect to the main conclusions drawn on the basis of the current analysis, there seems to be some disagreement on the adjustment to money market equilibrium errors. While Cassard et al. (1995) and Wesche (1998) find significant adjustment of money to deviations from lon-run money demand, in this study, this applies to long-run money supply. In case of Cassard et al. (1995), this difference can at least partly be attributed to the sample definition, which mainly provides information about the time before 1987. It would therefore be particularly informative to learn about the estimation performance over time. The findings of the second study cannot be explained by this reasoning. Moreover, both studies also cover the period prior to 1983 which had been assumed unsuitable for a standard money demand analysis due to incompatible institutional settings.

The study of Cassard et al. (1995) can be compared best to the current exercise because it deals with the French money demand in direct comparison to the German example and thus highlights a number of aspects the other studies are not capable of.[30] However, the main drawback of their analysis is that the cointegration space which consists of two cointegration relations remains unidentified with the direct consequence of being unable to even report standard errors for the estimated cointegration coefficients. Thus, the significant adjustment coefficient reported could, for instance, likewise be a reaction to lagged values of the income velocity of money. In any case, the extent to which the real money growth adjusts to deviations from which long-run equilibria remains largely unknown.

In contrast to Cassard et al. (1995) and Wesche (1998), but in accordance with the current investigation, Fagan and Henry (1999) and Clausen (1998) find no money demand function at all.

The central argument to explain the difficulties with a French demand for money function is that it cannot be identified econometrically because the market for broad money has been dominated by the long-run money supply function. The model by e.g. Bofinger et al. (1998) which has also been used by Nautz (2000) for the setting of European central banks can help to understand why the long-run money supply represents the money market outcome much better. They identify exactly one combination of monetary policy targets and shocks (demand or supply) to the market for broad money that results first, in a destabilizing effect on the demand for money function, and second, in a stabilizing impact on money supply. Such a situation occurs only if the monetary policy objective is the money market interest rate.[31] Thus, combining this result with the insight gained in the preliminary analysis yields exactly that outcome. The French central bank was bound to target exchange rates in order to maintain the parity with the Deutschmark and hence shocks to the money market were accommodated in such a way to keep the desired interest

[30] These would be giving an account of the history of monetary policy, hinting at currency substitution, sensitivity of the estimates with respect to data definition and estimation technique for example.

[31] See for example Nautz (2000) pp. 95 ff.

rate level which eventually established a more stable long-run money supply function.

This said, even the money supply function cannot be viewed really stable in the long-run due to the change in the exchange rate regime in 1987. This is also reflected in the time varying coefficients of the long-run relationships.

4.4 Summary and Conclusion

During the period prior to EMU a stable long-run money supply function was found. Adding this finding to the results of the preliminary analysis, evidence accumulates which implies that the demand for money function was destabilized at the expense of stabilizing the supply function. This is part of the consequences of the exchange rate regime introduced in 1987 when the French Franc was devaluated against the Deutschmark for the last time. Some newly developed tools which are designed to account for changes in the cointegration relationships had to be applied in order to cope with the impact of the 1987 events on the data generating process. A comparison to estimates obtained when ignoring the break in 1987 hinted at the superiority of the alternative approach.

When comparing the recent results to those found by other authors, the largely contradictory outcomes can be explained by the differences in the definition of the sample period, by the infeasibility of a just comparison on grounds of missing information about the properties of the competing results and by the widespread ignorance of the change in the FF/DM exchange rate regime.

The long-run money supply function derived from the attempt to model a money demand function is consistent with e.g. the theoretical model by Bofinger et al. (1998) and was found to coincide with the implications of their framework.

Finally, with respect to the prospects of France for the European Monetary Union, it has to be pointed out that so far, French monetary policy has not been built on the existence of a stable money demand relationship. This is a direct consequence of France's care for the exchange rate which made it infeasible to target money at the same time. Thus, underlining the positive aspects of that setting, it could be argued that due to the introduction of the Euro and the delegation of the monetary policy decisions to the ECB, France will regain some sovereignty about monetary policy because it can make its voice heard at the board meetings. But even if the demands by France would not count, the situation can hardly worsen because France has already sustained a long period during which monetary policy had been imported from abroad, i.e. Germany.

Nevertheless, in case the ECB puts emphasis on its first pillar of monetary policy, which is monetary targeting, the lack of knowledge about the features of a French money demand will introduce some need for experimenting before the uncertainty originating from the missing facts will be eradicated.

The next chapter will address the same problem using a different approach in that it will assume a comprehensive currency area ignoring national borders and individual monetary policy conduct.

4.A Data, Tables and Figures

The data has been downloaded from Humboldt University's copy of the 1998 International Statistical Yearbook which includes the IMF data stream and OECD data bases.

Table 4.22. Data Sources

Data description and source code

item	description	code	source
nominal money	M3 seasonally adjusted , billions FF	132 39MCC	IMF
real output	Gross domestic product, 1995 prices, seasonally adjusted, 1000 billions FF	141037NSA	OECD
French price level (1)	harmonized index of consumer prices; base year 1995	133 64...	IMF
French price level (2)	index of consumer prices; base year 1990	132 64	IMF
repo rate	repurchasing agreements	132 60A	IMF
call money rate	call money rate	146207D	OECD
3-mth interest rate	PIBOR 3-month or 90 day rates (Interbank)	146225D	OECD
6-mth interest rate	LIBOR 6-month	132 60EB.	IMF
bond rate	10 yrs bond guaranteed by the government	146281D	OECD
forward rate	3-months forward rate, Frankfurt/M (averages), FF/DM	WU5046	Bundesbank
spot rate	official exchange rate, monthly averages (FF/DM)	132 RH	IMF

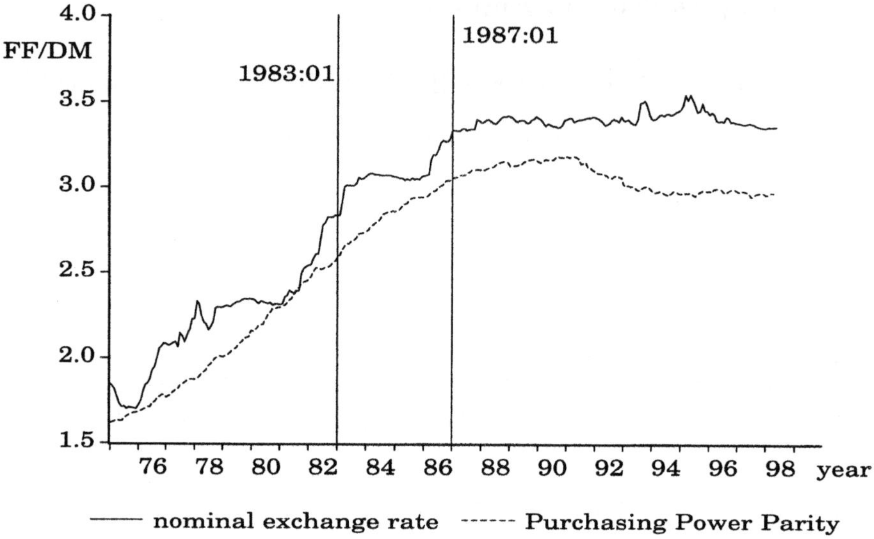

The purchasing power parity is the ratio of the French CPI and the German CPI based on 1990 prices times the purchasing power indicator for the same year according to an OECD statistic.

Figure 4.10. Nominal Exchange Rate and Purchasing Power Parity Line

Table 4.23. Residual Analysis of Unrestricted Reduced Form Estimations

1) Constant Coefficient Model[a] (see Table 4.11)

Test[b]	Dependent variable (equation) $\Delta(m-p)_t$	Δy_t	Δi_t^l	Δi_t^{cm}	$\Delta \pi_t$
correlation and	**1.007**	·	·	·	·
	-.04	**.379**	·	·	·
standard	.17	-.02	**.379**	·	·
	-.01	.01	.23	**.863**	·
deviation	-.32	.11	.35	-.05	**1.091**
AR(1-5)	1.21	1.20	2.30*	.95	.71
	[.32]	[.32]	[.06]	[.46]	[.62]
Vec. AR(1-5)	1.01; 125, 113 [.47]				
Nonnormality	7.87*	0.33	1.33	20.02**	1.97
	[.02]	[.85]	[.51]	[.00]	[.37]
Vec. Nonnormality	32.69**; 10 [.00]				
ARCH (4)	2.20	3.51	4.95	1.02	4.40
	[.70]	[.48]	[.29]	[.91]	[.35]
Vector ARCH (2)	485.27; 450 [.12]				

2) Time Varying Coefficient Model[a] (see Table 4.15)

Test[b]	Dependent variable (equation) $\Delta(m-p)_t$	Δy_t	Δi_t^l	Δi_t^{cm}	$\Delta \pi_t$
correlation and	**.756**	·	·	·	·
	.02	**.441**	·	·	·
standard	.18	.02	**.398**	·	·
	.03	.04	.20	**.855**	·
deviation	-.30	.17	.39	.04	**1.146**
AR(1-5)	1.18	1.28	1.86	1.04	1.91
	[.33]	[.29]	[.12]	[.40]	[.11]
Vec. AR(1-5)	.95; 125, 113 [.62]				
Nonnormality	2.97	2.42	.87	17.88**	1.70
	[.23]	[.30]	[.65]	[.00]	[.43]
Vec. Nonnormality	28.09**; 10 [.00]				
ARCH (4)	3.40	1.23	1.40	1.49	4.73
	[.49]	[.87]	[.84]	[.83]	[.32]
Vector ARCH (2)	485.27; 450 [.12]				

[a] Models with α, Γ_i unrestricted, β restricted.
[b] See explanations in table 4.18 on page 150.
Entries report the value of the test statistics, degrees of freedom and the p-values in brackets.

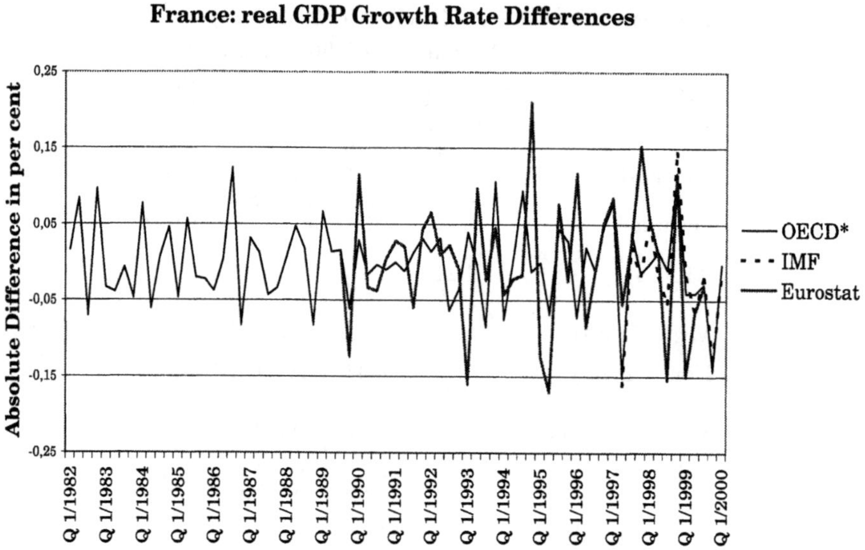

Percentage difference of alternative data to the data set used in the analysis.

Figure 4.11. Differences in GDP Growth Rates of Various Data Sources

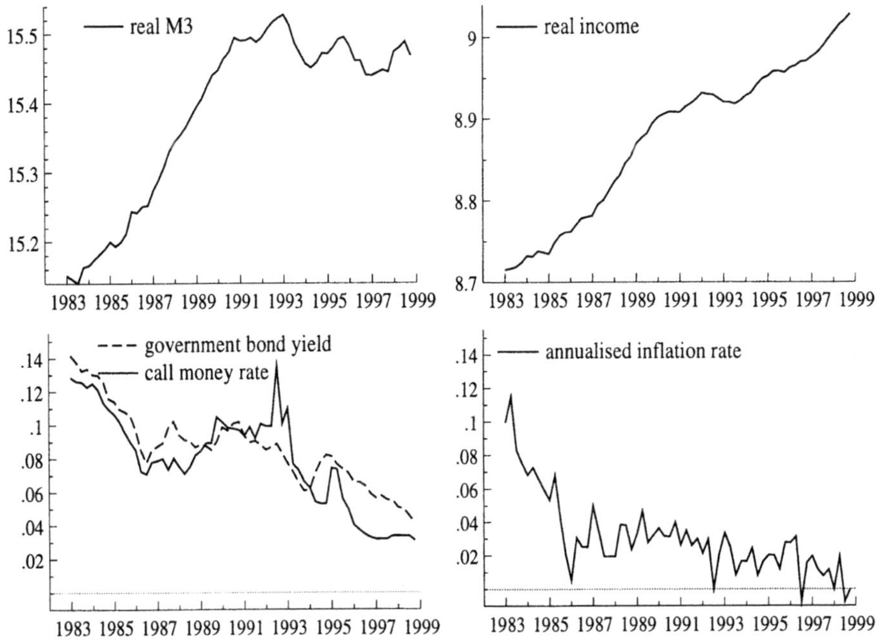

Money and income in logs, interest and inflation rates in annual decimals.

Figure 4.12. Data Graphics

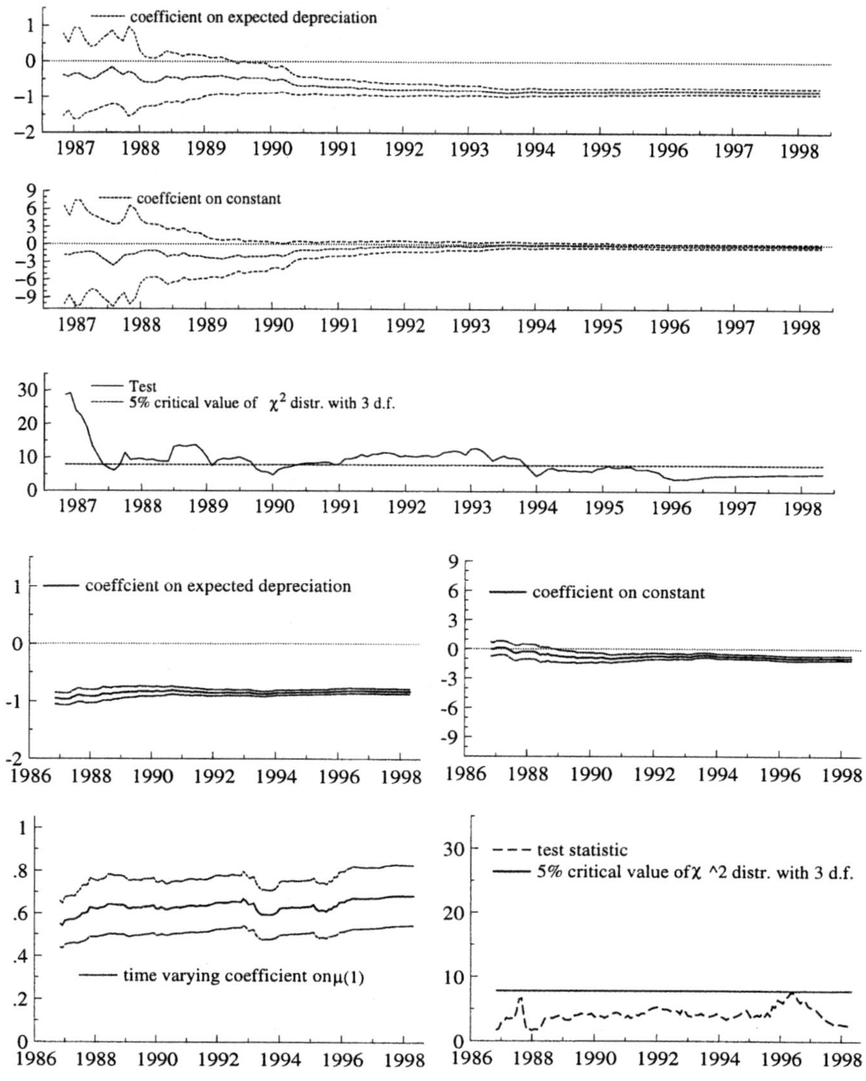

Sample: 1983-1998, short-run re-estimated, point estimates with two-standard error bands, recursive test statistic on restrictions.
Rows 1-3: restrictions according to H_0^2 imposed.
Rows 4-5: restrictions according to H_0^4 imposed, a smooth shift function is applied ($f_t^3(\vartheta, T_1)$, see chapter 3).

Figure 4.13. CIP Analysis: Comparison of Recursive Long-run Estimates

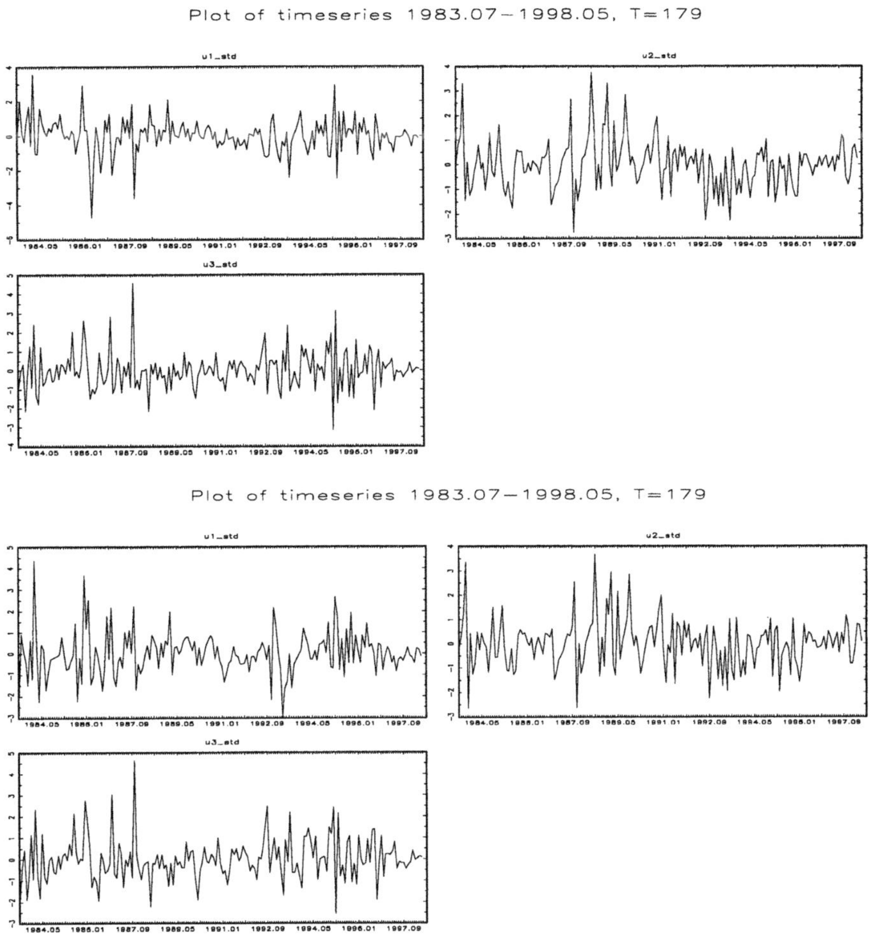

Standardized residuals of the constant coefficient model (top) and of the time varying coefficient model (bottom).

Sample: 1983-1998, restrictions according to H_0^2 (three top panels) and H_0^4 (three bottom panels) imposed, parameter estimates as in 4.6. For each panel in the top left: residuals from $\Delta i^s_{F,t}$ equation, top right: residuals from $\Delta i^s_{G,t}$ equation, bottom left: residuals from ΔE_t equation.

Figure 4.14. CIP Analysis: Standardized Residuals

5

Money Demand in Europe: Evidence from the Past

5.1 Introduction

Complementary to the previous chapter, this part of the thesis investigates the monetary conditions on a supra-national level. Europe is regarded as an entity which is subject to both the same economic shocks and the same monetary policy. The general objective of the empirical analysis is to find a good statistical model which may also say something about structural, economically meaningful relationships within the data, and which might also be used for the conduct of monetary policy.

The chapter partly draws on Müller and Hahn (2001). That paper has been significantly extended to cover more recent developments within the Euro countries as well. A distinctive feature of the investigation is the precise and detailed description of the data sources and aggregation methods applied, to form a basis for comparison to other studies.

The structure of the analysis is as follows. After a brief overview of the topic, advantages and drawbacks of relying on aggregated artificial data referring to the time prior to the European Monetary Union will be discussed. Then, the analysis outlines in detail data sources and aggregation methods used to collect a data set for studying money demand properties in the area of the EMU member states. As a result, it does not appear to be reasonable going back in history much further than 1984 because data quality and availability deteriorates rapidly prior to that date.

The second part is a cointegration analysis of money, income, long and short-term interest rates, and prices within a Vector Autoregressive Error Correction Model. The focus will be on long-run money demand, which will be identified and, furthermore, found to be stable. It turns out however, that a slightly different, yet statistically equally valid identification scheme, leads to partly different conclusions about the long-run relations. Moreover, this alternative statistical model appears to be superior in some aspects. Therefore, both model variants will be looked at and compared to each other.

Finally, an economic interpretation is provided along the scheme suggested in chapter 2.

5.2 Preliminary Considerations

When the idea of a single currency for Europe won more and more followers, economists shifted the focus of their research to the conditions under which a European monetary policy would likely have to be conducted. One of the research interests focused on whether or not European money demand is stable and whether or not a more stable money demand on a European level compared with national findings can be regarded as a statistical artefact (see e.g. Artis, Bladen-Hovell and Zhang (1992), Arnold (1994), Arnold and de Vries (2000)).

By now, there is widespread acceptance that European policy decisions have to be based upon the data available so far, regardless of the impact of a possible change in agents behaviour which could have been induced by the start of the European Monetary Union. However, such a change in conditions will become apparent after some time only. Therefore, from an empirical viewpoint, the best one can do is to look at Europe as an economic union which, in principle, works like a large national economy.

For the first time Kremers and Lane (1990) estimated European money demand by aggregating national data sources. For a long time, most studies have focused on a limited set of countries, mainly the larger or core countries of the then future EMU.[1] Here, a money demand function for the eleven EMU-countries which joined EMU from the very beginning is estimated. When the first version of this analysis was completed, only Gottschalk (1999) and Coenen and Vega (1999) had chosen the same group of countries. Meanwhile, a few more authors have dealt with the same selection (see inter alia Trecroci and Vega (2000), Brand and Cassola (2000), Gerlach and Svensson (2001), Fagan, Henry and Mestre (2001)).

5.2.1 Problems Related to Aggregation

Aggregation Approach

Economists who attempt to estimate a money demand function for the EMU face a number of special problems. These have arisen because the EMU only just began in 1999. Therefore, no long time series data is available. One common solution is to rely on artificially constructed EMU data generated by aggregating the national data of the participating countries for the time prior to the EMU. In constructing the data one faces on the one hand problems with the availability and the quality of the data used, and on the other hand special problems concerning the appropriate aggregation method.

The question of the appropriate aggregation method did not arise for the present money demand investigation because it uses the official monetary aggregate for the EMU constructed by the European Central Bank itself. Paying attention to consistency when aggregating different data series, the construction of the other EMU series is performed in the same way as the monetary aggregate. Therefore, no detailed discussion of the advantages and disadvantages of different aggregation methods will be conducted.

[1] See e.g. Wesche (1998), Hayo (1999), Monticelli and Strauss-Kahn (1993), Fagan and Henry (1999) to name only a few.

Availability and Quality of the Data

Estimating money demand for the EMU means estimating an aggregated money demand that comprises the data of 11 countries.[2] Providing sufficient time series which cover long periods for all variables included in the money demand is hampered because for some EMU countries no extensive and detailed statistics are available at all. Therefore, a considerable amount of interpolation, particularly in the earlier part of the data sample was unavoidable.

Furthermore, distortions in the EMU data are an important issue. Different sources of impairment can be identified for the EMU data. First, they can be biased because the underlying national series by themselves are distorted by, for example, structural breaks. A second reason for distortion in the aggregated data is that it often refers to non-harmonized national sources. The national time series are based on national data definitions which can vary significantly between countries. For instance, the aggregated EMU data is based on different calculation methods of GDP or different maturities of the assets the interest rates refer to. Further harmonization problems arise because non-seasonally adjusted national data is not published for all countries joining the EMU, and different procedures of seasonal adjustment are applied in different countries.

5.2.2 Interpretation Problems

The interpretation of the results achieved with the artificial EMU data has to be taken with caution. It remains open how relevant the results and conclusions are for the time period after the start of EMU. Two aspects are to be distinguished. The first is the relevance of the results based on past data for the time after a potential structural break in general, while the second is the relevance of the results referring to the artificially generated aggregated EMU data for the Euro era in particular.

[2] These countries are Belgium, Spain, France, Ireland, Italy, Luxembourg, Austria, the Netherlands, Portugal, Finland, and Germany.

Inference for EMU from Past Data

A general statement concerning the transferability of the results obtained before a regime shift to the time period following the regime shift, is related to the Lucas (1976) critique. It implies that since a regime shift like the start of a common monetary policy in the EMU countries can induce changes in agents' behaviour, it is not compelling that conclusions drawn on the basis of past data are also valid for the time period after the regime shift. Using this approach, it follows that results obtained from historical data for the money demand in the EMU have to be interpreted carefully.

A potential source of a structural break in agents' behaviour is a change in the monetary conditions present in the countries joining the EMU. For example, Arnold and de Vries (2000) argue that fixing the exchange rate leads to increased correlation between the price inflation rates within Europe, thereby replacing the source of pre-EMU variation which they hold to be the variation in the exchange rate. If this was true, the apparently better properties of money demand functions on a European level were simply owed to the offsetting effects of currency substitution in the aggregate. That is why Arnold and de Vries (2000) do not regard stability as a reliable property of an EMU demand for money function. A European money demand function has been observed to be more stable than many national functions by e.g. Kremers and Lane (1990), Monticelli and Strauss-Kahn (1993), Artis et al. (1992), and Monticelli (1996). The convergence process of monetary conditions between countries participating in the EMU took place within the time period that underlies this investigation - the years 1984 to 2000.[3] This implies that a change in the behaviour of individuals might have taken place within the

[3] This can easily be seen by comparing, for instance, the inflation rates or the interest rates between the EMU countries both at the beginning and at the end of the period under consideration. At the beginning enormous differences show up while at the end convergence seems to be achieved.

estimation sample which could exert an influence on money demand and its stability properties.

Against that, the monetary conditions at the end of 1998 resemble those after the start of the EMU. A change in the behaviour of individuals at the very day of the introduction of the Euro due to changing monetary conditions does not seem to be likely. Subsequently, the results obtained should provide some evidence about the conditions beyond that date.

Further arguments in favour of the relevance of the results based on past data for the EMU regime are brought up by Hayo (1999). First, he suggests that the start of the EMU could bring about an economic shock on money demand which could possibly be only of temporary nature. Similar statements have been made with respect to the shock due to the German monetary union. In such a scenario, monetary policy in the EMU can rely on the results achieved on the basis of the past data. Secondly, he assumes that people adjust their behaviour to the new monetary environment only very slowly. If this behavioral inertia proves right, past experiences will be applicable to the EMU regime at least for some time.

Inferring from Aggregated Artificial EMU Data

Besides the general problem of transferring results achieved before a (potential) structural break to the time after, evaluating the money demand and its properties in EMU on the basis of artificially aggregated data is accompanied by additional difficulties.

A special property of money demand functions for country aggregates seems to be that they exhibit better stability properties compared to national functions.[4] This leads to the question whether the enhanced stability prop-

[4] See e.g. Kremers and Lane (1990), Monticelli and Strauss-Kahn (1993), Artis et al. (1992), Monticelli (1996), Tullio et al. (1996) and Spencer (1997) in favour of that hypothesis and Arnold (1994), Arnold and de Vries (2000) in opposition to it.

erties will be maintained after the start of EMU, since EMU money demand exerts in some way properties similar to national functions.

One possible explanation for the better stability properties of EMU money demand we observe could be that negatively correlated national shocks compensate each other (Spencer, 1997). However, if this should prove to be the reason for the enhanced stability properties, the stability of money demand is likely to deteriorate after the start of the EMU since national shocks, especially monetary shocks, will occur more synchronized within a monetary union. Others relate this effect to the heavy weight attached to the German component in constructing the aggregated series leading to a reflection of the German money demand properties in the aggregate (see Tullio et al. (1996)).

The allegedly better stability properties of the aggregated EMU money demand could also be due to a superior specification of aggregated money demand functions compared to national functions. The specification bias caused by omitted variables such as currency substitution which constitutes a frequent source of distortions for national money demand functions is of minor importance for aggregated money demand functions, since for larger areas foreign influences are often included automatically. For instance, for the aggregated EMU money demand, the problem of currency substitution, as far as it refers to European currencies, is solved solely on the basis of the new definition of the monetary aggregate M3 of the ECB.

It is unclear, however, if the better stability properties of EMU money demand owed to a superior specification will remain after the EMU has started. Future instability can certainly not originate from currency substitution between Euro countries, yet may be introduced by substitution between the EMU area and the rest of the world.

Furthermore, the introduction of a single currency in Europe enhances competition between countries not only on the goods market by improving price transparency, but also on the financial markets. This spurs the development of financial innovations within the EMU, which could exercise a negative effect on the stability of money demand in the future as well (see Hayo (1999)).

5.3 Constructing European Data

The estimation and test results are sensitive to the construction of the data in general and the employed aggregation method in particular. Therefore, the construction and aggregation procedure of the EMU data underlying this investigation is an important feature and is described precisely in the following.[5] The analysis is based on quarterly data for the time period from 1984(1) to 2000(4). To cater for lags and differenced variables, the estimation sample starts at 1984(1). This period can be divided into two different periods one of which covering the estimation period of the paper by Müller and Hahn (2001) (until 1998(2)), the second one ending in 2000(4). The data has been generated in two different ways for these periods and therefore, both these ways are dealt with in the next paragraphs starting with the calculations for the period 1985(1)-1998(2).

The monetary aggregate is the official aggregate M3 of the ECB. A historical time series of this data was published by the European Central Bank (1999a). The definition of the monetary aggregate M3 of the ECB corresponds to a very broad monetary aggregate. It is broader than the aggregate M3 that was used previously, for example by the German Bundesbank.[6] As the ECB implemented a new definition for M3 containing different and new components such as money market funds and money market paper "a considerable

---

[5] An exact overview of the national data sources and of the time periods for which national data is estimated as well as the applied estimation methods, is given in the Tables 5.13 to 5.17 in the appendix.

[6] The monetary aggregate M3 of the ECB comprises currency in circulation, overnight deposits, deposits with an agreed maturity up to 2 years, deposits redeemable at notice up to 3 months, repurchase agreements, money market fund shares, and money market paper, and debt securities up to 2 years.

amount of estimation was necessary, particularly for earlier dates" (European Central Bank (1999a), p. 41). Furthermore, the ECB adjusted the national series for important structural breaks. For example, the impact of the German unification was straightened out of the time series. The national M3 series were then converted into Euro by the ECB using the irrevocably fixed conversion rates vis-à-vis the Euro which were determined on December 31, 1998. Thereafter, the national series were added up. The M3 data was published as non-seasonally adjusted end-of-month data. It was transformed from the end-of-month data into end-of-quarter data by using the last month of each quarter as quarterly data. In the last step, the M3 data was seasonally adjusted applying the Berlin Method (BV4).[7] Seasonal adjustment of M3 had to be applied for reasons of a consistent data set (see GDP construction below).

The main data source for the national real and nominal GDP data is Eurostat. Real and nominal GDP was calculated, and the resulting implicit GDP deflator served as a price measure. In periods where no national data was available, estimations had to be carried out. If, for example, during a certain period Eurostat data for one country was missing, but data from the Organisation for Economic Cooperation and Development (OECD) was available, then the level of the Eurostat GDP data in the missing period was calculated using the growth rate of the OECD data. The national data relies on the European System of Accounts going back to 1979 (ESA 79) because for the harmonized and therefore more appropriate European System of Accounts after the convention of 1995 (ESA 95), no long time series are at hand. Furthermore, for some countries, such as France, only seasonally adjusted GDP data exists. Therefore, it was decided to use seasonally adjusted GDP data for all countries.

[7] BV4 is the abbreviation of the German name Berliner Verfahren Version Nummer 4 which stands for Berlin Method version number 4. See Nourney (1993) for a description.

In analogy to the calculation of the monetary aggregate M3 by the ECB, the GDP series was adjusted for the impact of the German unification. The GDP data series for the whole of Germany starts in 1989(1). Before that date, no such data is available. Therefore, the GDP data for Germany for the period before 1989(1) was estimated assuming the growth rates of the West German GDP data. All national GDP series are then transformed into Euro currency using the fixed conversion rates vis-à-vis the Euro. After adding up the national GDP series, the EMU-GDP time series were obtained.

The national data of the long and short-term interest rates are taken from the OECD Main Economic Indicators. The long-term interest rates represent the yield of long-term government bonds. Unfortunately, the rates of return of the government bonds published by the OECD for different countries do not reflect exactly the same maturities. For example, for Germany the yield on public sector bonds with 7 to 15 years duration is taken while for Italy the yield on treasury bonds of maturity of one year or more is included.

Against that, the short-term interest rates refer exactly to the same maturities in all countries. They measure the yield of three-month inter bank deposits which is represented for instance in Germany by the three-month FIBOR or in France by the three-month PIBOR. The national interest rate series are constructed as end-of-quarter data. They are weighted with their current share of real EMU-GDP to obtain the EMU interest rate series. In years where no interest rate data for a particular country was available, the interest rate of this country does not enter the calculation. Inflation is measured as a quarter-on-quarter increase of the GDP deflator.

In order to obtain results for the most recent years, the data set described above has been complemented by data published after 1998(2). To that aim, the official ECB data on the money aggregate, nominal and real income, as well as on the interest rates where taken from the ECB data bases available on the internet. The income series were extended using the growth rates of the ECB data to obtain values for 1998(3) and later, while no such procedure was necessary for the interest rates. In a separate analysis investigating the properties of the ECB data and my own calculations, it was found that the correlation of the corresponding growth rates of the variables income, interest and inflation rates is no less than 70 percent. Thus, extending the data by this procedure seems to be acceptable.

A final remark is in order with respect to the aggregation weights. A number of studies like Wesche (1998) and Ericsson, Hendry and Tran (1994) among others highlight the advantages of using fixed rates as opposed to time varying weights, like nominal exchange rates, for converting assets of different denomination into a variable with the same unit of measurement. The intuition behind this procedure is that fixed weights are equivalent to linearly combining the original time series. In the framework of cointegration analysis this is important because all linear cointegration relations can be linearly transformed without loosing the property of cointegration. The cross country aggregation of the data with fixed conversion rates should therefore preserve the property of cointegration. Statements about other aspects of the cointegration characteristics like weak exogeneity and so on are much harder to derive (Ericsson et al., 1994). In contrast, Beyer, Doornik and Hendry (2000) advocate variable weights for adding first differences in log-levels where the weights are derived from relative sizes of the components measured in a common currency. The weights thus vary with the exchange rates. This of course, is only approximately a linear transformation of the data series.

5.4 Cointegration Analysis

This section applies the standard approach towards money demand analysis discussed in chapter 2. After analyzing the stationarity properties of the variable set, the general modelling approach will be briefly reviewed. Then, the cointegrating rank of the system is determined, and finally, the cointegration vectors are identified as well as their stability properties investigated.

5.4.1 Uni-variate and Multi-variate Data Properties

Knowledge about the stationarity properties of the data underlying the investigation is crucial to the choice of the appropriate econometric methods. Therefore, unit root tests are conducted for the five variables under consideration to discriminate between trend stationary and difference stationary variables.

From the results obtained with the Augmented Dickey-Fuller tests shown in Table 5.1, it can be concluded that all variables are integrated of order one.[8]

The non-stationary time series are analyzed in the standard setup of equation (2.9) with $\nu_1 = 0$, $(Y_t = [(m-p)_t, y_t, i_t^l, i_t^s, \Delta p_t]')$ and $T = 64$ observations. The appropriate lag length of the corresponding *VAR* representation for the whole system seems to be two according to the Hannan-Quinn, the Akaike Information and the Final Prediction Error (FPE) criteria. Therefore, the general, unrestricted *VAR*(2) appears to be an appropriate starting point for further statistical analysis.

Estimating the unrestricted $VAR(2)$ gives the opportunity to perform a number of specification tests to check whether or not the residual properties can be regarded satisfactory for further statistical analysis (see Table 5.2). Keeping in mind that the data had to be seasonally adjusted, the test statistics focus on order five, when it comes to checking autocorrelation within the residuals. It turns out, that no major problems prevail apart from a rejection at the ten percent level of the null of no autocorrelation in the inflation equation. The same equation is an exception when the null of normality is tested, while neither the vector of all residuals nor any other single equation gives rise to concern with respect to the quality of the model.

[8] Calculations were performed with the software packages *PcFiml* (see Doornik and Hendry (1997)), *GAUSS for NT* and *JMulti*. The Data is plotted in Figure 5.6 in the appendix.

Table 5.1. Unit Root Tests for EMU Data

Sample: 1985(1) - 2000(4), $T = 64$

variable	setup[a]	ADF[b]	crit. values[c]		decision
$(m-p)_t$	μ_0,t,1-5	-1.69	-3.41	-3.13	I(1)
$\Delta(m-p)_t$	μ_0,3,4	-2.83*	-2.86	-2.57	
y_t	μ_0,t,1-5	-2.16	-3.41	-3.13	I(1)
Δy_t	μ_0,1,4	-2.79*	-2.86	-2.57	
Δp_t	μ_0,1-4	-1.05	-2.86	-2.57	I(1)
$\Delta^2 p_t$	μ_0,1-4	-5.74**	-2.86	-2.57	
i_t^l	μ_0,1	-1.58	-2.86	-2.57	I(1)
Δi_t^l	μ_0,1	-4.26**	-2.86	-2.57	
i_t^s	μ_0,1	-1.53	-2.86	-2.57	I(1)
Δi_t^s	μ_0,2	-4.66**	-2.86	-2.57	
$(i^s - i^l)_t$	μ_0,1	-2.33	-2.86	-2.57	I(1)
$\Delta(i^s - i^l)_t$	μ_0,1	-4.62**			
$(i^l - \pi)_t$	μ_0,1	-2.91*	-2.86	-2.57	I(0)
$(i^s - \pi)_t$	μ_0,1	-2.10	-2.86	-2.57	I(1)
$\Delta(i^s - \pi)_t$	μ_0,2	-4.70**	-2.86	-2.57	

[a] μ_0: constant, t: trend, the integers indicate the lags of differenced dependent variables included in the regression. AIC order selection criterium is applied.
Small letters indicate logarithms except for i_t^l and i_t^s. $\pi_t = 4\Delta p_t$ with p is the logarithm of the implicit deflator of the GDP.
[b] Augmented-Dickey-Fuller test statistic with * and ** indicating significance at the five and one percent level respectively.
[c] Five (column 5) and ten (col. 6) percent critical values according to MacKinnon (1991).

The overall outcome of the tests is generally satisfactory, in particular because the unwanted AR-effect is only found in one equation. Most of the other tests like those for normality, general mis-specification as well as the test for presence of autoregressive conditional heteroscedasticity do not indicate problems.

Economic structure enters when the sample of integrated variables exhibits cointegration features such as for example in equation (2.11). That means,

Table 5.2. Residual Analysis of the Unrestricted *VAR*(2)

$$Y_t = \nu_0 + A_1 Y_{t-1} + A_2 Y_{t-2} + \varepsilon_t$$

Test[a]	Residuals of single equations						Vector	
	d.f.	$(m-p)_t$	y_t	i_t^l	i_t^s	π_t	d.f.	Y_t
observ.	-	64	64	64	64	64	-	-
AR(1-5)	$\chi^2(5)$	1.60 [.18]	.96 [.45]	1.32 [.27]	1.34 [.26]	2.12* (.08)	$F(125,123)$	1.16 [.20]
NORM	$\chi^2(2)$	1.14 [.57]	1.21 [.32]	.38 [.82]	.50 [.73]	2.39* [.06]	$\chi^2(10)$	6.85 [.74]
ARCH(1-4)	F(4,45)	.16 [.96]	.56 [.69]	.18 [.95]	.38 [.82]	.69 [.60]	-	-
Mis-spec	F(20,22)	.70 [.80]	.77 [.73]	.69 [.80]	.55 [.92]	.39 [.98]	F(300,260)	0.61 [1.00]

[a] AR(1-5) tests significance autocorrelation of up to five lags, ARCH(1-4) tests for presence of autoregressive heteroscedasticity in the residuals up to order 4, NORM is the Jarque-Bera test for normality, Mis-spec tests for general mis-specification. The marginal levels of significance are given in brackets
*, ** indicate significance at the ten and five percent significance level respectively.

in order to find long-run relationships between the variables, it has to be checked whether or not they comply to the concept of money demand, for example. Thus, the matrix Π potentially contains information about long-run relationships of the variables under consideration.

From a theoretical perspective, three linearly independent cointegration relationships can be expected (see chapter 2). The uni-variate tests already pointed to stationarity of the real long-term interest rate, a result which will be taken into account when it comes to the identification of the cointegrating relations below.

Noting the dependence of the performance of cointegration tests on the number of observations available, not only one test at a certain lag length is performed but also at varying numbers of lagged endogenous variables, and subsystems are considered.[9] That is, starting with a maximum lag length of

[9] See Reimers (1991), Yap and Reinsel (1995), Saikkonen and Luukkonen (1997) and Hubrich et al. (2001) on the properties of cointegration tests with varying

three, which seems to be reasonable given 68 observations in the sample and five variables under investigation, the number of lags is reduced down to one and this is done so for five models.[10] These are the full model (five variables), a model which excludes inflation, one which excludes inflation and short-term interest rates, one without short-term interest rates, and the fifth comprises real money and real income only.

Table 5.3 on page 187 reports the cointegrating ranks chosen in a sequential test procedure by three different tests at the five and ten percent level of significance. The three tests are the well known Johansen (1995a) likelihood-ratio test (LR^i, trace statistic), another LR test with trend adjustment (LR^i_{ta}), and Lagrange multiplier type tests (LM^*, $LM^1_2(it)$, LR^{GLS}_{ta}), which have been suggested by Lütkepohl and Saikkonen (2000). The relative performance of all these tests has been analysed e.g. by Hubrich et al. (2001). In Table 5.3 it can be seen that the cointegrating rank of the full system could easily be put at either one or two, depending on the cointegration test and the level of significance.[11] While the $LM^1_2(it)$ and the LM^{GLS}_{ta} find cointegrating rank one only, the Johansen test (LR^i) as well as the LR^i_{ta} and the LM^* indicate the presence of two cointegrating relations, although partly at the ten percent level only.

In the light of the uni-variate analysis, the long-term interest rate as well as the inflation rate are of particular interest. If the real long-term interest rate was really stationary, then the exclusion of either of these variables would lead to a reduction of the evidence for cointegration. This seems indeed to be the case according to the second section in Table 5.3 where the same tests are applied to a system without inflation. As a tendency, those tests which previously found cointegrating rank one now find rank zero while those which

lag order and dimension. A general outcome is the remarkable deterioration of power when the lag length and/or dimension of the system becomes larger.

[10] We have 64 observations from 1985(1) to 2000(4) and four pre-sample data points.

[11] All test statistics and critical values for the full system can be found in Table 5.11 in the appendix.

indicated rank two for the full model, report rank one only. Again, the details depend on the significance level chosen. Interestingly, while excluding both inflation and short-term interest rate does not have such a strong impact as omitting inflation alone. When excluding only the short-term interest rate the results are almost identical to the full system outcomes. Thus, the short-term interest rate seems to be of minor importance for the cointegrating properties.

Finally, cointegration between the real money and the real income is looked at. For this combination there is also weak evidence for cointegration as indicated by the LR^i at one and three lags, and $LM_2^1(it)$, LR_{ta}^{GLS} at one lag and the ten percent level of significance. The Johansen test (LR^i) finds cointegration between these two variables most consistently for all but one lag orders. Here, lag order four is the preferred choice. Apart from the Johansen test, $LM_2^1(it)$ indicates cointegration at the five percent level of significance.

A second series of tests considers the relations between the interest rates and the inflation rate only. It should be recalled that the ADF test pointed to stationarity of the difference between the long-term interest rate and inflation. Therefore, the system cointegration test with these three variables should produce at least cointegrating rank one. As the first section of Table 5.4 indicates, cointegration hardly finds any support at all. Apart from the LR_{ta}^i and the LR_{ta}^{GLS} test statistics, the hypothesis that the rank is zero cannot be rejected. This result appears robust with respect to both variations in the level of significance as well as changing the lag order. The following sections, namely parts three and four of Table 5.4, provide some evidence for this to be a power problem though. In particular there seems to be support for one cointegration relation to exist between the short-term interest rate and the inflation rate. At the same time, a combination of long-term interest and inflation rate also is found stationary at the five percent level by the LR^*, LR_{ta}^{GLS} and at the preferable lag order. These two results are quite puzzling, however, because if both these combinations were really stationary, there would have to exist

Table 5.3. Cointegration Test: Ranks Selected by Various Tests (1)

Sample: 1985-2000 $\Delta Y_t = \nu_0 + \alpha\beta' Y_{t-1} + \Sigma_{j=1}^{p-1} \Gamma_j \Delta Y_{t-j} + \varepsilon_t$

p	LR^i	LR^i_{ta}	LM^*	$LM_2^1(it)$	LR^{GLS}_{ta}
$Y_t' = ((m-p)_t, y_t, i_t^l, i_t^s, \pi_t)$, full model					
1	2(3)	2	2	2	2
2	**1(2)**	**0(2)**	**2**	**1**	**1**
3	1	0(2)	2	2	0
$Y_t' = ((m-p)_t, y_t, i_t^l, i_t^s)$, π_t excluded					
1	2	1	1	1	1
2	**1**	**0**	**1**	**0(1)**	**0**
3	1	0	1	1(2)	0(1)
$Y_t' = ((m-p)_t, y_t, i_t^l)$, π_t and i_t^s excluded					
1	1	1	1	1	0(1)
2	**0**	**0**	**1**	**0**	**0**
3	0(1)	0	1	0	0
$Y_t' = ((m-p)_t, y_t, i_t^l, \pi_t)$, i_t^s excluded					
1	1	1	1(2)	1	1
2	**1(2)**	**1(2)**	**2**	**1**	**1**
3	1	0	1(2)	0	1
$Y_t' = ((m-p)_t, y_t)$, i_t^s, i_t^l and π_t excluded					
1	1	0	0	0(1)	0(1)
2	0	0	0	0	0
3	1	0	0	0	1
4	**1**	**0**	**0**	**1**	**0**

The columns 2-6 report the ranks selected at the 5 % level of significance and at the 10% level in parentheses if there is a difference. A sequential test procedure is applied.
LR^i_{ta} and LM^* refer to Saikkonen and Lütkepohl (2000a), p. 381, eq. (3.12) and eq. (3.10) respectively. Lütkepohl and Saikkonen (2000) at p.186 , eq. (4.10) present $LM_2^1(it)$ with the two-step procedure for estimating μ_0 and μ_1, it indicates iterative variant. LR^{GLS}_{ta} can be found in Saikkonen and Lütkepohl (2000c), p. 442, eq. (4.7).

Explanations continued in Table 5.4.

Table 5.4. Cointegration Test: Ranks Selected by Various Tests (2)

Sample: 1985-2000

$\Delta Y_t = \nu_0 + \alpha\beta' Y_{t-1} + \Sigma_{j=1}^{p-1} \Gamma_j \Delta Y_{t-j} + \varepsilon_t$

p	LR^*	LR^i_{ta}	$LM^1_2(it)$	LR^{GLS}_{ta}
$Y_t' = (i_t^l, i_t^s, \pi_t)$, $\mu_1 = 0$, Fisher and spread				
1	0	0(1)	2	1
2	**0**	**0**	**0**	**0(1)**
3	0	0	0	0
$Y_t' = (i_t^l, i_t^s)$, $\mu_1 = 0$, spread				
1	0	0	0	0
2	**0**	**0**	**0**	**0**
3	0	0	0	0
$Y_t' = (i_t^l, \pi_t)$, $\mu_1 = 0$, Fisher (1)				
1	0	0	1	1
2	**1**	**0**	**0**	**1**
3	0	0	0	0(1)
$Y_t' = (i_t^s, \pi_t)$, $\mu_1 = 0$, Fisher (2)				
1	0(1)	1	2	1
2	**0(1)**	**0**	**1**	**0**
3	0(1)	1	1	0

The columns report the ranks selected at the 5 percent level of significance and at the 10 percent level in parentheses if there is a difference. A sequential test procedure is applied. LR^i and LR^* refer to Johansen (1991). Critical values are available e.g. in Johansen (1995b) Tables 15.3. (for LR^i) and 15.2. (for LR^*). Only LR^* takes into account the restriction $\mu_1 = 0$ (if imposed).
Bold face marks the results of the preferable lag order (AIC criterium), maximum lag order considered: five.

See also explanations in Table 5.3.

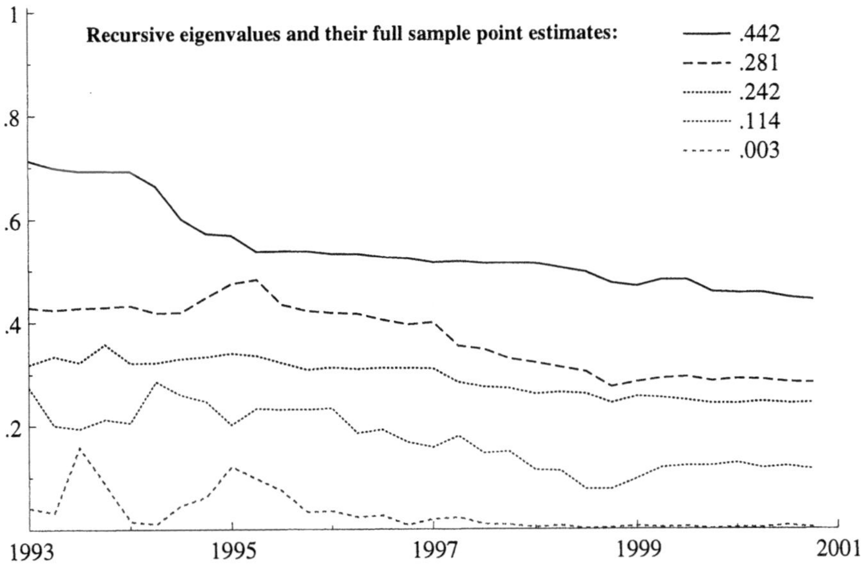

Largest to smallest eigenvalues, recursively estimated together with their point estimates for the sample 1985-2000. The underlying model is the Unrestricted EMU-11 *VECM*(1) model. These estimates are the basis for the Johansen test (see Table 5.11 on page 213 in the appendix).

Figure 5.1. Recursively Estimated Eigenvalues

a linear combination of short and long-term interest rates which is likewise stationary as long as the inflation rate itself is integrated of order one.

The results are mixed, to say the least. But judging on the aggregate of evidence, imposing the restriction of cointegrating rank two can certainly be justified. Figure 5.1 sheds some light on the difficulties when taking this decision. It plots the recursively estimated eigenvalues of the unrestricted *VECM*(1). The largest eigenvalue is estimated as .442 and certainly far enough away from zero to be associated with cointegrating rank one. In contrast, the second and third largest eigenvalues (estimated .281 and .242 respectively) can hardly be distinguished from each other. Some arbitrariness in choosing any rank between one and three therefore appears unavoidable.

To sum up the results obtained so far, arguments can be put forward to continue the analysis under the assumptions that the system is cointegrated of order two, and that long-term interest rate as well as the inflation rate do play an important part in being able to impose that restriction.

5.4.2 Identification of Cointegration Vectors

The next step of the analysis is the identification of the cointegrating vectors. As in the previous chapter, this procedure starts with exactly identified cointegration relations. Then, further restrictions are added depending on the $t-$ratios of the estimated coefficients. Parameters were dropped, when their standard deviation clearly exceeded half the absolute value of the point estimate. When a coefficient is dropped, its value is set to zero. In this case as well as in the cases where parameters serve scaling purposes, or are set to equal certain values, no standard deviation is reported. Each of these restrictions will be subject to a likelihood ratio test which checks whether or not the restrictions are too strong compared to the unrestricted model. The level of significance to be chosen for that procedure is five percent.[12]

It will turn out that two competing final specifications of the long-run relations can be derived. Therefore, both these outcomes will be scrutinized further in parallel and their implications discussed.

To begin with, Table 5.5 reports the results for the first identification scheme. In each step, the restriction added is indicated by putting the respective coefficient(s) in bold face. It is easy to see that at the third step already the marginal level of significance of the over identification test statistic is found to be very close to the five percent margin. Thus, the exclusion of the short-term interest rate from the second cointegrating relation is just accepted. Step four attempts to establish the uni-variate unit root test result of a stationary real long-term interest rate which fails however. This is indicated by the corresponding test statistic which is significant at the one percent level. Therefore, the hypothesis of the Fisher relation to hold with the coefficients $(1\ -1)$ has to be rejected. From step 5 onward, the hypotheses

[12] The testing procedure is that of Johansen (1995b), section 7.2.

to be tested also include restrictions on the adjustment coefficients, α. The zeros of the final step (step 7) indicate that both the interest rates are weakly exogenous with respect to both the cointegrating relationships. A similar hypothesis (weak exogeneity of real money) referring to the monetary aggregate is clearly rejected (see step 8 in Table 5.5).

Accepting the hypothesis in the 7th step, the following long-run dynamics are obtained (standard errors in parenthesis):

$$\alpha\beta' Y_t = \begin{pmatrix} \alpha_1 & \alpha_2 \end{pmatrix} \begin{pmatrix} \beta_1 \\ \beta_2 \end{pmatrix} Y_t$$

$$= \begin{pmatrix} \underset{(.02)}{-.05} & 0 \\ \underset{(.02)}{.11} & \underset{(.04)}{-.17} \\ 0 & 0 \\ 0 & 0 \\ 0 & \underset{(.07)}{.28} \end{pmatrix} \begin{pmatrix} 1 & \underset{(.05)}{-1.57} & \underset{(.38)}{2.22} & \underset{(.32)}{-1.87} & 0 \\ 0 & 0 & 1 & 0 & \underset{(.22)}{-1.55} \end{pmatrix} \begin{pmatrix} (m-p) \\ y \\ i^l \\ i^s \\ \pi \end{pmatrix}_t , \tag{5.1}$$

where the relation of main interest displays all features of a money demand as discussed in the introduction

$$(m-p)_t = 1.57 y_t - 2.22 i^l_t + 1.87 i^s_t + ec_{m,t}.$$

The long-term interest rate can be interpreted as an opportunity cost measure because an increase will lead to a reduction in the demand for real balances while the short-term interest rate is associated with real money in the opposite way. The latter fact is compatible with the view that interest rates on assets within the monetary aggregate provide an incentive to supply short-term credits and hence increase the demand for the broad monetary aggregate. The second relationship,

$$i^l_t = 1.55 \pi_t + ec_{F,t}$$

is of the Fisher type, where the coefficient on the inflation rate indicates that a one percent increase in the (expected) inflation rate is met by a 1.55 percentage increase in the nominal interest rate. Some authors attribute such a behaviour to tax effects because an increase in the nominal interest rate means higher nominal income which is subject to taxation. Therefore, some of the income tax is passed on to the nominal market price.[13]

It may be worthwhile to comment on the estimated adjustment coefficients as well. The error correction terms, $ec_{m,t}$ and $ec_{F,t}$ indicate deviations from the respective equilibrium path which would eventually have to lead to an adjustment of the variables involved if the labels money demand and Fisher type relation are attached correctly. As can be seen from (5.1) this indeed seems to be the case. Moreover, although being rather small, the coefficient on the $ec_{m,t}$ term in the equation for changes in real money is significantly different from zero, and has the correct sign. Thus, positive deviations of the observed real money from the long-run demand curve in one period will be followed by a slowdown in real money growth in the following period. Eventually, the money stock will approach its long-run equilibrium level again. In addition to the money stock, real income also adjusts. In that case, excess real money measured by large values of $ec_{m,t}$ foreshadow a rise in the real income and thereby move the demand curve towards the disequilibrium point. This observation is compatible with a real balance effect.

As indicated above, the identification of the money demand curve hinges on the crucial decision of removing the short-term interest rate from the second cointegrating vector. It could likewise be argued that in the third step, one of the interest rates should be deleted from the first relationship instead. This is particularly reasonable since the respective t-ratios are .23 (for i^l in the first relation, step 2) and 6.8 (for i^s in the second relation, step 2). Doing so leads to a different identification which is reported in Table 5.6, steps 3a to 6a. It turns out that according to the likelihood ratio statistics, both interest rates

[13] See for example Jaschke, Stehle and Wernicke (2000) on the German case.

Table 5.5. EMU: Identifying Cointegration Relationships

$$\Delta Y_t = \nu_0 + \alpha\beta' Y_{t-1} + \Gamma_1 \Delta Y_{t-1} + \varepsilon_t$$
$$Y_t = ((m-p)_t \; y_t \; i_t^l \; i_t^s \; \pi_t)'$$

step	*vector*	$(m-p)_t$	y_t	i_t^l	i_t^s	π_t	*d.f.*	χ^2
1	β_1	1	−1.49	.01	.05	0		
			(.05)	(.30)	(.26)			
	β_2	−.13	0	1	−7.97	14.15		
		(.18)			(1.23)	(2.16)		
2	β_1	1	−1.52	.07	−.12	0	1	.12
			(.05)	(.31)	(.24)			[.73]
	β_2	**0**	0	1	−9.77	19.57		
					(1.43)	(2.87)		
3	β_1	1	−1.54	1.79	−1.43	0	2	5.52
			(.04)	(.32)	(.27)			[.06]
	β_2	0	0	1	**0**	−1.58		
						(.19)		
4	β_1	1	−1.53	2.59	−1.35	0	3	10.99**
			(.04)	(.30)	(.23)			[.01]
	β_2	0	0	1	0	**-1**		
5	β_1	1	−1.55	1.81	−1.48	0	3	5.65
			(.04)	(.33)	(.28)			[.13]
	β_2	0	0	1	0	−1.56		
						(.22)		
	α_1'	−.06	.11	.009	−.06	−.08		
		(.02)	(.03)	(.03)	(.05)	(.06)		
	α_2'	**0**	−.15	−.06	.09	.38		
			(.04)	(.06)	(.08)	(.09)		
6	β_1	1	−1.58	2.25	−1.88	0	6	9.49
			(.05)	(.38)	(.32)			[.15]
	β_2	0	0	1	0	−1.53		
						(.19)		
	α_1'	−.05	.11	**0**	**0**	**0**		
		(.02)	(.02)					
	α_2'	0	−.18	−.06	.01	.28		
			(.04)	(.04)	(.06)	(.07)		

Columns 3-7: Parameter estimates and their corresponding standard errors (in parenthesis). Column 8: Degrees of freedom of the χ^2 statistic. Column 9: χ^2 statistic and the corresponding marginal level of significance [in brackets].

Where no number in parenthesis is given the corresponding coefficient value had been imposed.

Table continued on page 194.

Table 5.5. EMU: Identifying Cointegration Relationships (cont.)

$$\Delta Y_t = \nu_0 + \alpha\beta' Y_{t-1} + \Gamma_1 \Delta Y_{t-1} + \varepsilon_t$$
$$Y_t = ((m-p)_t \; y_t \; i^l_t \; i^s_t \; \pi_t)'$$

step	*vector*	$(m-p)_t$	y_t	i^l_t	i^s_t	π_t	*d.f.*	χ^2
7	β_1	1	−1.57 (.05)	2.22 (.38)	−1.87 (.32)	0	8	12.19 [.14]
	β_2	0	0	1	0	−1.55 (.20)		
	α_1'	−.05 (.02)	.11 (.02)	0	0	0		
	α_2'	0	−.17 (.04)	**0**	**0**	.28 (.07)		
8	β_1	1	−1.67 (.07)	**2.71** (.56)	**-2.71** (.47)	0	9	19.01* [.03]
	β_2	0	0	1	0	−1.62 (.24)		
	α_1'	0	.08 (.01)	0	0	0		
	α_2'	0	−.001 (.0004)	0	0	.23 (.06)		

Columns 3-7: Parameter estimates and their corresponding standard errors (in parenthesis). Column 8: Degrees of freedom of the χ^2 statistic. Column 9: χ^2 statistic and the corresponding marginal level of significance [in brackets].
Where no number in parenthesis is given the corresponding coefficient value had been imposed.

and inflation can be removed from one of the cointegration relations while the second relationship will be made of the short-term interest rate and inflation alone. It should also be noted however, that the respective coefficient on the inflation rate in the second relationship exceeds unity by one. This might be the reason for not finding a stationary real short-term interest rate in the univariate analysis. Again, hypotheses on the adjustment coefficients can also be tested which produces the following long-run structure (standard errors in parentheses):

Table 5.6. EMU: An Alternative Identification Sequence

$$\Delta Y_t = \nu_0 + \alpha\beta' Y_{t-1} + \Gamma_1 \Delta Y_{t-1} + \varepsilon_t$$
$$Y_t = ((m-p)_t \; y_t \; i_t^l \; i_t^s \; \pi_t)'$$

step	*vector*	$(m-p)_t$	y_t	i_t^l	i_t^s	π_t	*d.f.*	χ^2
3*a*	β_1	1	−1.52	**0**	−.07	0	2	.13
			(.05)		(.16)			[.94]
	β_2	0	0	−.14	1	−1.95		
				(.14)		(.20)		
4*a*	β_1	1	−1.52	0	−.08	0	3	.44
			(.04)		(.15)			[.93]
	β_2	0	0	**0**	1	−2.15		
						(.17)		
5*a*	β_1	1	−1.51	0	**0**	0	4	.58
			(.03)					[.97]
	β_2	0	0	0	1	−2.12		
						(.15)		
6*a*	β_1	1	−1.51	0	0	0	9	3.86
			(.02)					[.92]
	β_2	0	0	0	1	−2.07		
						(.16)		
	α_1'	−.11	.09	**0**	−.11	**0**		
		(.02)	(.03)		(.04)			
	α_2'	**0**	−.13	**0**	**0**	.29		
			(.04)			(.07)		

Columns 3-7: Parameter estimates and their corresponding standard errors (in parenthesis). Column 8: Degrees of freedom of the χ^2 statistic. Column 9: χ^2 statistic and the corresponding marginal level of significance [in brackets].
Where no number in parenthesis is given the corresponding coefficient value had been imposed.

$$\alpha\beta' Y_t = \begin{pmatrix} -.11 & 0 \\ (.02) & \\ .09 & -.13 \\ (.03) & (.04) \\ 0 & 0 \\ -.11 & 0 \\ (.04) & \\ 0 & .29 \\ & (.07) \end{pmatrix} \begin{pmatrix} 1 & -1.51 & 0 & 0 & 0 \\ & (.02) & & & \\ 0 & 0 & 0 & 1 & -2.07 \\ & & & & (.16) \end{pmatrix} \begin{pmatrix} m-p \\ y \\ i^l \\ i^s \\ \pi \end{pmatrix}_t . \tag{5.2}$$

In this instance, the long-term interest rate does not enter either of the long-run relationships and it does not seem to be affected by them. This implies that efficient estimation of the long-run relationships could have been made without modelling Δi_t^l at all.

According to (5.2), the short-term interest rate is not longer weakly exogenous with respect to money, and income and the equilibrium in the money market now only depends on the level of income

$$(m - p)_t = 1.51 y_t + ec_{v,t}.$$

If the coefficient on income was exactly one, it could be argued that the income velocity of money, defined as $(m-p)_t - y_t$ was stationary in the long run. With the coefficient on income being larger than unity, it can be reasoned that this measure tends to decline over time. Without the interest rates entering this long-run relationship, a money demand curve cannot be defined in the interest - real money stock space. Therefore, no behavioural long-run functional can be derived where interest or inflation rates are important. A long-run relationship of that kind is implied by the quantity theory of money and by the monetarist view.

The $ec_{v,t}$ term also feeds back into the short-term interest rate equation indicating that, at least in the short-run, there is potential for a link between interest rates and real money holdings. The negative coefficient is well-matching with the liquidity effect according to which excess money gives rise to a decline in the nominal interest rate. Second, the error correction term also enters the equation for real income. In particular, real money balances in excess of the long-run equilibrium spur income growth in the following period. This is what the real balance effect predicts, for example. Moreover, this finding is equivalent to saying that real income is not weakly exogenous with respect to the long-run demand for money function. For the standard version of the quantity theory of money that would imply imperfect control over the money stock by the central banks, because it is usually assumed that all determinants of money demand are given by exogenous relationships like supply and demand on the real goods markets, technology and so on. If this assumption would really hold, then the central bank could fix money supply, and the level of the nominal interest rate would result endogenously.

With income being at least partly determined by deviations from the long-run money demand equilibrium, and in turn a determinant of long-run money demand itself, it cannot be considered being exogenous for the long-run relationship. In effect, monetary targeting becomes much more complicated, and thus a less attractive policy option. It is worth mentioning that the latter reasoning also holds with respect to short-term interest rates which are also affected by money demand disequilibria. In addition, the argument also applies to the first identification result in (5.1) due to the feedback relation between money and income.

As before with the Fisher type relations for the long-term interest rate, a similar relationship can be written for the short-term interest rate

$$i_t^s = 2.07\pi_t + ec_{f,t}.$$

The interpretation is basically the same as for the first identification scheme. Both these disequilibrium measures, $ec_{F,t}$, $ec_{f,t}$ affect real income growth negatively which is consistent with the assumption that high levels of real interest will lower economic activity.

In the following, the two competing results for the identified cointegration relationships will be distinguished by the suffix (a) signifying the outcome given in (5.2). In both cases the cointegration relationships themselves are referred to as money demand and Fisher type relation for the first and second cointegrating vectors respectively.

5.4.3 Properties of the Long-run Dynamics in the System

Having identified not only two but four cointegrating relationships, certainly raises the question of how to evaluate the findings correctly. Since there is no clear cut evidence yet for preferring one result over the other, a number of comparative analyses will follow to asses the findings.

Before doing so a number of relevant criteria will be fixed: the stability of the estimated long-run relationships over the estimation period, the forecasting power, and the residual properties of the corresponding reduced form estimates. The starting point however, will be a descriptive comparison of the implicit disequilibrium measures. Figure 5.2 provides the necessary information. Both pairs of cointegration relations show an amazing degree of co-movement which could not be expected from the parameter estimates alone. With respect to the money demand relations this can certainly be attributed to the dominance of the common trend between income and money stock. It is interesting to note that these two relations differ from each other by the missing interest rates in the money demand (a) relation only. Thus, if the interest rates also had a common stochastic trend which could not be identified due to power problems of the statistical tests, this could explain the similarity of the two curves in the upper panel of Figure 5.2.

This argument also finds support by the second panel where the two Fisher type relations are plotted. Although they combine the inflation rate with two different interest rates, the graphs of the error correction terms are strikingly similar. Unfortunately, relying on the identification method applied above, and assuming cointegrating rank three leads to implausible results in that a cointegration relation between the short-term interest rate and real income can be identified.[14] That however, is a result of the particular sample period during which the interest rates and the inflation rate feature some exceptional trending behaviour matching the usual deterministic trend in the real income variable. For detecting the common stochastic trends it does not seem infor-

[14] Including a trend in the cointegrating space hardly provides evidence for cointegrating rank two.

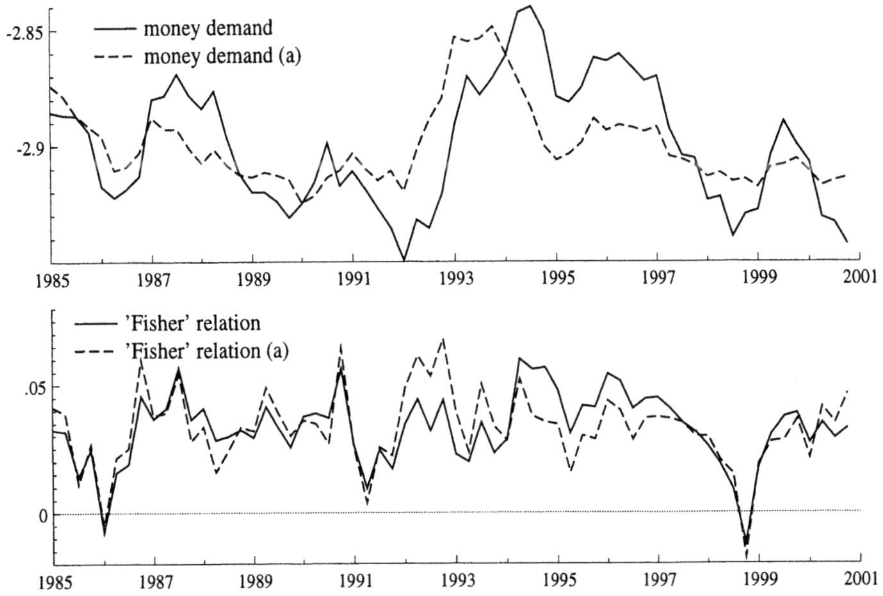

Error correction terms of the identified long-run relationships according to Table 5.5, steps 7 and Table 5.6, step 6a.

Figure 5.2. Comparison of Long-run Relationships in the EMU System

mative to replace them with their deterministic counterparts even though that would partly improve the model fit.[15]

From the plots of the error correction terms no further insight in the differences between the alternative cointegration relations is gained. Turning to the other criteria, joint recursive estimation of the long-run parameters (β) and the adjustment coefficients (α), provides some information about how stable the system has been during the sample period with respect to the long-run dynamics. Starting with the sample definition 1985(1) - 1993(1) the model is estimated with all restrictions on α and β according to the Tables 5.5 and 5.6, steps 7 and 6a respectively in place, then the observations for 1993(2) are

[15] See e.g. Trecroci and Vega (2000) and Gerlach and Svensson (2001) on a model for the same sample period with an exponential trend describing the decline in the (expected) inflation rate within the Euro area.

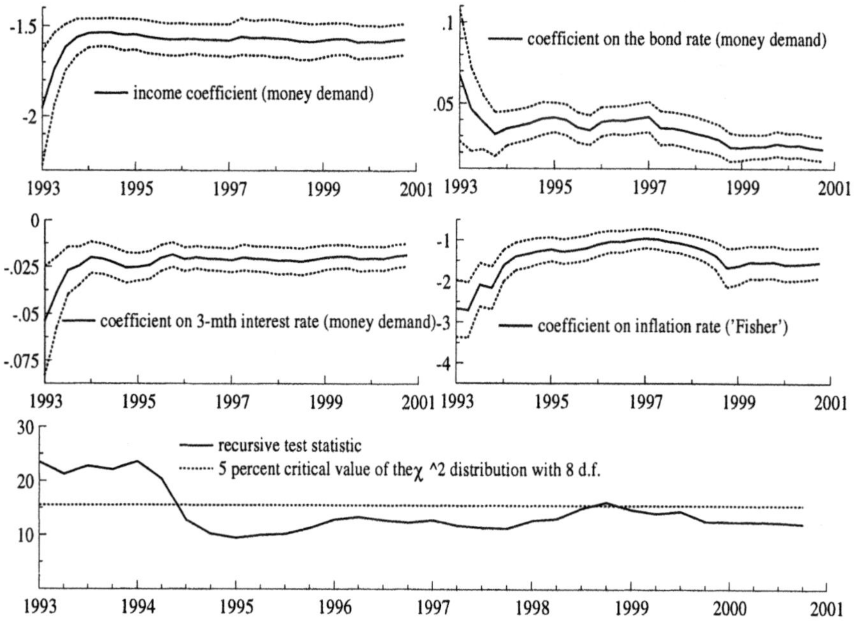

Recursively estimated coefficients together with two standard error bands on income, long and short-term interest rates and inflation for the identification scheme according to Table 5.5, step 7. Recursive test statistic for the validity of the identification restrictions imposed.

Figure 5.3. Stability of the Long-run Relationships over Time

added, the model is estimated again and so on until all observations are used. At each point, the estimates for the coefficients on β and the likelihood ratio test statistic for the over identifying restrictions are pinned down which eventually produces Figures 5.3 and 5.4. Stability is found if the freely estimated parameters do not vary significantly throughout the sample period and if the test statistic stays consistently below the critical value.

On both these accounts the model with the money demand (a) seems to do slightly better. The test statistic for the over identification restrictions is far from being significant at the five percent level of significance for most of the time in that case. For the first model however, the restrictions seem to suit

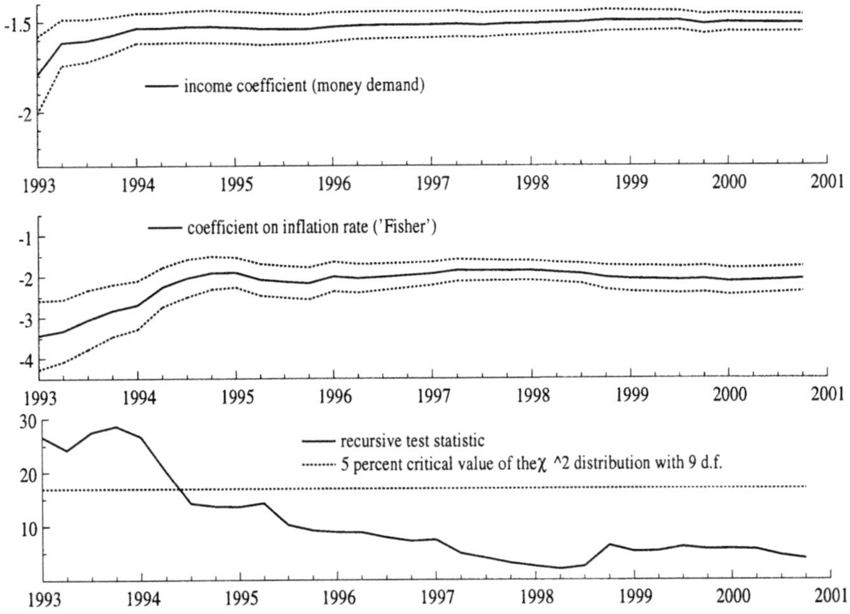

Recursively estimated coefficients together with two standard error bands on income and inflation for the identification scheme according to Table 5.6, step 6a. Recursive test statistic for the validity of the identification restrictions imposed.

Figure 5.4. Stability of the Long-run Relationships (a) over Time

the data less well over time as can be seen from the significant test statistic for the time just before the introduction of the new currency.

5.4.4 A General Comparison of Two Alternative Models

Residual Properties

The next evaluation will be based on the residual properties of the reduced form estimation results for both long-run dynamics. Two outcomes are generated. One of them considers the *VECM*(1) models while the other stems from a restricted reduced form model where additional restrictions are generated by the sequential elimination of regressors (SER) procedure already applied to the French data. Exactly the same method is used and the final specifications as well as the corresponding model evaluation statistics are tabulated. When adding restrictions to the short-run parameters other than the α coefficients, then the starting point is a *VECM*(2) model with the error correction terms of the previously described analysis as regressors. The idea for that is to capture some of the initially present autocorrelation in the error terms discussed before. Table 5.12 reports the residual properties of the reduced form *VECM*(1) models where the differences between the upper and lower part of the table arise from the different structure of $\alpha\beta'$ depending on the identification outcome referred to.

It is easy to check that except for the income growth and the long-term interest rate equations, the model referring to the money demand (a) does fit the data better than its rival. It also has an advantage because it indicates fewer remaining autocorrelations in the residuals. Both these features carry over to the comparison of the restricted reduced form estimation results (see Table 5.9).[16] Inspecting these two tables, it can be seen that the money demand model (a) is at least as good as its counterpart. It appears superior since less equations are subject to autocorrelation effects in the residuals. There is also less indication of non-normality within the set of residuals. Therefore, the comparison of the residual properties suggests to prefer the money demand model (a) over its rival.

Forecasting Power Comparison

Returning yet again to the comparison of the model performances, the standard errors of the residuals indicate a superior specification of the model due to the second identification outcome. This holds especially with respect to inflation and the monetary aggregate. These two variables certainly are the most interesting from the monetary policy maker's point of view. But it is not the modelling alone; the ability to base decisions about future monetary policy on the empirical investigation is what matters most.

[16] Tables 5.7 and 5.8 report the corresponding coefficient estimates.

Table 5.7. Restricted Reduced Form of the Money Demand Model

independent variable	lag	Coefficient estimates[a] of equations for $\Delta(m-p)_t$	Δy_t	Δi_t^l	Δi_t^s	$\Delta \pi_t$
$\Delta(m-p)_t$	1	.53	.32	.17		
		(.08)	(.08)	(.11)		
Δy_t	1		.31			
			(.10)			
	2		.25	.26	.46	.68
			(.09)	(.10)	(.16)	(.18)
Δi_t^l	1			.46	.35	−.47
				(.12)	(.15)	(.18)
Δi_t^s	1		.13	−.22		
			(.07)	(.09)		
	2		.09			
			(.06)			
$\Delta \pi_t$	1	−.16				−.25
		(.05)				(.11)
	2		−.09			
			(.05)			
intercept		−.13	.41	−.00	−.00	−.01
		(*n.a.*)	(*n.a.*)	(*n.a.*)	(*n.a.*)	(*n.a.*)
$ec_{m,t}$	1	−.04	.14			
		(.01)	(.01)			
$ec_{F,t}$	1		−.23			.26
			(.03)			(.06)

[a]Standard errors in parentheses.

To shed some light on this question, a limited forecast comparison is made. Taking the restricted reduced form models (RRFM), all coefficients including the β are estimated for the period 1985(1) to 1998(4). Then, these estimates are fixed and the corresponding model is solved for the endogenous variables.[17] That means, the values of the dependent variables in the first quarter of 1999 are calculated on the basis of past observations. In the next step, these past observations as well as the calculated numbers enter the same procedure for obtaining hypothetical values of 1999, second quarter, and so on. Thus, the model dynamically produces out-of-sample forecasts for the period after the introduction of the Euro. The only full sample information that enter are the

[17] The calculations were performed with *EView2.0*.

Table 5.8. Restricted Reduced Form of the Money Demand (a) Model

a) Estimation results

independent variable	lag	Equation (dependent variable) $\Delta(m-p)_t$	Δy_t	Δi_t^l	Δi_t^s	$\Delta \pi_t$
$\Delta(m-p)_t$	1	.55	.35	.17		
		(.08)	(.09)	(.10)		
Δy_t	1		.41			
			(.09)			
	2		.31	.27	.34	.74
			(.10)	(.12)	(.17)	(.17)
Δi_t^l	1			.45	.31	−.42
				(.12)	(.15)	(.09)
	2		.15			
			(.08)			
Δi_t^s	1	−.13		−.19		
		(.07)		(.09)		
$\Delta \pi_t$	1	−.15				
		(.04)				
	2		−.10			.19
			(.05)			(.09)
intercept		−.26	.31	−.00	−.23	−.01
		(*n.a.*)	(*n.a.*)	(*n.a.*)	(*n.a.*)	(*n.a.*)
$ec_{v,t}$	1	−.11	.12		−.09	
		(.02)	(.02)		(.04)	
$ec_{f,t}$	1		−.19			.34
			(.03)			(.05)

[a]Standard errors in parentheses.

over-identification restriction of the long-run specification as well as the zero restrictions imposed on the short-run coefficients (the Γ_i matrices in equation (2.9)).

Another interesting feature of this strategy is, that it imitates the situation of the ECB at the beginning of the Euro period in that it uses information from the past to foresee developments for the time after the rise of the Euro.

The root mean squared forecast error (RMSE) helps to assess the forecasting capabilities in two ways. The first evaluates the model demand (a) specification related to (5.2) in terms of the forecast performance of both alternatives. Let $\tilde{y}_{t+h,i}$ denote the forecast of the variable y_{t+h}, $h \geq 1$ periods

Table 5.9. Residual Properties of the Competing Money Demand Models

1) Demand for Money Model (see Table 5.7)

Test	Dependent variable (equation) $\Delta(m-p)_t$	Δy_t	Δi^l_t	Δi^{cm}_t	$\Delta \pi_t$
correlation and	**.339**	·	·	·	·
	.11	**.251**	·	·	·
standard	.09	.16	**.382**	·	·
	.28	.24	.36	**.544**	·
deviation[a]	-.43	.02	-.03	-.003	**.642**
AR(1-5)[b]	2.14*	1.77	1.92	3.82**	2.31*
	[.08]	[.14]	[.11]	[.01]	[.06]
Vector AR(1-5)[b]	.89; 125, 152 [.76]				
Nonnormality[c]	8.97**	5.20*	.51	.53	3.17
	[.01]	[.07]	[.78]	[.77]	[.21]
Vector Nonnormality[c]	12.43; 10 [.26]				
ARCH (4)[d]	1.79	.36	.86	.26	.01
	[.33]	[.84]	[.50]	[.90]	[.99]

2) Money Demand (a) Model (see Table 5.8)

Test	Dependent variable (equation) $\Delta(m-p)_t$	Δy_t	Δi^l_t	Δi^{cm}_t	$\Delta \pi_t$
correlation and	**.308**	·	·	·	·
	.11	**.260**	·	·	·
standard	.15	.08	**.382**	·	·
	.17	.22	.38	**.525**	·
deviation[a]	-.36	.04	-.03	.10	**.596**
AR(1-5)[b]	1.72	1.84	1.77	3.05**	2.19*
	[.15]	[.12]	[.10]	[.02]	[.07]
Vector AR(1-5)[b]	.73; 125, 152 [.96]				
Nonnormality[c]	2.48	13.77**	.55	1.12	3.25
	[.29]	[.00]	[.76]	[.57]	[.20]
Vector Nonnormality[c]	18.72; 10 [.04]				
ARCH (4)[d]	1.74	1.02	5.06	.50	.78
	[.78]	[.91]	[.28]	[.97]	[.94]

[a] Bold face numbers report 100 times the standard deviations, the off-diagonal entries refer to the correlations between the residuals of the corresponding equations (vertical = horizontal ordering).
*, ** significance at the 10 and 5 percent level respectively.
[b] Test for autoregressive residuals up to order 5. Single equation tests: 5 degrees of freedom (d.f.); χ^2 distribution.
[c] Test for (vector) normality of the residuals based on the estimated first two moments. See Lütkepohl (1993a), pp 155 ff. D.f. equal to number of estimated moments considered (vector: 5 times 2, two else); test statistic follows χ^2 distribution.
[d] Single (and vector) equation test for autoregressive heteroscedasticity of the residuals up to order 4 (2) with 4 (450) d.f.; χ^2 distribution.

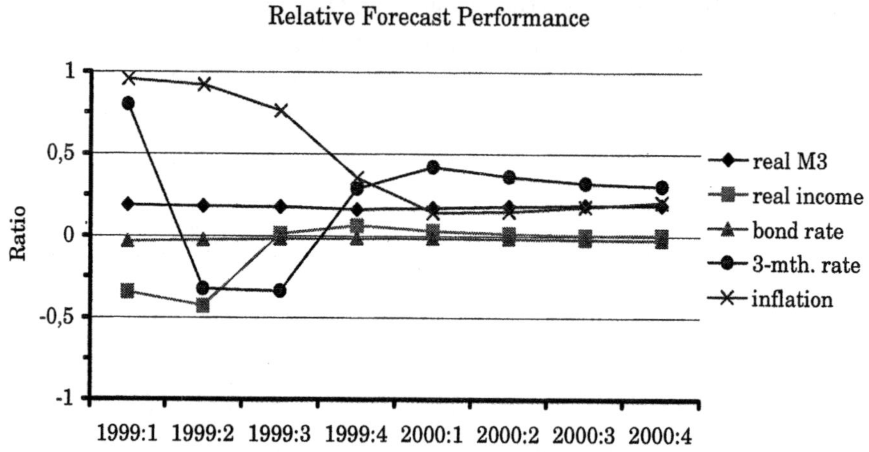

The vertical axis measure the relative *superiority* of the restricted reduced form model (RRFM) for the money demand (a) (step 6a in Table 5.6 on page 195) over the RRFM corresponding to the initial identification (step 7 in Table 5.5 on page 194).
The ratio is defined as the distance between the root mean squared forecast errors (RMSE) of the two RRFM, divided by the sum of both RMSE. All values above the zero line indicate better forecast performance of the RRFM of the long-run money demand (a) on average between 1991, first quarter and the quarter given on the horizontal axis.

Figure 5.5. Comparison of Forecast Capabilities

ahead of the current period, t. The i indicates the model on which this forecast is based with $i = 1$ signifying the first model, and $i = 2$ the second. Furthermore, define the squared forecast error,

$$\zeta_{h,i} = \left(y_{t+h} - \tilde{y}_{t+h,i}\right)^2$$

and the root mean squared error

$$\bar{\zeta}_{h,i} = \sqrt{\frac{1}{h}\sum_{m=1}^{h} \zeta_{m,i}}$$

to obtain the relative forecast performance measure

$$\varrho_h = \frac{\bar{\zeta}_{h,1} - \bar{\zeta}_{h,2}}{\bar{\zeta}_{h,1} + \bar{\zeta}_{h,2}} \; .$$

The parameter ϱ quantifies the extent to which the forecast based on the long-run money demand (a) specification outperforms the forecast by the initial model. Positive values indicate superiority and negative inferiority. The absolute value measures the weight of the difference between the forecast errors in the sum of them. Therefore, values close to one correspond to very large forecast errors obtained by the initial model relative to the error made by the demand for money (a) model.

The outcome of the exercise is plotted in Figure 5.5. It reveals, that the alternative identification is indeed preferable if the medium and longer horizon is concerned. In the short-run, however, the picture is more diverse which can be seen from the results for the real income and the short-term interest rate in early 1999. Apart from that, no gains can be made when relying on the model referring to the initial identification of the long-run structure. In particular, real money and inflation can be predicted much better, both over the medium and longer horizon. Because the cointegration relations determine long-run behaviour of the variables, the last finding certainly underlines the advantages of the demand for money (a) specification.

Table 5.10. RMSE of Dynamic Out-Of-Sample Forecasts

endogenous variable	RMSE × 100 money demand	money demand (a)	random walk
$(m-p)_t$	1.678	**1.146**	2.400
y_t	.877	**.866**	1.211
i_t^l	**1.629**	1.712	1.770
i_t^s	1.771	**.947**	1.791
π_t	.724	**.477**	2.075

The entries are the square root of the mean of the squared differences between the observed value and the multi-step out-of-sample forecasts (RMSE) for the period 1999(1)-2000(4). The minimum of each line is printed in bold face.

A second illustration of the average forecasting performance is provided over the whole two years horizon. The RMSE serves again as a rough and easy measure. As usual, a naive forecast based on the random walk hypothesis is also computed.[18] A brief look at Table 5.10 will close the comparison. It reveals that for none of the variables the random walk forecast is superior to the structured statistical models. Second, in line with most of the other criteria pointing to the superiority of the alternative long-run specification, this time it again has the edge. In four out of five variables, the RMSE is absolutely smaller when considering this variant.

Summarizing the evaluation section, the identified cointegration relationships as of (5.1) as well as of (5.2) can be considered valid restrictions on the cointegration space, and moreover, are stable over time. While there are minor indications of remaining problems with the statistical properties of the residuals of the final restricted reduced form model, the overall outcome seems acceptable. When it comes to discriminating between the alternative cointegration relationships none of the candidates is superior on all accounts, although the monetarist money demand function of equation (5.2) generally provides more satisfactory results. A possible explanation for the observed similarities between the approaches may lay in the fact that the limited sample size does not provide enough information to clearly identify the role of the interest rates in the cointegration space. Those effects not captured by the long-run coefficients in the money demand (a) relation, spill over to the short-run coefficients producing similar behaviour of both competing model variants in the end.

5.4.5 Interpretation of the Long-run Relationships

The empirical analysis of the previous sections produced four candidates for stable long-run relationships which however, can only be segregated in two types. One of them is a money demand, and the other is a stationary real

[18] Note that the forecasts are made for the growth rates and that therefore the random walk with drift and without trend is appropriate.

interest rate. The reason for this is owed to the fact that the actual error correction terms almost perfectly coincide.

Dealing with the stationary real interest rate first, the evidence points to a close link between the inflation rate and nominal interest rate levels. Generally, this is in line with the Fisher hypothesis which states that the nominal interest rate level also accounts for the expected future inflation. The remaining difference is then explained as a risk premium which should follow a stationary process. The corresponding error correction term enters the equation for the real income growth significantly with a negative sign as well as the equation for changes in the inflation rate with a positive coefficient. The first effect is consistent with the assumption that increasing real interest rates depress economic activity while the second signals that deviations from the long-run level contain valuable information about future inflation. The magnitude of the long-run coefficient on inflation is not in line with the theory, however. One of the suggestions to rationalize coefficient estimates like those in (5.1) and (5.2) is the effect of progressive taxes. The marginal tax rate increases with higher nominal income. Therefore, investors who have to pay taxes on the interest earned would not only demand higher nominal interest rates the higher the expected inflation rate is, but on top of that, they would want an extra premium for having to pay more taxes due to their increased marginal tax rate. This reasoning would of course require more detailed analysis in that direction to base it on firm grounds.

Brand and Cassola (2000) quote an alternative explanation. They hint at the possibility of a so-called peso problem. This may have occurred due to the steady decline in the inflation rate which might have led to permanent, systematic over prediction of the inflation rate. Consequently, homogeneity in the Fisher relation would disappear.

With respect to the money demand relation it should be noted that despite the different findings in equations (5.1) and (5.2), both these results point to the existence of a stable long-run relationship between income and real money. The corresponding equilibrium errors serve as indicators for future money growth because they feed back into the money growth equation in the correct way. The stability properties of these relationships, which also carry over to the time after the actual introduction of the Euro currency, provide evidence that they could be used for monetary policy conduct. This is because knowledge about what the long-run equilibrium relation looks like and what the consequences are of deviations therefrom, is valuable information independent of the actual monetary strategy.

When considering the differences between the alternative identification procedures, it turns out that they are less pronounced than are the similarities. This is firstly because the implied error correction terms do not differ much from each other, and secondly because the dynamic structure is very similar too. This can be concluded from the fact that in the money growth equation both the adjustment coefficients for deviations from the long-run equilibrium are in the range of $(-.04, -.11)$. Moreover, the long-run coefficients on money are of approximately the same magnitude. Additionally, deviations from long-run money demand (a) also explain the evolution of the short-term interest rate, which in turn serves as a significant regressor in the money growth equation. In the other model, the short-term interest rate is linked directly to real money growth because it features as a determinant of the long-run demand for money.

For the final exercise, the money demand (a) model is considered because of its overall better performance than the model related to the initial identification outcome. This last effort compares the current findings to the scheme suggested in chapter 2. Allowing for the minor adjustment of replacing the long-term interest by the short-term real interest rate found in the EMU data, leads to the following. The estimated long-run dynamics fall into the category (ii) with cointegrating rank two and presence of a money demand relation as well as a Fisher type relationship. In contrast to the statements given there, no direct link can be recognized between the policy interest rate and the money stock in the long-run dynamic structure. Instead, the adjustment coefficients are in accordance with a real balance effect ($\alpha_{1,y} > 0$), and a liquidity effect ($\alpha_{1,i^s} < 0$). Moreover, the real short-term interest rate is indicative of future inflation ($\alpha_{2,\pi} > 0$) as well as slowing down real income growth.[19] Looking from a different angle, real money cannot be thought of as being weakly exogenous, and that is why it can neither be strong nor super exogenous. As argued in the introductory chapter, this sheds serious doubt on the controllability of the European money stock by the ECB.

5.5 Conclusions

This last chapter made an attempt to produce evidence for the existence of long-run relationships between important European macroeconomic variables. The analysis was conducted before the difficult background of neither having practical experience nor well developed theoretical guidance for basing monetary policy for a newly created currency area as diverse as the EMU on information from the past. The basic assumption underlying this experiment is that European monetary policy will necessarily be conducted with aggregated data. This appears more likely than an approach that considers the history of a selection of national experiences alone. The second basic feature of the study is that it provides a transparent account of the data sources. Looking at the quality of the data sources it was felt that reliable data for the time before 1984 could not be produced and therefore, limitations in the sample length had to be accepted.

Despite all difficulties, applying the standard tools of money demand analysis and some special measures to circumvent the power problems induced by the small sample size, two long-run relationships could be identified. One of them resembles aspects of a money demand function, however, it is not quite

[19] Refer to Table 5.6, step 6a. The second subscript indicates the equation of the dependent variable the respective error correction term enters.

clear what part interest rates play. The second resembles a Fisher type relationship with the setback of partly unsatisfactory long-run coefficients. The latter is likely due to the sample period and the special effects observed in the run-up to the beginning of the Euro era.

Among the new results, which the precursory study of Müller and Hahn (2001) had not yet found, is the remarkable stability of both the long-run relationships which even carries over to the period after the introduction of the Euro. Although the main focus is on the long-run relationships, the model also seems to work well for short-run analyses as has been demonstrated by means of multi-step out-of-sample forecast evaluation.

As to implications for monetary policy, the results certainly support a rather cautious approach towards selecting a particular strategy. This warning applies especially to advocates of a monetary targeting strategy because the lack of necessary exogeneity properties on the part of the real money stock, calls into question the opportunity to control money in the long-run.

5.A Appendix: Tables, Figures and the Data

Table 5.11. Rank Tests

$$\Delta Y_t = \nu_0 + \alpha\beta' Y_{t-1} + \Gamma_1 \Delta Y_{t-1} + \varepsilon_t$$
$$Y_t = [(m-p)_t,\ y_t,\ i_t^l,\ i_t^s,\ \pi_t]'$$

Trace test statistics and critical values[a]

r_0	LR^i	5% crit. value	LR^i_{ta}	LM^*	5% crit. value	$LM_2^1(it)$	LR_{ta}^{GLS}	5% crit. value
0	84.12**	68.5	69.70**	102.2**	52.06	83.36**	76.41**	65.69
1	46.82*	47.2	39.23**	38.12**	33.64	39.26	38.32	45.12
2	25.67	29.7	19.33	13.65	20.66	9.60	16.88	28.47
3	7.92	15.4	6.34	2.03	9.79	2.57	8.90	15.92
4	0.17	3.8	–	–	–	.01	0.12	6.83

[a] The hypothesis $H_0 : rk(\beta') = r_0$ is tested sequentially with r_0 increasing. For the sources of the critical values see the notes in Table 4.9. The * and ** indicate significance at the ten and five percent level respectively.

Table 5.12. Money Demand in EMU: Residual Properties of Unrestricted Reduced Form Estimations

1) Model according to Table 5.5, step 7 (see p. 194).

Test[a]	Dependent variable $\Delta(m-p)_t$	Δy_t	Δi^l_t	Δi^s_t	$\Delta \pi_t$
correlation and	**.334**	·	·	·	·
	.12	**.282**	·	·	·
standard	.09	.27	**.392**	·	·
	.27	.30	.38	**.561**	·
deviation	-.35	.13	.07	.11	**.672**
AR(1-5)[b]	1.99*	4.16**	2.24*	3.06**	2.54**
	[.10]	[.05]	[.07]	[.02]	[.04]
Vector AR(1-5)[b]		.96; 125, 147 [.58]			
Nonnormality	6.95*	4.49	.09	3.42	1.32
	[.03]	[.11]	[.95]	[.18]	[.52]
Vector Nonnormality		11.59; 10 [.31]			
ARCH (4,48)[c]	1.49	.46	.13	.47	.57
	[.22]	[.76]	[.97]	[.76]	[.69]

2) Model (a) according to Table 5.6, step 6a (p. 195).

Test[a]	Dependent variable $\Delta(m-p)_t$	Δy_t	Δi^l_t	Δi^s_t	$\Delta \pi_t$
correlation and	**.313**	·	·	·	·
	.06	**.301**	·	·	·
standard	.13	.22	**.395**	·	·
	.15	.28	.40	**.536**	·
deviation	-.37	.20	.04	.17	**.676**
AR(1-5)[b]	1.63	1.11	1.32	1.37	2.24*
	[.17]	[.36]	[.27]	[.25]	[.06]
Vector AR(1-5)[b]		.85; 125, 142 [.82]			
Nonnormality	2.08	7.84**	.09	3.99	1.00
	[.35]	[.02]	[.95]	[.14]	[.61]
Vector Nonnormality		12.39; 10 [.26]			
ARCH (4,48)[c]	.24	.11	.13	.44	.92
	[.91]	[.98]	[.97]	[.78]	[.46]

[a] See explanations in Table 5.9 on page 205 except for:
[b] Test for autoregressive residuals up to order 5. Single equation tests: F-statistic with 1) 5,46 and 2) 5,51 degrees of freedom, and
[c] Single equation test for autoregressive heteroscedasticity of the residuals up to order 4 with 4 over 48 degrees of freedom; F distribution.

Table 5.13. Sources and Periods of Coverage of the Aggregate M3

Country	Source I MFI balance sheet statistics	Source II Best estimates of national contributions to the Euro area aggregates	Source III National monetary aggregates (national non-harmonized data)
Belgium	As from December 1996	January 1980 to November 1996	
Germany	As from January 1980		
Spain	As from January 1980		
France	As from January 1980		
Ireland	As from September 1997	December 1995 to August 1997	January 1980 to November 1995
Italy	As from December 1995	January 1980 to November 1995	
Luxembourg	As from September 1997	January 1980 to August 1997[a]	
Netherlands	As from December 1990	December 1982 to November 1990	January 1980 to November 1982
Austria	As from November 1996[b]	January 1980 to October 1996	
Portugal	As from January 1980		
Finland	As from January 1980		

[a] Estimated by applying the EU10 growth rates.
[b] Includes interpolations for the period from November 1996 to August 1997.
SOURCE: ECB (1999), Monthly Bulletin February, p. 42.

Table 5.14. Sources and Periods of Coverage of the Nominal GDP

Country	Source I Eurostat	Source II other
Belgium	As from 1985	The data for the year 1984 is calculated on the basis of the average growth rates of the other EMU countries.
Germany		The data has been supplied by the German Institute for Economic Research (DIW), Berlin. For the period prior to 1989 the data for unified Germany is calculated on the basis of the growth rates of the former West Germany.
Spain	All	
France	All	
Ireland		For the period before 1990 the data is calculated on the basis of the average growth rates of the other EMU countries. As from 1990 the data of the DIW is taken.
Italy	All	
Luxembourg		For the period prior to 1990 the data is calculated on the basis of the average growth rates of the other EMU countries. As from 1990 the data of the DIW is taken.
Netherlands	As from 1990	For the period before 1990 the data is calculated on the basis of the growth rates of Eurostat data.
Austria	All	
Portugal	As from 1986	For the period prior to 1986 the data is calculated on the basis of the average growth rates of the other EMU countries.
Finland	All	
Europe	As from 1998(3)	Growth rates of Gross Domestic Product are used to calculate the evolution of the data for 1985-1998(2) beyond that time (ECB Monthly Bulletin 08/2001, p. 40* col. 1)

Table 5.15. Sources and Periods of Coverage of the Real GDP

Country	Source I Eurostat	Source II other
Belgium	As from 1985	The data of the year 1984 is calculated on the basis of the growth rates of OECD data.
Germany		The data has been supplied by the German Institute for Economic Research (DIW), Berlin. For the period before 1989 the data for unified Germany is calculated on the basis of the growth rates of West Germany.
Spain	All	
France	As from 1990	For the period prior to 1990 growth rates of Eurostat data are used.
Ireland		For the period before 1990 the data is calculated on the basis of the extrapolated share of 9 EMU countries (EMU except for Ireland and Luxembourg). As from 1990 calculations of the DIW on the basis of indicators and the yearly GDP data of the OECD are used.
Italy	All	
Luxembourg		For the period prior to 1990 the data is calculated on the basis of the extrapolated share of 9 EMU countries (EMU except for Irland and Luxembourg). As from 1990 calculations of the DIW on the basis of indicators and the yearly GDP data of the OECD are used.
Netherlands	As from 1990	For the period before 1990 the data is calculated on the basis of the growth rates of Eurostat data.
Austria	As from 1990	For the period prior to 1990 the data is calculated on the basis of the growth rates of Eurostat data.
Portugal	As from 1988	For the period before 1988 data is calculated on the basis of growth rates of International Monetary Fund data.
Finland	All	
Europe	As from 1998(3)	Growth rates of GDP are used to calculate the evolution of the data for 1985-1998(2) beyond that time (ECB Monthly Bulletin 08/2001, p. 40* col. 10)

Table 5.16. Definitions of the National Long-term Interest Rates

Country	Long-term interest rate
Belgium	Yield of government bonds (6-years and over) on the secondary market.
Germany	Public sector bond yield, that refers to long-term public bonds (7 to 15 years duration) on the secondary market.
Spain[a]	Yield on 10 year government bonds, with the exception of 1994 for which the data refers to 9 year government bonds.
France	Yield on long-term public sector bonds on the secondary market.
Ireland	Yield on government securities of 15 years to maturity.
Italy	Yield on Treasury bonds of maturity of one year or longer.
Luxembourg	No data available.
Netherlands	Yield on the five longest term central government bonds.
Austria	Yield on bonds of maturity of one year or more on the secondary market.
Portugal[b]	Yield on 10-year government debt bonds on the secondary market.
Finland[c]	Yield of 3 to 6 year taxable central government bonds on the secondary market.
Europe[d]	Yield on 10-year government debt bonds

SOURCE: OECD (1997) Main Economic Indicators, Sources and Definitions, July.
[a]Data not available for the period 1984(1) - 1986(4).
[b]Data not available for the period 1984(1) - 1994(4).
[c]Data not available for the period 1984(1) - 1987(4).
[d]For 1998(3)-2000(4): Source: Monthly Bulletin of the ECB, August 2001, p. 27*, column 5.

Table 5.17. Definitions of the National Short-term Interest Rates

Country	Short-term interest rate
Belgium	3-month Treasury Certificates
Germany	3-month FIBOR
Spain	3-month interbank loans
France	3-month PIBOR
Ireland	3-month interbank rate
Italy	3-month interbank rate
Luxembourg	No data available.
Netherlands[a]	3-month AIBOR
Austria[b]	3-month VIBOR
Portugal[c]	86-96 day interbank rate
Finland[d]	3-month HELIBOR
Europe[e]	3-month money market rates

SOURCE: OECD (1997) Main Economic Indicators, Sources and Definitions, July.
[a]Data not available for the period 1984(1) - 1985(4).
[b]Data not available for the period 1984(1) - 1988(4).
[c]Data not available for the period 1984(1) - 1985(2).
[d]Data not available for the period 1984(1) - 1986(4).
[e]For 1998(3)-2000(4): Source: Monthly Bulletin of the ECB, August 2001, p. 26*, column 3.

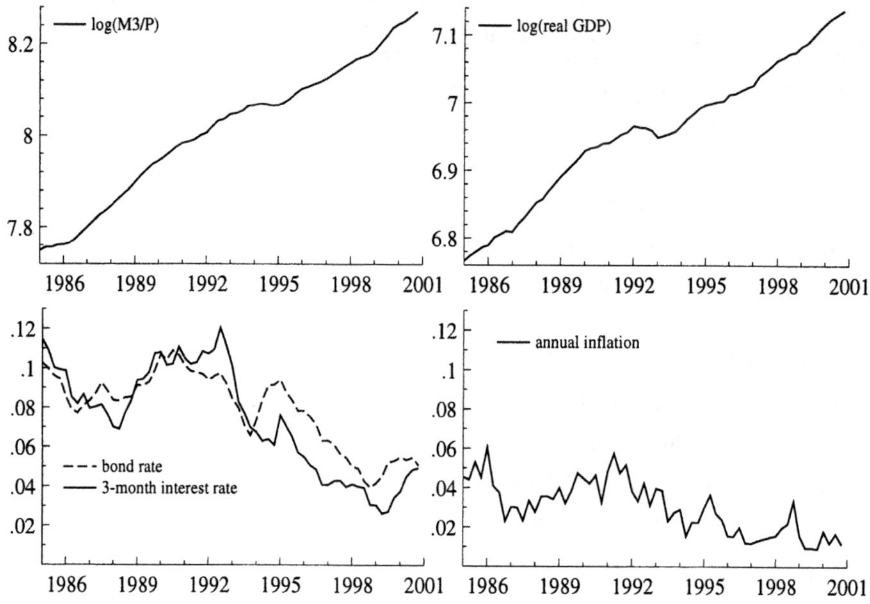

Figure 5.6. Data Graphics

6

Summary and Outlooks

System cointegration analysis of the demand for money function has proven to be fruitful since these econometric models frequently fit the data very well. It is therefore hoped that they resemble the true data generating process quite accurately. In contrast, economic interpretation of the entirety of the outcomes - among those presence or absence of weak exogeneity - often remains rather vague. The scheme of chapter 2 tried to provide a starting point for a systematic approach in that direction. For instance, with respect to the adjustment to the long-run relations, the importance of the role of expectations has been pointed out. A task for further research could be to isolate those implications of the underlying economic models more accurately which can be unveiled by econometric analysis. In a consecutive step, those economic concepts could then be found which comply best with the observable data.

However, even if the economic considerations are right, exogenous events may occur which hamper statistical analysis. One possible effect could be a shift in the mean value of a time series. A good example for this is the German monetary union which was followed by an upward shift of the stock of Deutschmark M3. Two recent proposals of testing for unit roots under these circumstances have been discussed in the second chapter and illustrated with macroeconomic time series. The discussion has included a suggestion for a concise proceeding of testing and model checking. A special feature of the new unit-root tests is that they allow for smooth transitions from the old to the new mean value. Moreover, when applied correctly, the distribution of the test statistic is independent of both the shape of the shift and its date of occurrence. Finally, those who are interested to apply the tests are provided with appropriate *GAUSS* procedures.

Preparing for the common currency required great efforts on the part of all EMU member states. These efforts are also reflected in their respective monetary policies. While for many European countries the standard money demand estimation approach delivers reasonable results, France has been found not to fit in that framework. The techniques discussed in the third chapter helped to shed some light on the particularities of the French case. In an auxiliary analysis the change in the exchange rate policy has been modelled as a non-linear transition process of the mean risk on the market for short-term credits. The need for modelling the policy shift carried over to the cointegration analysis of the French monetary system. In accordance with the theoretical explanations of the money supply process in European economies, the long-run money supply function was found more stable than the demand function, and could hence be identified. However, the consequences for the prospect of the common monetary policy are still not well understood, and they therefore provide an interesting area for future research.

The fourth chapter started with the assumption that all eleven EMU member states may be looked at as an economic entity even before the Euro era. Paying attention to the "first pillar" of the ECB's monetary strategy, the properties of a European demand for money function were derived on the basis of pre- and actual EMU data. The money demand function is important because it provides a guidance for calculating the "reference value" for money growth. In contrast to earlier findings, no prominent role could be assigned to the interest rates. Therefore the results lend support to the classical quantity theory of money, or the monetarist views. Nevertheless, a long-run demand for money function exists and this specification appeared superior to a competing approach that included interest rates in the formulation of the long-run relation.

However, the impact of monetary policy decisions, or any other shock, cannot be derived from the money demand function alone. Therefore, further scrutiny of the cointegration models, perhaps in the spirit of Johansen and Juselius (2000), appears worthwhile. They put forth the question of how to control certain target variables in cointegrated systems. The models derived in the chapters 3 and 4 suit their framework, and thus can be applied in further studies.

Not coincidentally, the last remark is partly at odds with the earlier hope for a more detailed research in the match of economic and econometric concepts. This is because the control rules can be derived purely agnostically. Therefore, the pursuit of both of these approaches promises to become an exciting field of future research.

List of Tables

List of Figures

References

Arize, A. C. and Shwiff, S. S. (1993). Cointegration, Real Exchange Rate and Modelling the Demand for Broad Money in Japan, *Applied Economics* **25**(6): 717 – 26.

Arnold, I. J. M. (1994). The Myth of a Stable European Money Demand, *Open Economics Review* **5**: 249 –259.

Arnold, I. J. M. and de Vries, C. G. (2000). Endogeneity in European Money Demand, *European Journal of Political Economy* **16**: 587 – 609.

Artis, M. J., Bladen-Hovell, R. C. and Zhang, W. (1992). A European Money Demand Function, *in* P. R. Masson and M. P. Taylor (eds), *Policy Issues in the Operation of Currency Unions*, International Monetary Fund, Oxford, U.K., pp. 240 – 263.

Artus, P. and Salomon, R. (1996). The EMS Credibility, and Disinflation: The French Case, *in* P. de Grauwe, S. Micossi and G. Tullio (eds), *Inflation and Wage Behaviour in Europe*, Clarendon Press, Oxford, U.K., pp. 30 – 58.

Barnett, W. A. (1980). Economic Monetary Aggregates: An Application of Index Number and Aggregation Theory, *Journal of Policy Modelling* **14**(1): 11 – 48.

Bernanke, B. S. and Gertler, M. (1995). Inside the Black Box: The Credit Channel of Monetary Policy Transmission, *Journal of Economic Perspective* **9**(4): 27 –48.

Beyer, A., Doornik, J. A. and Hendry, D. F. (2000). Reconstructing Aggregate Euro-zone Data, *Journal of Common Market Studies* **38**(4): 613 – 24.

Bofinger, P., Reischle, J. and Schächter, A. (1998). The Money Supply Process, *in* E. Baltensperger (ed.), *Transmissionsmechanismen der Geldpolitik*, Schriften des Vereins für Socialpolitik 264, Duncker & Humblot, Berlin, pp. 29 – 54.

Boswijk, P. H. (1995). Identifiability of Cointegrated Systems, *Discussion Paper TI 7-95-078*, University of Amsterdam,Tinbergen Institute.

Brand, C. and Cassola, N. (2000). A Money Demand System for EURO Area M3, *Working Paper 39*, European Central Bank.

Brüggemann, R. and Lütkepohl, H. (2001). Lag Selection in Subset VAR Models with an Application to a U.S. Monetary System, *in* R. Friedmann, L. Knüppel and H. Lütkepohl (eds), *Econometric Studies: A Festschrift in Honour of Joachim Frohn*, LIT-Verlag, Münster, pp. 107 – 28.

Candelon, B. and Lütkepohl, H. (2000). Was There a Regime Change in the German Transmission Mechanism in 1983?, *Discussion Paper 17*, Humboldt Universität zu Berlin.

Cannan, E. (1921). The Application of the Theoretical Apparatus of Supply and Demand to Units of Currency, *The Economic Journal* **31**(124): 453 – 61.

Cassard, M., Lane, T. D. and Masson, P. R. (1995). ERM Money Supplies and the Transition to EMU, *in* P. R. Masson (ed.), *France: Financial and Real Sector Issues*, International Monetary Fund, Washington, pp. 112 – 45.

Clausen, V. (1998). Geldnachfrage und Geldpolitik in Europa, *in* E. Baltensperger (ed.), *Transmissionsmechanismen der Geldpolitik*, Schriften des Vereins für Socialpolitik 264, Duncker & Humblot, Berlin, pp. 55 – 92.

Clower, Robert, W. (1967). A Reconsideration of the Microfoundations of Monetary Theory, *Western Economic Journal* **6**: 1 – 9.

Coenen, G. and Vega, J.-L. (1999). The Demand for M3 in the Euro Area, *Working Paper 6*, European Central Bank.

Doornik, J. A. and Hendry, D. F. (1997). *Modelling Dynamic Systems Using PcFiml 9 for Windows*, Timberlake Consulting, London.

Dornbusch, R. and Fischer, S. (1990). *Macroeconomics*, 5th edn, McGraw-Hill, New York.

Eitrheim, Ø. (1999). The Demand for Broad Money in Norway, 1969-1993, *in* H. Lütkepohl and J. Wolters (eds), *Money Demand in Europe*, Physica-Verlag, Heidelberg, pp. 73 – 88.

Elliott, G., Rothenberg, T. J. and Stock, J. H. (1996). Efficient Tests for an Autoregressive Unit Root, *Econometrica* **64**: 813 – 836.

Engle, R. F. and Granger, C. W. J. (1987). Co-Integration and Error Correction: Representation, Estimation and Testing, *Econometrica* **55**(2): 251 – 76.

Engle, R. F. and Hendry, D. F. (1993). Testing Super Exogeneity and Invariance in Regression Models, *Journal of Econometrics* **56**: 119 – 139.

Engle, R. F., Hendry, D. F. and Richard, J.-F. (1983). Exogeneity, *Econometrica* **51**(2): 277 – 304.

Ericsson, N. R. (1992). Cointegration, Exogneity, and Policy Analysis: An Overview, *Journal of Policy Modeling* **14**: 251 – 80.

Ericsson, N. R. (1998). Empirical Modelling of Money Demand, *Empirical Economics* **23**(3): 483–506.

Ericsson, N. R., Hendry, D. F. and Mizon, G. E. (1998). Exogeneity, Cointegration, and Economic Policy Analysis, *Journal of Business and Economic Statistics* **16**(4): 370 – 87.

Ericsson, N. R., Hendry, D. F. and Prestwich, K. M. (1998). The Demand for Broad Money in the United Kingdom, 1878-1993, *Scandinavian Journal Of Economics* **100**(1): 289–324.

Ericsson, N. R., Hendry, D. F. and Tran, H.-A. (1994). Cointegration Seasonality, Encompassing and the Demand for Money in the United Kingdom, *in* C. P. Hargreaves (ed.), *Nonstationary Time Series Analysis and Cointegration*, Oxford University Press, Oxford, U.K., pp. 179 – 229.

European Central Bank (1999a). *Monthly Bulletin, February*, European Central Bank.

European Central Bank (1999b). *Monthly Bulletin, January*, European Central Bank.

European Central Bank (2000). Monetary Policy Transmission in the Euro Area, *Monthly Bulletin, July* pp. 43 – 58.

Fagan, G. and Henry, J. (1999). Long Run Money Demand in the EU: Evidence for Area Wide Aggregates, *in* H. Lütkepohl and J. Wolters (eds), *Money Demand in Europe*, Physica-Verlag, Heidelberg, pp. 218 – 40.

Fagan, G., Henry, J. and Mestre, R. (2001). An Area-wide Model (AWM) for the EU11, *Working Paper 42*, European Central Bank.

Fisher, I. (1930). *The Theory of Interest*, Macmillan, New York.

Friedman, M. (1956). The Quantity Theory of Money - A Restatement, *in* M. Friedman (ed.), *Studies in the Quantity Theory of Money*, University of Chicago Press, Chicago, pp. 3–21, appendix, 252–7.

Friedmann, M. and Schwartz, A. J. (1982). *Monetary Trends in the United States and the United Kingdom: Their Relation to Income, Prices, and Interest Rates, 1867-1975*, University of Chicago Press, Chicago.

Gerlach, S. and Svensson, L. E. O. (2001). Money and Inflation in the Euro Area: A Case for Monetary Indicators ?, *Working Paper 98*, Bank for International Settlements.

Gottschalk, J. (1999). A Cointegration Analysis of a Money Demand System in Europe, *Kiel Working Paper 902*, The Kiel Institute of World Economics.

Hagen, J. v. and Fratianni, M. (1990). German Dominace in the EMS: Evidence from Interest Rates, *Journal of International Money and Finance* **9**: 358–75.

Hansen, B. E. (1992). Tests for Parameter Instability in Regression With I(1) Processes, *Journal of Business and Economic Statistics* **10**: 321–35.

Hansen, P. R. (2000a). Structural Breaks in the Cointegrated Vector Autoregressive Model, *Working Paper*, University of California, San Diego.

Hansen, P. R. (2000b). Testing for Structural Changes in Cointegration Relations, *Working Paper*, University of California, San Diego.

Hassler, U. and Wolters, J. (1999). Forecasting Money Market Rates in the Unified Germany, *Volkswirtschaftliche Reihe 24*, Freie Universität Berlin.

Hayo, B. (1999). Estimating A European Demand for Money, *Scottish Journal of Political Economy* **46**(3): 221–44.

Hendry, D. F. (1985). Monetary Economic Myth and Econometric Reality, *Oxford Review of Economic Policy* **1**(1): 72 – 84.

Hendry, D. F. and Mizon, G. E. (1999). Exogeneity, Causality, and Co-breaking in Economic Policy Analysis of a Small Econometric Model of the Money in the UK, *in* H. Lütkepohl and J. Wolters (eds), *Money Demand in Europe*, Physica-Verlag, Heidelberg, pp. 1 – 28.

Hubrich, K. (2001). *Cointegration Analysis in a German Monetary System*, 1st edn, Physica Verlag, Heidelberg.

Hubrich, K., Lütkepohl, H. and Saikkonen, P. (2001). A Review of Systems Cointegration Tests, *Econometric Reviews* **20**(3): 247 – 318.

Hwang, J. and Schmidt, P. (1996). Alternative Methods of Detrending and the Power of Unit Root Tests, *Journal of Econometrics* **71**: 227 – 248.

Issing, O. (1993). *Einführung in die Geldpolitik*, 5th edn, Franz Vahlen, München.

Jarchow, H.-J. (1993). *Theorie und Politik des Geldes: I Geldtheorie*, 9th edn, Vandenhoek & Ruprecht, Göttingen.

Jaschke, S., Stehle, R. and Wernicke, S. (2000). Arbitrage und die Gültigkeit des Barwertprinzips im Markt für Bundeswertpapiere, *Zeitschrift für die betriebswirtschaftliche Forschung* **52**: 440 – 468.

Johansen, S. (1988). Statistical Analysis of Cointegration Vectors, *Journal of Economic Dynamics* **12**: 231 – 54.

Johansen, S. (1991). Estimation and Hypothesis Testing of Cointegration Vectors in Gaussian Vector Autoregressive Models, *Econometrica* **59**(6): 1551 – 81.

Johansen, S. (1992). A Representation of Vector Autoregressive Processes Integrated of Order 2, *Econometric Theory* **8**: 188 – 202.

Johansen, S. (1995a). Identifying Restrictions of Linear Equation with Applications to Simultaneous Equations and Cointegration, *Journal of Econometrics* **69**: 111 – 132.

Johansen, S. (1995b). *Likelihood-based Inference in Cointegrated Vector Autoregressive Models*, Oxford University Press.

Johansen, S. (1997). Likelihood Analysis of the I(2) Model, *Scandinavian Journal of Statistics* **24**: 433 – 462.

Johansen, S. and Juselius, K. (1990). Maximum Likelihood Estimation and Inference on Cointegration - With Applications to the Demand for Money, *Oxford Bulletin of Economics and Statistics* **52**: 169–210.

Johansen, S. and Juselius, K. (2000). Controlling a Non-Stationary Variable in the Cointegrated Vector Autoregressive Model, *Discussion Paper draft*, Economics Department, European University Institute, Florence, http://www.econ.ku.dk/okokj/Papers/control.pdf.

Juselius, K. (1996). An Empirical Analysis of the Changing Role of the German Bundesbank after 1983, *Oxford Bulletin of Economics and Statistics* **58**: 791–819.

Juselius, K. (1998). Changing Monetary Transmission Mechanisms within the EU, *Empirical Economics* **23**(3): 456–481.

Juselius, K. (1999). Models and Relations in Economics and Econometrics, *Discussion Paper draft*, Economics Department, European University Institute, Florence, http://www.econ.ku.dk/okokj/Papers/Models99.pdf.

Juselius, K. and Gennari, E. (1998). Dynamic Modeling and Structural Shift: Monetary Transmission Mechanisms in Italy before and after EMS, *Discussion Paper draft*, Economics Department, European University Institute, Florence, http://www.econ.ku.dk/okokj/Papers/Italy.pdf.

Keynes, J. M. (1930). *A Treatise on Money*, Macmillan, London & New York.

Keynes, J. M. (1936). *The General Theory of Employment, Interest, and Money*, Macmillan, London & New York.

Kirchgässner, G. and Wolters, J. (1996). Determination of Long-term Interest Rates in the EMS, *in* P. de Grauwe, S. Micossi and G. Tullio (eds), *Inflation and Wage Behaviour in Europe*, Clarendon Press, Oxford, U.K., pp. 281 – 309.

Kleibergen, F. and Hoek, H. (2000). Bayesian Analysis of ARMA Models Using Noninformative Priors, *Discussion Paper 2000-027/4*, Tinbergen Institute, Erasmus University Rotterdam.

Kremers, J. J. M. and Lane, T. D. (1990). Economic and Monetary Integration and the Aggregate Demand for Money in the EMS, *Staff Paper 37*, International Monetary Fund.

Laidler, D. E. W. (1993). *Demand for Money: Theory, Evidence, and Problems*, 4th edn, Harper Collins College Publishers, New York.

Laidler, D. E. W. *(ed)*. (1999). *The Foundations of Monetary Economics, Volume I*, Edward Elgar Publishing, Cheltenham, UK and Northampton, USA.

Lanne, M., Lütkepohl, H. and Saikkonen, P. (1999). Comparison of Unit Root Tests for Time Series with Level Shifts, *Discussion Paper 88*, Sonderforschungsbereich 373 at Humboldt-Universität zu Berlin, http://sfb.wiwi.hu-berlin.de/papers/1999/DP88-99.ps.Z.

Lanne, M., Lütkepohl, H. and Saikkonen, P. (2001). Test Procedures for Unit Roots in Time Series with Level Shifts at Unknown Time, *Discussion Paper 39*, Sonderforschungsbereich 373 at Humboldt-Universität zu Berlin, http://sfb.wiwi.hu-berlin.de/papers/2001/DP200139.ps.Z.

Leybourne, S., Newbold, P. and Vougas, D. (1998). Unit Roots and Smooth Transitions, *Journal of Time Series Analysis* **19**(1): 83 – 97.

Li, H. (1995). A Reexamination of the Nelson-Plosser Data Set Using Recursive and Sequential Tests, *Empirical Economics* **20**: 501 – 18.

Lucas, R. E. (1976). Econometric Policy Evaluation: A Critique, *Carnegie Rochester Conferences on Public Policy 1*, North-Holland, Amsterdam, pp. 19 – 46.

Lütkepohl, H. (1993a). *Introduction to Multiple Time Series Analysis*, 2nd edn, Springer-Verlag, Berlin.

Lütkepohl, H. (1993b). The Sources of the U.S. Money Demand Instability, *Empirical Economics* **18**: 729 – 743.

Lütkepohl, H., Müller, C. and Saikkonen, P. (2001). Unit Root Tests for Time Series with a Structural Break when the Break Point is Known, *in* C. Hsiao, K. Morimune and J. L. Powel (eds), *Nonlinear Statistical Modeling*, Cambridge University Press, Cambridge, UK and New York, USA, pp. 327 – 348.

Lütkepohl, H. and Saikkonen, P. (2000). Testing for the Cointegrating Rank of a VAR Process with a Time Trend, *Journal of Econometrics* **95**: 177–198.

Lütkepohl, H., Saikkonen, P. and Trenkler, C. (2000). Comparison of Tests for the Cointegrating Rank of a VAR Process with a Structural Shift, *Discussion Paper 10*, Sonderforschungsbereich 373 at Humboldt-Universität zu Berlin, http://sfb.wiwi.hu-berlin.de/papers/2000/DPLSa00010.ps.zip.

Lütkepohl, H. and Wolters, J. (1998). A Money Demand System for German M3, *Empirical Economics* **23**(3): 371–386.

MacKinnon, J. (1991). Critical Values for Co-integration Tests, *in* R. Engle and C. Granger (eds), *Long-Run Economic Relationships*, Oxford University Press, Washington, pp. 267 – 67.

Mankiw, N. G. (1994). *Macroeconomics*, 2nd edn, Worth, New York.

Marshall, A. (1923). *Money, Credit and Commerce*, Macmillan, London.

Meltzer, A. H. (1963). The Demand for Money: The Evidence from the Time Series, *Journal of Political Economy* **LXXI**(3): June, 219 – 46.

Meltzer, A. H. (1995). Monetary, Credit and (Other) Transmission Processes: A Monetarist Perspective, *Journal of Economic Perspective* **9**(4): 49 –72.

Monticelli, C. (1996). EU-Wide Money and Cross-Border Holdings, *Weltwirtschaftliches Archiv* **132**(2): 215 – 235.

Monticelli, C. and Strauss-Kahn, M.-O. (1993). European Integration and the Demand for Broad Money, *The Manchester School* **LXI**(4): 345 – 366.

Müller, C. (1998). *Der Einfluss der Wahl der Ordnung eines Vektorautoregressiven Prozesses auf Kointegrationstests*, Diplomarbeit (master's thesis), Humboldt-Universität zu Berlin, Wirtschaftswissenschaftliche Fakultät.

Müller, C. (1999). Monetary Policy in France Prior to European Monetary Union, *Allgemeines Statistisches Archiv* **83**(4): 369 – 384.

Müller, C. and Hahn, E. (2001). Money Demand in Europe: Evidence from the Past, *Kredit und Kapital* **34**(1): 48 – 75.

Nautz, D. (2000). *Die Geldmarktsteuerung der Europäischen Zentralbank und das Geldangebot der Banken*, Physica-Verlag, Heidelberg.

Nautz, D. and Wolters, J. (1999). The Response of Long-term Interest Rates to News about Monetary Policy Actions: Empirical Evidence for the US and Germany, *Weltwirtschaftliches Archiv* **135**: 397 – 412.

Nelson, C. R. and Plosser, C. I. (1982). Trends and Random Walks in Macroeconomic Time Series: Some Evidence and Implications, *Journal of Monetary Economics* **10**: 139 – 162.

Nourney, M. (1993). Umstellung der Zeitreihenanalyse, *Wirtschaft und Statistik* **11**: 841 – 852.

Patinkin, D. (1966). *Money, Interest, and Prices: An Integration of Monetary and Value Theory*, 2nd edn, Harper and Row, New York.

Pentecost, E. J. (1993). *Exchange Rate Dynamics*, 1st edn, Edward Elgar, Cambridge.

Perron, P. (1989). The Great Crash, the Oil Price Shock and the Unit Root Hypothesis, *Econometrica* **57**(6): 1361 – 1401.

Phillips, A. W. (1958). The Relationship between Unemployment and the Rate of Change of Money Wage Rates in the United Kingdom 1861-1957, *Economica* **25**: 283 ff.

Pigou, A. C. (1917). The Value of Money, *The Quarterly Journal of Economics* **37**: 38 – 65.

Reimers, H.-E. (1991). *Analyse kointegrierter Variablen mittels vektorautoregressiver Modelle*, 1st edn, Physica-Verlag, Heidelberg.

Saikkonen, P. and Lütkepohl, H. (2000a). Testing for the Cointegrating Rank of a VAR Process with an Intercept, *Econometric Theory* **16**: 373–406.

Saikkonen, P. and Lütkepohl, H. (2000b). Testing for the Cointegrating Rank of a VAR Process with Structural Shifts, *Journal of Business and Economic Statistics* **18**: 451–64.

Saikkonen, P. and Lütkepohl, H. (2000c). Trend Adjustment Prior to Testing for the Cointegrating Rank of a VAR Process, *Journal of Time Series Analysis* **21**(4): 435–56.

Saikkonen, P. and Lütkepohl, H. (2001). Testing for Unit Roots in Time Series with Level Shifts, *Allgemeines Statistisches Archiv* **85**(1): 1 – 25.

Saikkonen, P. and Luukkonen, R. (1997). Testing Cointegration in Infinite Order Vector Autoregressive Processes, *Journal of Econometrics* **81**: 93 – 126.

Seo, B. (1998). Tests for Structural Change in Cointegrated Systems, *Econometric Theory* **14**: 222 – 59.

Sims, C. (1992). Interpreting the Macroeconomic Time Series Facts: The Effects of Monetary Policy, *European Economic Review* **36**: 975 – 1000.

Spencer, P. (1997). Monetary Integration and Currency Substitution in the EMS: The Case of a European Monetary Aggregate, *European Economic Review* **41**: 1403 – 1419.

Sriram, S. S. (1999). Survey of Literature on Demand for Money: Theoretical and Empirical Work with Special Reference to Error-Correction Models, *Working Paper 64*, IMF.

Svensson, L. E. O. (1985). Money and Asset Prices in a Cash-in-Advance Economy, *Journal of Political Economy* **93**(5): 919 – 44.

Svensson, L. E. O. (2000). Does the P* Model Provide Any Rational for Monetary Targeting?, *German Economic Review* **1**(1): 69 – 82.

Trecroci, C. and Vega, J. L. (2000). The Information Content of M3 For Future Inflation, *Working Paper 33*, European Central Bank.

Tullio, G., Souza, E. D. and Giucca, P. (1996). The Demand for Money Functions in Europe and in Germany before and after the Fall of the Berlin Wall, *in* P. de Grauwe, S. Micossi and G. Tullio (eds), *Inflation and Wage Behaviour in Europe*, Clarendon Press, Oxford, pp. 310 – 338.

Wesche, K. (1998). *The Stability of European Money Demand: An Investigation of M3H*, Doctoral Dissertation, Universität Bonn, Department of Economics.

Wolters, J. and Hassler, U. (1998). Die Zinsstruktur am deutschen Interbanken-Geldmarktsatz, *ifo Studien* **44**(2): 141 – 160.

Working, E. J. (1927). What Do Statistical Demand Curves Show? (reprint), *in* G. S. . K. Boulding (ed.), *Readings in Price Theory*, Allen and Unwin, 1953, London, pp. 333 – 389.

Yap, S. F. and Reinsel, G. C. (1995). Estimation and Testing for Unit Roots in a Partially Nonstationary Vector Autoregressive Moving Average Model, *Journal of the American Statistical Association* **90**(429): 253 – 267.

Zivot, E. and Andrews, D. W. K. (1992). Further Evidence on the Great Crash, the Oil-Price Shock, and the Unit-Root Hypothesis, *Journal of Business and Economic Statistics* **10**: 251 – 270.

GPSR Compliance

The European Union's (EU) General Product Safety Regulation (GPSR) is a set of rules that requires consumer products to be safe and our obligations to ensure this.

If you have any concerns about our products, you can contact us on ProductSafety@springernature.com

In case Publisher is established outside the EU, the EU authorized representative is:

Springer Nature Customer Service Center GmbH
Europaplatz 3
69115 Heidelberg, Germany

Batch number: 10725973

Printed by Printforce, the Netherlands